Emotions in Multiple Languages

Also by Jean-Marc Dewaele

OPPORTUNITIES AND CHALLENGES OF BILINGUALISM (*co-edited with Li Wei and A. Housen*)

BILINGUALISM: BASIC PRINCIPLES AND BEYOND (*co-edited with Li Wei and A. Housen*)

FOCUS ON FRENCH AS A FOREIGN LANGUAGE: MULTIDISCIPLINARY APPROACHES (*edited*)

NEW TRENDS IN CROSSLINGUISTIC INFLUENCE AND MULTILINGUALISM RESEARCH (*co-edited with G. De Angelis*)

Emotions in Multiple Languages

Jean-Marc Dewaele
Birkbeck College, University of London, UK

palgrave
macmillan

First published in hardback in 2010
This paperback edition first published in 2013 by
PALGRAVE MACMILLAN

Palgrave Macmillan in the UK is an imprint of Macmillan Publishers Limited, registered in England, company number 785998, of Houndmills, Basingstoke, Hampshire RG21 6XS.

Palgrave Macmillan in the US is a division of St Martin's Press LLC, 175 Fifth Avenue, New York, NY 10010.

Palgrave Macmillan is the global academic imprint of the above companies and has companies and representatives throughout the world.

Palgrave® and Macmillan® are registered trademarks in the United States, the United Kingdom, Europe and other countries.

ISBN: 978–1–403–94316–3 hardback
ISBN: 978–1–137–35476–1 paperback

This book is printed on paper suitable for recycling and made from fully managed and sustained forest sources. Logging, pulping and manufacturing processes are expected to conform to the environmental regulations of the country of origin.

A catalogue record for this book is available from the British Library.

A catalog record for this book is available from the Library of Congress.

Transferred to Digital Printing in 2014

To Katja and Livia

Contents

List of Illustrations

Tables

Figures

List of Abbreviations

AoA	Age of onset of acquisition
ANOVA	Analysis of variance
CA	Communicative anxiety
CS	Code-switching
CP	Critical Period
CPH	Critical Period Hypothesis
FL	Foreign language
FLA	Foreign language anxiety
IL	Interlanguage
L1, L2, L3, L4, L5	first, second, third, fourth, fifth language to have been acquired
LX	One of the languages of a multilingual acquired after the establishment of the L1(s) and undetermined in terms of chronology of acquisition or proficiency
NNS	Non-native speaker
NS	Native speaker
SLA	Second Language Acquisition
TEI	Trait Emotional Intelligence
TL	Target language

Preface and Acknowledgements

I very gratefully acknowledge the invaluable contributions of many friends, colleagues, students, reviewers of several of my papers on the topic and, especially, the many participants to the web questionnaire and the 20 participants who agreed to be interviewed.

Special thanks go to the co-author of the Bilingualism and Emotions web questionnaire (Dewaele and Pavlenko, 2001–2003), Professor Aneta Pavlenko, whose pioneering work in the field of multilingualism and emotion has been an inspiration to many researchers. Her insights and her judicious feedback on various manuscripts since our initial collaboration in 2000 have substantially contributed toward the development of my own thinking on the subject.

I am very grateful to her, Professor Li Wei and Emeritus Professor Arthur Van Essen, who read an earlier version of the present book and made excellent critical comments and suggestions for improvement.

I would also like to thank my friends and colleagues Professor Adrian Furnham, Dr Dino Petrides and Dr Rosemary Wilson for collaborating with me on various papers, some of which have been integrated into the present book.

Professor Jeanette Altarriba, Professor Catherine Caldwell-Harris, Professor Jasone Cenoz, Professor Vivian Cook, Dr Gessica De Angelis, Professor François Grosjean, Dr Zhu Hua and Professor Timothy Jay have also been rich sources of information and suggestions.

I would also like to express my gratitude to Dr Benedetta Bassetti for carrying out the interviews with 20 adult multilinguals in London. This particular project entitled "The communication of emotion in multiple languages" was funded by a Small Research Grant from the British Academy (SG-42593) in 2006.

I wish to thank the people from Palgrave Macmillan for their support, with special thanks to Ms Vidhya Jayaprakash and the proofreader for an excellent job.

I am also very grateful to Dr Amelia Huzum, Mr Adriell Nicolas, Dr Eszter Nucz, Professor Zoltán Kövecses, Dr Anna Ogarkova, Dr Jennifer Bown and Dr Marcella LaFever, who wrote insightful reviews about the first version of the book. I took on board their suggestions for this second edition.

I also thank my wife Katja and my daughter Livia for their unstinting support and for putting up with it all. Finally, I would like to thank my parents whose love and support allowed me to blossom.

Note on the Author

Jean-Marc Dewaele (MA French, MA Spanish, MA European & International Law, MA Eastern European Affairs, PhD in Romance Languages and Literature (Free University of Brussels, 1993)) is Professor of Applied Linguistics and Multilingualism at Birkbeck College, University of London. He has published widely on individual differences in psycholinguistic, sociolinguistic, pragmatic, psychological and emotional aspects of Second Language Acquisition and Multilingualism. He was president of the European Second Language Association (2007–2011) and Convenor of the AILA Research Network *Multilingualism: Acquisition and Use*. He is member of the editorial boards of *The International Journal of Multilingualism, Estudios de Linguistica Inglesa Aplicada, Vigo International Journal of Applied Linguistics,* the *International Journal of Language Studies*, the *Canadian Modern Language Review* and the *International Journal of Language and Culture*. He was Reviews Editor of *Sociolinguistic Studies* (2006–2010) and the *International Journal of Bilingual Education and Bilingualism* (2010–2012). He was Assistant Editor of *the International Journal of Bilingualism* (2006–2012) and became General Editor of the *International Journal of Bilingual Education and Bilingualism* (2013–).

Introduction

Emotions play a crucial part in the lives of monolinguals and multilinguals. Sharing emotions, whether in face-to-face interactions or through written communications, is a crucial social activity, and the ability to do so helps us maintain physical and mental health (Averill, 1982; Fussell, 2002).

Fussell points out:

> The interpersonal communication of emotional states is fundamental to both everyday and clinical interaction. One's own and others' affective experiences are frequent topics of everyday conversations, and how well these emotions are expressed and understood is important to interpersonal relationships and individual well-being. (Fussell, 2002: 1)

I personally discovered the importance of the social sharing of emotion (Rimé, 2009) when I found myself temporarily unable to do so because of language barriers.

At the end of my first year at the university of Brussels, I had enrolled for a month-long course at the University of Salamanca to kick-start my mastery of Spanish. Travelling down to Salamanca, I was struck by how monolingual the Spanish were, and my attempts at obtaining information using French and English were often unsuccessful. Being a complete beginner, I struggled to get a foot on the linguistic ladder, even more so because the teaching was in Spanish and translating and retranslating words with the help of my little dictionary was excruciatingly slow. Although I made some progress, I was unable to share my sense of frustration or my exhilaration with my host family as they were monolingual Spanish speakers. I could not tell jokes and I was unable to say anything that sounded remotely interesting, to my ears. I discovered that it is hard to socialise using emotionless textbook phrases. I took consolation from the fact that the experience would make me stronger psychologically. This experience was particularly unsettling because as a French-Dutch bilingual from birth, living in a country where multilingualism is the norm, I had never experienced a near total inability to communicate across the full emotional spectrum. Although my Spanish improved as the month went on, and little phrases drifted into my inner speech, I looked forward to being back in a familiar environment where I could share my experiences effortlessly with my friends and family. I think this experience may have contributed to my present interest in the communication of emotions in the various languages of a multilingual.

Reading Daniel Everett's (2008) riveting account of his arrival as a missionary and anthropologist among a small tribe of Pirahas in central Brazil in 1977, I was reminded of how perplexing it can be to be immersed in an unfamiliar language, culture and world view. Everett discovered that the Pirahas did not engage in phatic communication. They did not use any of the small talk ("how are you? Hello; you're welcome; sorry; thank you") that we use to maintain social and interpersonal channels: "Piraha sentences are either requests for information (questions), assertions of new information (declarations), or commands, by and large" (2008: 11). Pirahas also laugh about everything: "They laugh when they catch a lot of fish. They laugh when they catch no fish (...) I have been impressed with their patience, their happiness, and their kindness" (p. 85). The Piraha language, which Everett set out to describe, turned out to be unique in many ways, such as the five channels of discourse that have a unique cultural function: "whistle speech, hum speech, musical speech, yell speech, and normal speech – that is, speech using consonants and vowels" (pp. 185–186). Everett's growing understanding of the Piraha language and culture led to a personal epistemological and religious crisis:

> The Pirahas made me question concepts of truth that I had long adhered to and lived by. The questioning of my faith in God, coupled with my life among the Pirahas, led me to question what is perhaps an even more fundamental component of modern thought, the concept of truth itself. (p. 272)

What Everett's experiences show is that contact with a new language and culture can have profound consequences that go far beyond the purely linguistic aspect of second language learning. As Cook (2002) points out, "the minds, languages and lives of L2 users are different from those of monolinguals" (p. 9).

From birth, the monolingual child learns to communicate emotions and organise its needs in one single language: "hunger, physical pain, need for warmth, protection, to have its surrounding explained) and different feelings (e.g., wonderment, feeling of wellbeing, love, happiness, sadness, discomfort)" (Javier, 2007: 23). The experience of expressing emotions and needs in a language forces the monolingual child to develop specific linguistic modes of organising and categorising these experiences (p. 24). These linguistic-specific organisations and categorisations will be reorganised if that child starts attending a school where a different language is spoken. This new environment might pose some particular challenges for the monolingual child, who might be unable at first to communicate an experience or an emotion in the new language and could be left with a general feeling that he/she cannot totally and fully express itself in the new language (Javier, 2007). On the other hand, a multilingual child has several linguistic codes available at all times to organise and process his or her perceptions of various kinds, and is thus aware of the wide array of means to express or decode a specific emotion. He/she is more aware of the diversity in the world and able to consider it through the prism of its different languages and cultures (cf. Javier, 2007; Xiao-Lei Wang, 2008). A word of caution is needed here. I think it would be wrong to view the opposition "monolingual" versus "multilingual" child in Manichean terms, as the monolingual may well master various sociolects or dialects.

Xiao-Lei Wang (2008) offers a fascinating portrait of the dynamic sense of self of her two biracial and trilingual boys in New York where the boys speak French with their Swiss father, Chinese (Putonghua) with their mother and English with their friends outside home. They travel regularly to Switzerland and China to boost their linguistic and cultural skills and to maintain ties with their family members there. This allows the boys to develop their different languages and worldviews and to build a unique, hybrid cultural, national and ethnic identity which may shift according to the place where they are and who they are talking with.

Xiao-Lei Wang's (2008) book offers food for thought on the terminological problems concerning the labelling of multilinguals' languages. The common practice in applied linguistics is to number multilinguals' languages chronologically (L1, L2, L3...), according to their first contact with a language (Hammarberg, 2009). This linear numbering practice works fine when applied to individuals who grew up with one language and acquired foreign languages consecutively. It becomes slightly more complicated in cases of simultaneous bilingual or trilingual acquisition, as is the case in the Wang family. If the boys have three "first" languages, L1a, L1b, L1c, would their first "foreign" language learnt at school be their "L2", or should it be considered their "L4"? The other problem is that of intermittent or alternating acquisition (Hammarberg, 2009: 4). The first contact with a language might have been followed by a relatively short period of exposure, with renewed exposure many years later. I was, for example, exposed to English as a baby when my parents – who have always spoken French with me – decided to spend a year in the US after my father obtained a Fulbright exchange grant. Although English was all around me, I do not seem to have picked up much, and would certainly not list English as an L1. I did, however, pick up some English back in Belgium when trying to decipher what my parents were saying to each other when they did not want to be overheard. Also, English music and films in the original version provided sporadic exposure to the language until the age of 13 when I started learning English at school in Belgium. Multilinguals might thus learn a language gradually over different periods of life, making it hard to determine an exact "starting point", and thus a linear time scale. Hammarberg (2009) also raises the question of scanty knowledge of a language. In other words, how much knowledge of a language should one have before claiming to master that language? And how should languages be judged for which a person only has a particular type of knowledge, such as reading competence in a dead language?

Researchers have used the labels L1, L2, L3 differently according to their own specific research orientation. The L1 is conventionally defined as the language(s) that was (were) established up to a certain level before the age of 3 (McLaughlin, 1984: 10). The L2 would then refer to any language acquired after that. Mitchell and Myles (1998), for example, use the word "second" as an umbrella term for all "foreign" languages: "because [...] the underlying learning processes are essentially the same for more local and for more remote target languages, despite differing learning purposes and circumstances" (p. 2).

Cook (2002) uses the word in "second" in the same way when introducing the concept of the L2 user, which he distinguishes from the L2 learner. The proficiency of L2 users in their different languages may vary widely: "Some of them use the second language as skilfully as a monolingual native speaker, like Nabokov writing whole novels in a second language; some of them can barely ask for a coffee in a restaurant" (Cook, 2002: 3). Whether they are highly proficient or not, L2 users are legitimate users of that L2:

> One motivation for this usage is the feeling that it is demeaning to call someone who has functioned in an L2 environment for years a "learner" rather than a "user". A person who has been using a second language for twenty-five years is no more an L2 learner than a fifty-year-old monolingual native speaker is an L1 learner. (Cook, 2002: 4)

Cook is obviously not interested in a finer-grained distinction between the languages acquired after the L1(s), and thus labels them all L2s.

Researchers who are specifically interested in the acquisition of new language after the second language feel that this acquisition may be qualitatively different from the acquisition of the L2 have used the term "L3" (Hammarberg, 2009). Not being particularly focused on potential differences between the acquisition of the L3 and later languages, trilingualism researchers use the term "third" as an umbrella term referring to "third or additional languages" (De Angelis, 2007).

As I am interested in adult individuals who have learnt second, third, fourth and even fifth languages at various times during their life and who reflect on their experiences in communicating emotions in these different languages, I have decided to distinguish between the different ones learnt after the L1(s), using the traditional order of acquisition of the languages. The reason is practical rather than theoretical. As the main instrument for data collection was a web questionnaire, it became imperative to keep the length down, and make it as simple as possible (see the chapter on methodology). The same questions were thus repeated for every language, according to their order of acquisition (L1, L2, L3, L4, L5). The data thus collected allow comparisons between languages, as well as separate analyses on the effect of various independent variables. A linguistic background question on the onset of acquisition of every language made it possible to identify participants who had acquired languages simultaneously.

I will be using the term "LX" to refer non-specifically to one of the languages of the multilinguals learnt after an L1 had been established. To avoid the use of the rather lengthy formula "bi- and multilinguals", I will generally refer to them as multilinguals, even though multilinguals are usually defined as knowing three or more languages (Hammarberg, 2009: 6). The terms "L1, L2, L3, L4, L5" will be used whenever more specificity on a particular language is needed, while keeping in mind that this classification forces an individual' s complex linguistic biography into a Procrustean bed. When considering the number of languages as an independent variable, I will use the more specific terms "bilinguals", "trilinguals", "quadrilinguals" and "pentalinguals".

All participants in the study will be referred to as multicompetent "LX users", "exploiting whatever linguistic resources they have for real-life purposes" (Cook, 2002: 10). Cook's (1991) notion of "multicompetence" is extremely useful because it considers the knowledge of multilinguals as an integrated "compound state of a mind with two grammars" (Cook 1991: 112). In a later publication, Cook expanded the definition of multicompetence, describing it as the "knowledge of two or more languages in one mind" (Cook, 2003: 2). He pointed out:

> Since the first language and the other language or languages are in the same mind, they must form a language super-system at some level rather than be completely isolated systems.

In other words, an individual's knowledge of two languages will be different from that of monolinguals in those two languages. Moreover, any newly acquired language will affect the use of the other languages (Cook, 2003).

A final distinction that needs to be highlighted is the opposition between native speaker (NS) and Non-native speaker (NNS). Multicompetence led Cook (1999) to a re-evaluation of the concept of the NS. Cook observed that in Second Language Acquisition (SLA) research, L2 users' performance was almost always compared with that of the NS, whether overtly or covertly.

This monolingual bias has been strongly criticised (see also Pavlenko, 2005), as indeed LX users should be not be considered as deficient users of a language. I will occasionally use the distinction when discussing existing research, but the design of the empirical study is not based on this categorical distinction (see the chapter on methodology). I see the NS as someone who learnt a language in early childhood, who continued using the language regularly, and who is recognised by other NSs as belonging to their speech community.

I am specifically interested in two dimensions of emotion in an LX. First, I will consider the experiences of LX users in their communication of positive and negative emotions in LXs. I am certainly not claiming that there is a one-to-one association between one set of emotions in one language and another set in another language. I will focus on how multilinguals express emotions differently in different languages. Second, I will look at the affective factors linked to the use of LXs and try to identify those that influence them.

The communication of emotion in an LX can be particularly difficult because LX learners and users may not have the linguistic and pragmatic means to express the full range of their emotions in a way that would satisfy their communicative needs and be considered appropriate by their interlocutors (Dewaele, 2008a). It usually takes some time before LX users can be relatively confident that their communicative intentions in expressing emotions will be correctly decoded and that their capacity to infer the emotions expressed by their interlocutors is sufficient. I have underlined the need for longitudinal studies on affective socialisation in an LX and on the rate of conceptual development in adulthood (Dewaele, 2008b).

Metaphorically the communication of emotion in an LX could be compared to trying to hold a bar of soap in a bathtub. It requires a relentless effort to overcome multiple failures and to achieve smooth emotional interactions. The difficulty lies in the fact that communicating emotions in an LX, i.e. with limited communicative competence, is very hard because as L1 users we are usually able to express our own emotions precisely, and we want to be able to understand other people's emotions unerringly. Understanding emotional outbursts in a listener's LX may also be more difficult because they may contain less conventional implicatures that are more difficult and take longer to interpret than more conventional ones. Taguchi (2005) reported that there is a strong proficiency effect for accuracy in interpretation of both types of implicature.

My colleagues and I have argued that knowledge of the degree of emotionality of a word and of its affective valence is just as important as knowledge of that word's grammatical class, or its gender (Altarriba and Bauer, 2004; Dewaele, 2008b; Pavlenko, 2005, 2008a). An inaccurate or incomplete understanding of the emotionality and valence of an emotion word, or an emotion-laden word, in the LX might have unwanted illocutionary effects

(Sbisa, 2001), which might be far more embarrassing than phonological, morphological or syntactical errors (Dewaele, 2008b).

Fussell's (2002) insistence on the importance of expressing and understanding emotions "well" explains why expressing emotions in an LX is probably the ultimate challenge for LX learners and LX users. An LX learner who uses that LX for the first time outside the comforting walls of the classroom soon realises that conversations about emotional topics that never posed a problem in the L1 suddenly become fraught with obstacles in authentic interactions, specifically with NSs. Communicating with NSs who may speak a local dialect, who do not make a special effort to articulate clearly and who speak too quickly, can be discouraging to the new LX user. An NS may not realise, or simply not care, that the NNS seems to have trouble following him/her. The new LX user is therefore forced to sink or swim from the moment of his/her first authentic interaction. If the emotion is not expressed as would be expected by NSs, the LX user might be misunderstood. I pointed out in Dewaele (2008a) that NSs themselves could consciously deviate from the norm when expressing emotions but that this did not have the same pragmatic consequences as for LX users.

Since LX users are legitimate, multicompetent users of an LX, it seems only fair to grant them the right to deviate from the L1 norm as NSs enjoy. As an LX user of English, I could not agree more. However, I have realised that my LX user's sense of being a legitimate language user has not always been shared my British interlocutors. I discovered that NSs do not always perceive and interpret LX users' deviations from the NS norm in the same way as deviations by L1 users. An utterance, a swearword or a risqué joke uttered by an NS may be judged appropriate by NS peers, but the same words in the mouth of someone who sounds foreign risk being judged as inappropriate or even gross by NS interlocutors.

I experienced this "double standard" when using a swearword in Spanish (my L4) with Spanish friends at a doctoral course during a night out in Malaga. Wine and swearwords had been flowing freely all evening, yet when – after considerable internal deliberation – I uttered the highly common swearword "joder" ("fuck") to show my strong feelings on a topic, my friends looked at me in stunned silence. They explained that my swearword sounded "funny" in their ears and that I should not use it (Dewaele, 2004b: 85). In other words, the word that they had used all evening was deemed inappropriate and off-limits when it came from me. My first thought was that this was totally unfair. Why could NSs use swearwords in their L1 without batting an eyelid and yet deem my own use of these words inappropriate? I later realised that foreign language users do not enjoy the same pragmatic and discursive freedom as NSs. Violations of the norm are interpreted differently when they are committed by a member of the in-group rather than by an LX user with a foreign accent. I encountered similar reactions in the UK when I ventured some sarcastic remarks to my neighbour – a well-educated, white, native English lady about the sudden mass hysteria surrounding the death of Princess Diana. My neighbour warned me sternly to avoid making jokes about something I could not possibly understand as a foreigner.

It thus seems that even when an LX user has the linguistic and sociopragmatic means to produce a conscious deviation from the TL norm for some special effect, or some violation of "politically correct" ways of thinking and speaking, an NS may judge it differently than a comparable deviation by a fellow NS and may assume that the LX user does not grasp the full meaning of his/her words. In sum, LX users have less latitude compared to L1 users in deviations from the L1 norm (Dewaele, 2008a).

So far I have only discussed the challenge of communicating emotions in LXs. Taking a completely different perspective, the emotions that underlie the learning of LX s and their subsequent use can also be considered. Daniel Everret's story about his experience among the Pirahas is a nice illustration of the fact that language learning itself can create intense emotion because of the close connection between language, culture and identity (Noels, Pon and Clément, 1996).

MacIntyre (2002) observes that emotion has not been given sufficient attention in the second language learning literature, with the exception of the study of language anxiety. He argues that: "emotion just might be the fundamental basis of motivation, one deserving far greater attention in the language learning domain" (p. 45).

Indeed, applied linguists have focused only on specific emotions that might be linked to the successful acquisition and subsequent use of the LX (Dörnyei, 2005; Gardner, 1985; Shoaib and Dörnyei, 2005; Skehan, 1989; Dörnyei and Ushioda, 2009). The concepts that have been examined most thoroughly are attitudes toward the LX, motivation to study the LX and anxiety in using the LX. Variations in attitudes, motivation and communicative anxiety have been linked to differences in progress and ultimate attainment in the LX.

The reasons why learners differ in degree of passion, dedication, motivation and fear of using the LX are complex and multifaceted (Dewaele, 2009d; Pavlenko, 2013). As MacIntyre (2002: 60) points out: "the link between motivation and emotion is strong, intricate and fascinating". Some reasons are obvious, such as the learning situation (it is hard to develop a passion for an LX if the only source of that language is a hated teacher), while others are more subtle and linked to the general sociopolitical climate, to historical events and to direct and indirect contact with the LX (teachers' and parents' accounts of what the LX speakers and their cultures are like) (Csizér and Kormos, 2009).

Attitudes toward the LX can also be affected by random events. Indeed, some learners may have experienced an unexpected "trigger event" that suddenly pushed the learning of the LX to the number one priority. Others may not have experienced such an event and therefore muddled on at a much slower pace without much passion and without too much worry about the ultimate goal. Novels and autobiographical texts offer us some excellent insights and illustrations about the contradicting emotions that an LX learner or user can experience when coming into contact with an LX, and then using it for authentic communication.

Pascal Mercier (2007) describes such an event in his novel *Night Train to Lisbon*. His main character, Raimund Gregorius, is a Swiss-German teacher of Latin, ancient Greek and Hebrew with little interest in modern languages. He loved Latin sentences "because they bore the calm of everything past. Because they didn't make you say something". (p. 15). His former wife, Florence, was a fluent speaker of Spanish but when hearing her speaking Spanish on the phone "he had to close the door" (id.). However, one morning on his way to school, he encounters a mysterious woman about to jump off a bridge. He manages to distract her and after an initial conversation in French, he asks her what her mother tongue is. The answer: "*Português*" has the effect of a magical formula on him: "The *o* she pronounced surprisingly as a *u*; the rising, strangely constrained lightness of the *é* and the soft *sh* at the end came together in a melody that sounded much longer than it really was, and he could have listened to all day long" (p. 7). The moment marks a milestone in his life and the start of his infatuation with Portuguese. Listening to the first record of a Portuguese language course at home "he repeated the same sentences again and again to narrow the distance between his stolid enunciation and the twinkling voice on the record"(p. 22). His rapid progress in Portuguese also alters his perception of the language: "*Português*. How different the word sounded now! Before it had possessed the magic of a jewel from a distant inaccessible land and now it was like one of a thousand gems in a palace whose door he had just pushed open" (p. 23). Gregorius abandons his former life in dramatic fashion and embarks on a journey to Lisbon, where he is forced to develop his basic Portuguese interlanguage quickly in order to find out more about the author of the amazing second-hand book he bought earlier in his hometown. He manages to overcome his communicative anxiety in Portuguese and becomes both braver and wiser as a person.

Emotion is thus clearly the driving force behind Raimund Gregorius' acquisition of Portuguese. His passion for Portuguese pushes him forward on the way to mastery of the language, but it also alters his sense of self. He is exhilarated and experiences a great liberation from self-imposed limitation. Indeed, learning a new language is like opening a new window on an unseen, and maybe even unimagined, part of the world. By doing so, a learner realises that the experience of learning a new language and a new culture is likely to open his/her mind and to alter his view of the world and of other cultures. This may be a slightly scary experience. Guiora et al., (1975) pointed out that one's language ego in a first language is shattered in the face of an empathetic relationship with a foreign language: "To speak a second language authentically is to take on a new identity. As with empathy, it is to step into a new and perhaps unfamiliar pair of shoes" (p. 48).

Fear, frustration, anxiety in the LX

The burning question is thus how LX users express their emotions "appropriately" in an LX when their blood is boiling with love or anger or frozen by frustration and despair? In this section I will present a few short examples of the types of difficulties LX users may encounter in communicating these specific emotions.

While fear is generally considered as a basic emotion, anxiety is not. However, it is this complex interaction of negative emotions and feelings that Eva Hoffman describes in her autobiography *Lost in translation: A life in a new language* (1989). Eva was born in Krakow, Poland and emigrated with her family to Canada in 1959 at the age of 13. She deeply regrets the loss of her sophisticated and confident Polish self in her interactions with native speakers of English. Speaking English shortly after her arrival fills her with dread, fear and rage. She is particularly incensed about her loss of control over her voice, and, as a consequence suffers from this (temporary) social handicap:

> It takes all my will to impose any control on the sounds that emerge from me. I have to form entire sentences before uttering them; otherwise, I too easily get lost in the middle. My speech, I sense, sounds monotonous, deliberate, heavy – an aural mask that doesn't become or express me at all. (...) I don't try to tell jokes too often, I don't know the slang, I have no cool repartee. I love language too much to maul its beats, and my pride is too quick to risk the incomprehension that greets such forays. I become a very serious young person (...). I am enraged at the false persona I'm being stuffed into, as into some clumsy and overblown astronaut suit. I'm enraged at my adolescent friends because they can't see through the guise, can't recognize the light-footed dancer I really am. (pp. 118–119)

Eva Hoffman did overcome her fear and anxiety in English: she obtained a PhD in the United States, became editor for *The New York Times*, published several books in English and settled down in Hampstead, in London, UK.

Jemma, one of the British participants in our web questionnaire (Dewaele and Pavlenko, 2001–2003), relates a similar experience of fear and frustration after being plunged in a new linguistic and cultural environment. She arrived in Germany for a year of study abroad after years of formal instruction in German at university. She reports:

> During my year in Germany I felt for the first few months that I had completely lost my identity. I was slow to understand, I could not express precisely what I meant and could not shape my verbal persona nor could

> I make jokes or entertaining remarks as I had no shared frame of context. I felt alienated and painfully frustrated and became very depressed. By the time I had finished my year however, I had sufficient command of the language to express myself and my character, to make jokes and even use comic catchphrases.

After the initial shock, Jemma seems to have been able to overcome her communicative deficit and her sense of alienation. This phenomenon is well documented by researchers working within a post-modern perspective. Study abroad has been described as an "identity-destabilizing" experience (Block, 2002, 2009; Kinginger 2008, 2009). Jemma gradually became more fluent in German and her lack of an affective repertoire became her focus of attention. She claims to have eventually overcome this hurdle as she developed an ability to communicate her feelings "appropriately" and to project a more accurate image of herself. Jemma's socialisation in German allowed her to recognise cues to communication of emotions in her interlocutors' behaviour and she became able to express her own feelings in ways that were considered appropriate by Germans (cf. Schiefflin and Ochs, 1986).

Love in the LX

The one thing that nobody would wish to get wrong is a declaration of love. Yet, this is exactly what happened to the young Milan Kundera, the successful Czech novelist who lives in Paris and writes in both French and Czech. In his book *L'immortalité,* he reminisces about a particularly embarrassing episode in which, as a young man with good "high school" French, but a limited grasp of sociocultural conventions and pragmatic rules in French, he mistook a standard politeness formula at the end of a letter, addressed to him by a female secretary working for the publishing house Gallimard, for a genuine declaration of love:

> Pour conclure une lettre, un Français vous écrit "Veuillez agréer, cher Monsieur, l'assurance de mes sentiments distingués". Quand j'ai reçu pour la première fois une telle lettre, signée par une secrétaire des Editions Gallimard, je vivais encore à Prague. De joie, j'ai sauté au plafond: à Paris, il y a une femme qui m'aime! Elle a réussi, dans les dernières lignes d'une lettre officielle, à glisser une déclaration d'amour! Non seulement elle éprouve pour moi des sentiments, mais elle souligne expressément qu'ils sont distingués! Jamais une Tchèque ne m'a rien dit de pareil! Bien plus tard, quand je me suis installé à Paris, on m'a expliqué que la pratique épistolaire offre tout un éventail sémantique de formules de politesse; elle permettent à un Français de choisir, avec une précision de pharmacien, le sentiment qu'il veut, sans l'éprouver, exprimer au destinataire; dans ce très large choix, les "sentiments distingués" représentent le plus bas

> degré de la politesse administrative, confinant presque au mépris. (Milan Kundera, 1990 : 242_243)
>
> [To conclude a letter, the French write "Please accept, dear sir, the assurance of my distinguished feelings". When I first received such a letter, signed by a secretary from the publisher Gallimard, I was still living in Prague. I jumped for joy: in Paris, a woman loves me! She managed to insert a declaration of love into the last lines of an official letter! Not only does she harbour feelings for me, but she states explicitly that these feelings are distinguished! Never before had any Czech woman told me anything similar! Much later, once I was settled in Paris, I was told that a whole semantic range of politeness formulas are used in correspondence; they allow the French to choose, with the precision of a pharmacist, which feeling they wish to express to the addressee – without actually experiencing it. In this vast assortment, the "distinguished feelings" represents the lowest degree of administrative politeness, close even to contempt.]

Love is one of a series of emotions that all humans share but it may resist exact linguistic translation because of the uniqueness of the specific verbal and non-verbal manifestations and expressions across languages and cultures (Altarriba 2003; Derné, 1994). Communicating love and recognising an emotion script of love in an LX is therefore extra challenging if it has to be channelled through narrow and imperfect discourse. Individuals do not like to be too obvious, and may have secret communicative intentions. If the secret intention is to make someone fall in love with you, you will try to create a favourable impression through a variety of verbal and non-verbal means. In other words, there is no immediately identifiable "love" script.

What may be produced is an idiosyncratic blend of apologies, jokes, compliments, gazes, sighs and touches, but the word "love" itself might not be uttered.

Anger in the LX

Do L2 users have a preferred language for angry outbursts? Can they "channel" angry feelings into any language in which they are proficient with equal ease? Bilinguals' autobiographies suggest that there are constraints in language choice for the expression of anger. One such author, Nancy Huston, a Canadian from Calgary who as a young adult went to Paris, where she stayed and published a string of novels in French, notes the following about the expression of anger in an LX:

> (...) il y a toujours quelque chose de ridicule à s'emporter dans une langue étrangère: l'accent s'empire, le débit s'emballe et s'achoppe... on emploie

> les jurons à tort et a travers – et, du coup, on doit s'ingénier à trouver des moyens plus raffinés pour exprimer sa colère". (Huston and Sebbar, 1986: 23)
>
> [there is always something ridiculous about getting carried away in a foreign language: the accent gets worse, the rhythm runs off and stumbles ... you use the wrong swear words in the wrong way – and, as a result, you have to work at finding more refined ways to express your anger]. (the quote and its translation come from the study on Huston by Kinginger, 2004b: 172)

I have shared Huston's views on the difficulty of expressing anger in an LX since the following personal experience reported in Dewaele (2006: 119). Coming back from the Second International Vigo Conference on Bilingualism in 2002, I found out that flights out of Vigo were delayed because of dense fog. In order to catch a connecting flight to Madrid a colleague and I were advised to take a taxi, and we were driven at high speed to the nearest airport, Porto, across the Portuguese border. We arrived at the gate a few minutes before the plane's take-off. My colleague went through unhindered after waving his ticket but I wasn't so lucky. My ticket lacked a validation code, which meant that I couldn't board the plane to Madrid. Fuming, I went to the Iberia counter to complain. After a halting start in Spanish (which I had been using a lot in the previous days), I realised that my boiling frustration and indignation could not be channelled into proper Spanish sentences. Although I would have preferred French or Dutch, I decided to switch to English, the language of my daily professional and social life, in which I could express anger much more appropriately. Thinking back to that episode, I realise that I lacked the specific script for anger in Spanish and that also I lacked the fluency needed to gain the upper hand in this linguistic confrontation. Listening to my halting sentences in Spanish, I realised that my grammatical, lexical and sociopragmatic errors would undermine the pragmatic effects I was seeking, i.e. an apology from the Iberia representative and an offer for help to catch a different flight (which I did get in the end). I realised in a flash that I could not project the image of a legitimately angry customer demanding compensation in Spanish. I certainly did not want to be perceived as an abusive foreigner, to whom all assistance would be refused and who might even end up in jail for inappropriate language and behaviour, hence the switch to a safe "middle ground" for my interlocutor and myself, i.e. English. When engaging in a linguistic confrontation, one needs to be quite sure of oneself, linguistically, culturally and pragmatically. Rusty armour with chinks is worthless (Dewaele, 2006: 119).

The anecdotes presented so far offer a glimpse of the complex issues underlying both the emotions of foreign language learners and users and the specific problem of recognising and expressing positive and negative emotions in an LX. I will attempt to present these issues in a more systematic way in the following chapters by relying on empirical data that I collected with the help of my colleague Aneta Pavlenko (Dewaele and Pavlenko, 2001–2003).

Overview of the book

The field of emotions in LXs is by nature highly interdisciplinary including neurobiology, psycho-evolutionary theory, cognitive psychology, social and cultural psychology, anthropology, cognitive linguistics and various areas of applied linguistics and multilingualism research, pedagogy, didactics and literary research. As an applied linguist, I will adopt an applied linguistic perspective and point to concepts and theories from adjacent areas that can shed light on the phenomena under consideration.

Chapter 1 starts off with a brief presentation of different areas of research into emotion in monolingual and multilingual contexts. The word "monolingual" does rarely occur in the research literature, because monolingualism is generally assumed to be the default setting and researchers assume that the language issue is unrelated to the study of emotion. Pavlenko (2005) has strongly criticised this monolingual bias in emotion research. I will point to neurobiological research in this area, to social constructivist approaches and to the work of cultural psychologists. The review of neurobiological literature will be short because it belongs to a strand of research that is quite separate from the one in which the present study is situated. Indeed, I will not focus on physiological measures in reaction to certain language stimuli, but rather on self-reports from multilinguals about their expression of emotions in different languages.

After that, I will briefly mention some of the seminal research on the emotions of LX learners and on the specific area of the communication of emotions in an LX. This chapter is relatively short because I felt that it would be more appropriate to present specific literature reviews at the start of every chapter.

Chapter 2 discusses the epistemological and methodological issues that guided my research on emotion and LXs. This includes a discussion of the advantages and disadvantages of emic and etic perspectives, of qualitative versus quantitative research, of the dilemma that researchers face of whether to focus on individuals or groups and finally of the benefits of interdisciplinarity in the field of emotions and LXs.

Chapter 3 presents the sources of data and the sociobiographical profiles of the participants who provided the data on which the analyses will be based. This includes the *Bilingualism and Emotion Questionnaire* (Dewaele and Pavlenko, 2001–2003) and the *Multilingual Lives* interview corpus. It also includes a reflection on the advantages and disadvantages of using web-based questionnaires to collect data. The chapter concludes with a presentation of the general research question and nine hypotheses that will be tested in the following chapters.

Chapter 4 lays out the different independent variables that have been selected for the analyses. A first cluster comprises the "history of learning" variables such as the chronology of acquisition of different languages and resulting number of languages known, age of onset of learning the various languages and the context in which these languages were acquired. A second cluster consists of "current practice" variables such as frequency of use of the language and the network of interlocutors. A third cluster contains sociobiographical and psychological variables such as gender, age, education level and trait Emotional Intelligence.

Chapter 5 introduces the analyses of the first dependent variable, self-perceived competence in speaking, comprehending, reading and writing in the LXs.

Chapter 6 looks at the effect of the independent variables on the communication of feelings in LXs.

Chapter 7 focuses on individual variations in frequency of choice of LX for communicating one particular emotion, namely anger, including swearing.

Chapter 8 considers individual variation in participants' attitudes toward their different languages and the perception they have of the emotional force of swearwords in these different languages.

Chapter 9 looks at the emotions that LX users experience when using the LX, and more specifically foreign language anxiety. Here again the various hypotheses about the effect of the independent variables are tested.

Chapter 10 differs from the previous chapters in that it does not look at individual variations within a single language but rather at intra-individual variations, namely the self-reported frequency of code-switching in different situations while discussing emotional and non-emotional topics.

Chapter 11 recapitulates the findings from the different chapters in a more general discussion about possible causes for the variation patterns that were observed in the data. It also presents some tentative implications of the findings for the teaching of foreign languages and concludes with a brief reflection about the strengths and limitations of the research design.

1
Perspectives on Emotion

We may have an intuitive understanding of emotions, but their sheer complexity makes them difficult to define. What exactly is an emotion? Should it be differentiated from cognition? Can emotions be measured through observation of brain and body? These three questions have been hotly debated in the research literature. According to some, the differentiation between cognition and emotion is becoming more and more foggy, and underlines the need for new, less fuzzy, concepts (Rimé, 2009). Other researchers hold on to a more traditional Western view of "emotion as physicality", and "emotion as natural fact" (Lutz, 1986: 294–295). Those who adopt an empirical view of emotion, as Solomon (2003: 119) puts it, are "desperate for the observables and something to measure".

The neurobiological perspective

Unsurprisingly, empiricists are mostly found within the discipline of affective neuroscience that is concerned with the neural and neurochemical mechanisms underlying emotion and mood (Borod, 2000; Dalgleish, Dunn and Mobbs, 2009). The neurologists try to distinguish emotional from cognitive processes, arguing that to make progress in understanding the neurobiological nature of emotions experimental strategies need to be used that are different from those that are common in cognitive science (Panksepp, 1998, 2003). In a review of the research in the field, Panksepp (2000) suggests that the neurobiological systems that mediate the basic emotions (anger, fear, surprise, sadness, joy, disgust) are constituted of genetically coded, but experientially refined executive circuits situated in subcortical areas of the brain (specifically the prefrontal dorsolateral cortex) that can coordinate the behavioural, physiological and psychological processes that need to be recruited to cope with a variety of survival needs and that provide the individual with fundamental values for the guidance of behaviour. Several parts of the subcortex having been identified as playing a part in processing emotions: the hippocampus, the thalamus, the hypothalamus and the amygdala (Dalgleish, Dunn and Mobbs, 2009; Goldberg, 2006; LeDoux, 1996; Rosenthal, 2002).

The role of the hippocampus has been reconsidered after research by LeDoux (1996) suggested that it is more involved in registering and decoding perceptual patterns. It does however process emotional meaning, and is involved in learning (Fanselow, 1999; Goldberg, 2006) as it transfers information to the long-term memory (LeDoux, 1996; Linden, 2007).

The hypothalamus regulates autonomic and endocrine functions (Linden, 2007) and controls the body's fight-or-flight response (Linden, 2007; Rosenthal, 2002). It is also the control centre of gender-related behaviour and aggression (Linden, 2007).

The thalamus transmits sensory information between the cerebrum and the body's muscles (Linden, 2007). It shares a nerve knot with the hippocampus, namely the two amygdalae, which are responsible for emotions and anxiety (Goldberg, 2006). The amygdalae judge emotions expressed in voices and faces extremely fast (LeDoux, 2002). They play an important role in supplying unattended and attended emotional stimuli in working memory (LeDoux, 2002) and have therefore been dubbed man's warehouse of unconscious emotional memory (LeDoux, 1996). LeDoux describes the amygdala as the brain's emotional sentinel (LeDoux, 1996, 2002). The prefrontal lobes of the neocortex control the amygdala. The prefrontal lobes, decision-taking centres, can dampen the strong emotional impulses through rational, cognitive analysis, allowing the individual to reappraise the situation and adapt his/her reactions (LeDoux, 2002).

Harré (2009) argues that the study of emotions is interdisciplinary because it links cognitive, cultural and physiological phenomena. He sees emotions as "cognitive-affective-somatic hybrids", in other words, emotions involve "bodily perturbations, judgements of meanings, and the social force of emotion displays" (p. 294).

Research on the conceptualisation and expression of emotion has revealed that descriptions of emotional experience correspond with "bodily perturbations", i.e. physiological changes (i.e. autonomic and somatic activity levels) associated with emotional arousal. Harris (2004) argues that this "brain-based" perspective has a heuristic value as incongruence between psychophysiological measures and the subjective reports "would falsify the brain-based perspective or would force one to develop an explanation for why subjective and physiological reports differed" (p. 225). The present study is based on the assumption that a physiological link exists between basic emotions and the language that codes and expresses them.

A cognitive linguistic approach

A debate has been raging between researchers who defend a more universalist perspective on emotions and others who feel that emotions should be investigated using a more relativist perspective, with a focus on the differences across languages and cultures (Pavlenko, 2008a). These researchers typically view emotions as an assortment of socially and culturally shared scripts, which allow members of different cultures to differentially interpret similar physiological, subjective and behavioural processes. This view is well captured by Michelle Rosaldo, for whom emotions are "self-concerning, partly physical responses that are at the same time aspects of a moral and ideological attitude; emotions are both feelings and cognitive constructions, linking person, action, and sociological milieu" (cited by Levy, 1983, p. 128).

Wierzbicka and Harkins (2001) accept that technological advances allow researchers to identify with increasing detail the areas of the brain and the specific wave patterns that are linked with emotional states. Yet they express concern about the fact that the outcomes of this research, carried out in predominantly English-speaking research environments, are seen as universal, not just applicable to speakers of a particular language or members of a particular cultural group. The authors do not deny that emotions are linked to physiological processes, but stress that the study of emotions needs input from a variety of languages. Language plays a crucial role because "whatever the conditions that produce an emotion like anger, whether or not it is visibly expressed, and whatever physiological responses accompany it, it is only through language (if at all) that we can know that what is experienced is anger" (pp. 2–3).

In other words, cognitive linguists do not reject the idea that emotions have a physiological substrate. Rather, they argue that despite the degree of technical sophistication in research into the neuropsychology of human emotion, researchers seem unaware of absolutising their own language (with its built-in culture and concepts), i.e. of making universal claims on the basis of language-specific categories, whether cognitive or cultural or both. As a consequence, writes Ye (2001), they are like a frog in a well (*jingdiziwa*, a Chinese idiomatic expression), unable to jump out and seeing only "the little circle of sky above his well, imagining it to be the whole world" (p. 359). These Anglophone researchers tend to forget that the walls of the well are built with the bricks of specifically Anglophone values and judgements.

Wierzbicka and Harkins (2001) accept that there may be a basic human experience of something like "anger", yet argue that it would be problematic to claim that such an experience would be precisely equivalent to the English "anger", or to its translation equivalents or synonyms in other languages. They also point to the inherent variability in emotional responses between people in similar contexts: what one person might find harmless could be perceived as offensive by another. Even a single individual might react differently at different moments in time.

Moreover, the way emotions are displayed is highly variable: "one may turn red with anger, glower and shout in one situation and appear white-faced, expressionless and icily polite in another" (Wierzbicka and Harkins,

2001: 2). It is not clear whether neurological patterns are similar in both cases. This variation in the display of emotions is also linked to social and cultural factors.

Cultural psychological approaches

Markus and Kitayama (1991) are also situated within the "relativist camp". They link differences in the display of emotion between Eastern and Western societies to different views of the self: "While in the West the self is viewed as independent, self-contained, and autonomous, it is considered interdependent in Asian, African, Latin-American and many southern European cultures" (p. 225). For those with independent selves, emotional expressions may literally "express" or reveal the inner feelings such as anger, sadness and fear. For those with interdependent selves, however, an emotional expression may more often be regarded as a public instrumental action that may or may not be related directly to the inner feelings (p. 236). While in the West emotions that derive from and promote an independent view of the self can be openly displayed, in societies where the self is considered interdependent, overt expression of emotion is avoided (p. 236). While in Western society showing anger can be appropriate, "in Japanese society, the overt expression of anger and verbal attack is interpreted as evidence of immaturity and childishness" (p. 281). It is important to point out that this reference to "the West" is a generalisation, as there are cultural differences in the display of emotions, i.e. between the allegedly more reserved British, for example, and the more jovial Irish.

A social constructivist approach

Equally relativist is the social constructivist approach defended by Averill (1982). He proposes "to situate the emotions within the hierarchy of behavioral systems" (p. 4). He opposes those researchers who base their definition of emotion on some essential characteristic such as "a pattern of physiological arousal, a neurological circuit, a feeling or even a kind of cognitive appraisal" (p. 4). He points out that emotions can be analysed at social, psychological and/or biological levels: "at each level, it is also possible to distinguish broader systems of behaviour, of which emotions are part. Thus, we can analyze the emotions in relation to social systems, psychological systems and biological systems" (p. 19). In his constructivist approach, Averill emphasises the social level of analysis. He presents the following definition of emotions: "emotions may be defined as socially constituted syndromes (transitory social roles) which include an individual's appraisal of the situation and which are interpreted as passions rather than as actions" (p. 6). Averill does not use the word "syndrome" in a pathological sense, but rather with the meaning of "subsystem of behaviour". These subsystems are composed of elements: "physiological changes, expressive reactions, instrumental responses, and subjective feelings" (p. 19). He distinguishes emotions from other transitory social roles on the basis of the cognitive appraisals involved: "each emotion is based on a particular set of appraisals or evaluative judgements" (p. 19). He also distinguishes emotions from other social roles because he interprets them as passions rather than as actions.

Averill also distinguishes between three broad (and idealised) classes of emotion: impulsive, transcendental and conflictive emotional states. Anger belongs in the last category. He warns however that "an emotion is not just the sum of its parts" (p. 19) and that, as a consequence, the grounds are never sufficient in themselves for attribution of emotion: "The attribution of emotion also depends on the nature of the appraised object and on the meaning of the emotional role (i.e. how the emotional role relates to broader systems of behaviour, primarily at the social level of analysis)" (p. 19). Averill further argues that emotions reflect "the thought of an epoch, the secret of a civilisation. It follows that to understand the meaning of an emotion is to understand the relevant aspect of the sociocultural system of which the emotion is a part (subsystem)" (p. 24).

Social constructivist theorists tend to criticise universalist approaches by emphasising variability instead of common response (Barrett, 2006).

The emotions of LX learners and users

While emotion has been considered in functional and anthropological linguistics (Hymes, 1972; Sapir, 1921), emotion has received relatively little attention in the SLA literature (see however Brown, 1973; Curran, 1976; Krashen, 1981; MacIntyre, 2002; Rintell, 1990). Scovel (1978) pointed out that the role of affect in SLA is probably the least understood. A major textbook in SLA, Gass and Selinker (2008), devotes only a portion of one chapter (out of a total of 14) to affect and motivation, while Doughty and Long (2003) in their handbook of cognitive approaches to SLA, chose not include a single chapter on the role of emotion in language acquisition.

The only "emotional" variable to have been extensively researched in SLA is language learning motivation (cf. Dai and Sternberg, 2004; Gardner and Lambert, 1959). The crucial antecedent for motivation is generally considered to be attitudes and direct or indirect intercultural contact (Csizér and Kormos, 2008). However, MacIntyre (2002) has argued that that attitudes alone are not sufficient to support motivation, and that in order to understand the differences between the engaged and the non-engaged learner researchers need to delve into the emotions students experience during language learning. MacIntyre concludes that: "a better understanding of emotion has the capacity to explain cases where students endorse orientations but might not be energized to take action, and also cases where action is prevented by emotional arousal, either present or anticipated"

(2002: 63). MacIntyre and Gregersen (2012, p. 193) argue that "positive emotion facilitates the building of resources because positive emotion tends to broaden a person's perspective, opening the individual to absorb the language". They conclude that: "The emotion system is an engine for the positive-broadening power of the imagination" (p. 193).

Schumann (1997) has delved into the possible neurobiological substrate of motivation and affect. He points out that an individual's development of preferences and aversions constitutes a subform of experiential selection. Any individual is born with innate biases such as homeostatic value (i.e. maintaining stability in bodily systems, regulating hunger, thirst, ...) and sociostatic value (the tendency for all humans to seek out facial, vocal and tactile contact, as well as interaction with others). These innate, survival-enhancing tendencies lead to the formation of preferences and aversions (Schumann, 1997). Schumann (1997) argues that it is this sociostatic bias that prepares human infants to acquire language by making the voices and faces of caregivers targets of automatic attention. According to Schumann, these preferences and aversions are not innate, but are acquired during the life time of the individual. This value system or stimulus appraisal system (Leventhal and Scherer, 1987; Schumann, 1997) assesses internal and environmental stimuli on the basis of five criteria: novelty, pleasantness, goal significance, self and social image and coping potential (Schumann, 2004). This appraisal system is centred specifically in the amygdala and the orbitofrontal cortex (Rolls, 1999; Schumann, 1997). An individual remembers affective reactions to agents, events and objects, and can use that information to evaluate future stimuli (Leventhal, 1984). The uniqueness of each person's experience leads to highly variable neural preference systems across individuals (Schumann, 1997, 2004). Affective appraisal is thus at the core of cognition, and it drives the decision-making processes. Emotion is thus at the basis of any learning, or absence of learning. When a stimulus is positively assessed in a learning situation, it will have a positive effect on the amount of attention and effort a learner will be prepared to devote to it. It will also encourage the learner to approach similar stimuli in the future. However, when a stimulus is negatively assessed in a learning situation, less attention and effort will be devoted to it, and negative affective assessment may promote avoidance in the future. In other words, "patterns of appraisal may underlie what has been considered motivation in SLA" (Schumann, 1997: 8). Schumann saw the foreign language classroom as a typical environment of sociostatic regulation. Relations between teacher and students, but also between students, affect their sense of well being. A good classroom atmosphere might enhance students' desire to create and preserve these particular social affiliations. On the other hand, a bad atmosphere might be interpreted by students as threatening and might push them toward ending their membership of that classroom community (Schumann, 1997).

It is therefore not surprising that researchers in SLA and in language teaching research have focused on ways to create a positive learning environment in order to enhance language learning motivation. Different elements have been singled out as playing crucial parts in creating a well-functioning classroom community: the teacher's personality, ideology and pedagogical approach (Dörnyei, 2001; Ewald, 2007; Frantzen and Magnan, 2005; von Wörde, 2003; Williams and Burden, 1997). The progress of an L2 learner could be linked to the chemistry that develops between the learner, the group of learners and the teacher. Borg (2006) investigated the specific traits exhibited by effective language teachers. One crucial trait was "an ability to communicate freely and to radiate positive feeling" (p. 23). An ability to develop close relationships with students was also reported as a particular trait shared by effective language teachers (Borg, 2006). This finding reflects the conclusion of an earlier study on effective teachers of all subjects, namely their ability to create a supportive and caring emotional environment (Walls, Nardi, von Minden and Hoffman, 2002). Pedagogical practices and classroom environment have also been linked to students' motivation levels. Pertinent and appealing subject matters combined with non-threatening techniques create a positive language learning experience, support and promote group solidarity and lower levels of FLA in the classroom (Arnold, 2011; Chambers, 1999; Dörnyei, 2001; Ewald, 2007, von Wörde, 2003; Williams, Burden, Poulet and Maun, 2004).

Garrett and Young (2009) present an analysis of the testimony of the former who reported on her own learning process during a Portuguese course for beginners to the latter, in order to understand her "affective responses to the language learning process, the events from which her affect sprang, and her affective trajectory over the 8 weeks" (p. 209).

The authors point out that their study is original in the sense that previous longitudinal research on individual language learners typically focused on the development of linguistic ability or communicative competence in the target language rather than on emotion (p. 220). Garrett's affective responses to events were categorised into four groups: (a) her awareness of her own knowledge of Portuguese, (b) her own professional teacher's voice, (c) her responses to the Brazilian culture to which she was exposed and (d) social relations with other students and teacher (pp. 212–213). Quantitative analysis revealed that Garrett's remarks centred on social relations, followed by her teacher's voice, linguistic aspects of Portuguese and cultural information. Only the comments on cultural aspects were overwhelmingly positive; the comments in the other categories were more evenly divided (p. 213).

One striking finding is how dynamic emotion is and how variable across categories. Her interest in the structure of Portuguese language quickly declined after the start of the course while her interest in cultural instruction increased: it "helped keep her motivated to get through the intensive course" (p. 222) because it allowed her to communicate with more advanced speakers: "She felt she could better cope with her linguistic limitations with the help of culture learning" (p. 222). She also discovered how sociostatic value develops in class: after starting to form a group of "cool women" (p. 222) she reports an improvement in her feeling of general well-being. However, she struggled with FLA because she felt herself to be less proficient than other students, which did not improve her self-image. She also felt frustrated at the start of the course by her inability to ask for help using the target language. While her frustration diminished as she became more proficient, she reported a fear of falling behind toward the end of the course and of being "overstuffed with grammatical information", which hindered her ability to communicate (p. 216). Her FLA did not dissipate and the total number of negative comments related to language awareness exceeded the positive (p. 216).

She reported relatively little respect for the non-native-speaking teaching assistant who taught the class in the afternoons, because of his mixed use of Portuguese and English, but this changed completely toward the end of the course.

Interestingly, the emotional responses to the course were not the presumed focus of the study beforehand. After transcription and analysis, Garrett and Young found that the "emotional responses to the language learning experience (mostly in the classroom but occasionally outside of it) were the most salient features of her learning endeavour" (p. 221).

Bown and White (2010) published a study in the same vein, using a qualitative approach (semi-structured interviews and narrative journals) to investigate the regulation of emotion by independent, new learners of Russian. The study draws on social cognitive theory (Bandura, 2002; Martinez-Pons, 2001) and research on the intelligent processing of emotions (Goetz, Frenzel, Pekrun and Hall, 2005). The authors argue for the importance of understanding the individual and social antecedents of emotions, and the relationship between emotion and cognition in SLA. From the material gathered, Bown and White found that emotions played a pivotal role in students' social relationships, thoughts, actions and decision-making. Emotions also affected their cognitive appraisals of tasks, teachers, the learning environment and themselves. Students' relationships with teachers and the power relations that emerged were particularly salient features of the learning environment, and acted as significant emotional antecedents in the individualised instruction setting. Bown and White found that students' cognitive appraisals of situations mediated their experiences of emotions, and that they applied their cognitive abilities to self-regulate their emotions during the language learning process (Bown and White, 2010). Bown and White (2010) concludes that intelligent processing of emotions can have a positive impact on the experience of language learning.

Another study on the emotional experience of learners in the foreign language classroom was carried out by Mercer (2006). She considered advanced tertiary level learners over the course of one semester. The learners kept a journal focusing on their emotional experience of the language classroom. Mercer then constructed a questionnaire on the basis of an initial analysis of the journals. This questionnaire provided meta-feedback on the use of journals from the learners' perspective and allowed a detailed study of their beliefs and emotions. Some students appreciated having to write down their emotions in the foreign language: "I really enjoyed keeping the diary because it was a new experience for me to express my thoughts and feelings in a foreign language" (p. 75).

In more recent work Mercer has looked at the development of tertiary learners' foreign language self-concepts and self-beliefs, i.e. beliefs learners have about themselves that are thought to affect their behaviour and attitudes (Mercer, 2009).

Using the data gathered with the Bilingualism and Emotion Questionnaire (BEQ hereafter) (Dewaele and Pavlenko, 2001–2003), Pavlenko (2006) looked whether multilinguals feel that they become different people when they change languages. She also investigated how they make sense of these perceptions, and what prompts some – but not all – multilinguals to see their language selves as different (p. 6). An analysis of the feedback from 1039 multilinguals on the open question about "feeling different in a foreign language" revealed that a majority (65 per cent) reported feeling different when using another language compared to only a quarter of participants who reported not feeling different, with the remaining 10 per cent giving ambiguous responses (p. 10). Pavlenko noticed four main sources of perceptions of different selves: "(1) linguistic and cultural differences; (2) distinct learning contexts; (3) different levels of language emotionality; (4) different levels of language proficiency" (p. 10). She concluded that the perception of different selves is not restricted to late or immigrant multilinguals, but is a more general part of multilingual experience. She cautions that "similar experiences (e.g., change in verbal and non-verbal behaviours accompanying the change in language) may be interpreted differently by people who draw on different discourses of bi/multilingualism and self" (p. 27).

Wilson (2008) used the data from 1414 respondents to the BEQ, a corpus of 27,938 words, to identify the most common themes in the feedback from participants who declared feeling different in a foreign language. The most frequent response was that of feeling more confident and being more outgoing in a foreign language. Participants noted changes in body language, mannerisms and voice but also reported deeper levels of disguise through references to putting on a mask or taking on another role.

One typical comment was: "It is kind of liberating. You can reinvent yourself and be what you want to be or who you really are. (Paloma – 31- Spanish, English, French)" (p. 103). Comments also highlighted differences in self-expression in different languages and a feeling of having different identities in each language. Wilson (2008) developed a 29-item questionnaire on feelings about foreign language use with five-point Likert scales based on the themes that she had identified in the BEQ. Statements described different aspects of "feeling different" when using a foreign language, such as "I sometimes feel as though it's someone else speaking this language and not me" and, "I am more confident when I speak a foreign language because I don't mind making mistakes".

Wilson then correlated the scores of 108 adult foreign language users on her questionnaire with the scores of the same participants on five personality traits (Openness, Conscientiousness, Extraversion, Agreeableness and Neuroticism). She found that introverts who rated their proficiency at intermediate level or above reported feeling different when operating in a foreign language. Gender and age had no effect on feeling different but a lower educational level was linked to a higher likelihood of feeling different. Participants with higher levels of perceived L2 proficiency who had started learning their L2 at a younger age were more likely to say they felt different. The type of instruction received in the L2 was also linked to "feeling different" scores on the questionnaire, with mixed and naturalistic learners scoring higher than taught learners. Wilson (2013) used her data from 2008 to argue that SLA should focus much less on negative emotions and more on positive emotions and the sense of freedom that comes with using an L2. Dewaele and Nakano (2013) looked at perceived shift on five scales of feelings across four languages known to 106 adult multilinguals. Results showed that compared to L1 use, participants felt gradually less logical, less serious, less emotional and increasingly fake when using their L2, L3 and L4 (p. 107).

The communication of emotion in an LX

When I started my research on the communication of emotion in an LX in the 1990s, I was extremely surprised to discover that very little research in the field of interlanguage pragmatics had been carried out on how LX users recognise and express emotions in their LX. The surprise came from the fact that pragmatics is typically defined as "the study of language from the point of view of users, especially of the choices they make, the constraints they encounter in using language in social interaction and the effects their use of language has on other participants in the act of communication" (Crystal, 1997: 301). The communication of emotion thus seems to fit perfectly in this definition of pragmatics. Also, SLA researchers such as Kasper and Rose (2001, 2002) chose Crystal's definition of pragmatics as the basis of their study on pragmatics and second language teaching. They argue that Crystal's view of pragmatics as the study of communicative action in its sociocultural context is perfectly suited to an SLA context. The term "communicative action" is broad enough to cover a wide range of variables, including speech acts, but it also includes "engaging in different types of discourse and participating in speech events of varying length and complexity" (p. 2).

The category "emotion" is usually absent in pragmatic research designs on LX acquisition and use. The preferred unit of analysis is the speech act: "the minimal unit of communication is not a sentence or other expression, but rather the performance of certain kinds of acts, such as making statements, asking questions, giving orders, describing [...] etc." (Searle, Kiefer and Bierwisch, 1980: vii). Indeed, most research in interlanguage pragmatics has focused on apologies, requests and compliments in the LX (Warga, 2007).

However, a few pragmaticists have crossed disciplinary boundaries and engaged in interdisciplinary research on the communication of emotion by LX users. One such pioneer is Ellen Rintell, who happened to share an office with a psychologist (personal communication). In Rintell (1984) she examined the perception and expression of emotion as an illocutionary act in the speech of LX learners and users. The researcher asked 127 foreign students, enrolled in the Intensive English Program at the University of Houston, to identify which emotion – pleasure, anger, depression, anxiety, guilt or disgust – best characterised each of 11 tape-recorded conversations played to them. They were also asked to rate the intensity of each emotion on a Likert scale. Their responses were compared to those of 19 native English speakers, among whom there was a high level of agreement. The statistical analysis of the data demonstrated that there were no effects for either age or gender. In contrast, linguistic and cultural background and language proficiency played an important role in the students' performance. The strongest effect was that of language proficiency, whereby the scores of the beginner group were significantly lower than the scores of the intermediate and advanced students. However, even the most advanced subjects in the sample, who identified the emotions conveyed in the conversations only about two-thirds of the time, did poorly. In addition, when learners of three major language groups were compared to each other, it was found that Chinese students had more difficulty with the task; their scores were consistently different from those of the Arabic- and Spanish-speaking students. Additional analysis of correct identifications demonstrated that, for both native speakers of English and ESL learners, disgust and pleasure were easier to identify than depression, anxiety, guilt and anger.

Graham, Hamblin and Feldstein (2001) reported similar findings concerning the effect of cultural competence on the recognition of emotion in English voices by 54 native Japanese speakers and 38 native Spanish speakers learning English as an L2. The participants were asked to identify the emotion portrayed in eight audio recordings (anger, fear, joy, sadness, depression, hate, nervousness and no emotion). A control group of 85 native English speakers obtained an average rate of correct identification of 59 per cent across all eight conditions. This was significantly higher than the judgements of the native Spanish speakers (Mean = 42 per cent) and the native Japanese speakers (M = 38 per cent). An analysis of the misjudgements revealed a mostly systematic pattern across related pairs of emotions (anger confused with hate and vice versa) for the English and Spanish native speakers. The Japanese L2 users of English showed many more non-systematic confusions than the Spanish L2 users. However, the level of proficiency of the L2 users did not significantly affect the percentages of correct judgements of emotions. Average scores were 44.2 per cent for the advanced Spanish L2 users of English, compared to 43.8 per cent for the less proficient ones. Similarly, the advanced Japanese L2 users of English obtained average percentages of 41 per cent compared to 40 per cent for the low proficiency group.

Grabois (1999) compared word associations for a number of concepts including love, fear and happiness, provided by the following five groups of speakers: (1) monolingual speakers of Spanish, (2) monolingual speakers of English, (3) acculturated L2 users of Spanish or late English-Spanish bilinguals who had lived in Spain for three or more years, (4) American L2 learners of Spanish enrolled in a study abroad programme and (5) FL learners of Spanish enrolled in Spanish courses in an American university. Statistical analysis of the data demonstrated that associations supplied by the two groups of native speakers differed both in terms of the type of preferred associations (i.e. symbolic, metaphoric, related to sensory cues, etc.) and in terms of which specific words were elicited. For instance, in response to love, native speakers of English exhibited a greater preference for indirect (metaphoric and symbolic) associations, while native speakers of Spanish showed a preference for sensory and referential associations. Among the non-native speakers of Spanish, acculturated L2 users consistently achieved higher correlations with the associations provided by native speakers of Spanish than any other group.

Pavlenko, in a series of ground-breaking studies, has investigated the relationship between emotions and multilingualism (2002a, 2002b, 2004, 2005, 2006, 2012a, 2012b) using multiple data sources, including the autobiographical writings of bilingual authors and feedback on questionnaires. Her psycholinguistic work has focused on conceptual representations in bilinguals and on emotion and emotion-laden words in the bilingual mental lexicon (1999, 2005, 2008a, 2008b, 2008c). She has insisted that future models of the bilingual lexicon need to acknowledge not just the linguistic and cognitive, but also the affective aspects of the lexicon (2008a: 147). She argues that there is sufficient evidence to prove that on the lexical level, emotion and emotion-laden words need to be considered as a separate class of words in the mental lexicon. Pavlenko refers to research by Altarriba (2003) that showed that emotion and emotion-laden words are represented, processed and recalled differently from abstract and concrete words. Pavlenko argues that future models need to consider the conceptual level, and address cross-linguistic differences in emotion concepts. One crucial need is to establish to what extent "bilinguals' representations may differ from those of monolingual speakers" (2008a: 147). Finally, Pavlenko defends a stronger focus on the processing level: "models need to incorporate the affective processing dimension, recognizing affective priming effects and differences in emotionality across bilinguals' languages and word types" (p. 147).

One of Pavlenko's major findings has been the different patterns of lexicalisation and conceptualisation in Russian and English (Pavlenko, 2002b, 2005, 2009; Pavlenko and Driagina, 2007). Comparing emotional discourse produced by bilinguals with that of monolinguals in both languages, she established that Russian speakers prefer emotion verbs and adverbial constructions while English speakers opt for adjectival constructions. L2 learners thus need to acquire new lexico-syntactic frames: English speakers of

Russian have to learn to use verbs and adverbial constructions, presenting emotions as processes, and Russian learners of English need to use adjectival constructions, presenting emotions as states. Learners also need to understand the differences in the content and boundaries of conceptual categories linked to emotion words (Pavlenko, 2008a: 94). They have to establish whether Russian emotion words are conceptually equivalent to the English word, or only partially equivalent ("when there is only partial overlap between prototypical referents of the two translation equivalents") or non-equivalent (p. 95).

Pavlenko (2008a) defines emotion concepts as:

> prototypical scripts that are formed as a result of repeated experiences and involve causal antecedents, appraisals, physiological reactions, consequences, and means of regulation and display. These concepts are embedded within larger systems of beliefs about psychological and social processes, often viewed as cognitive models, folk theories of mind, or ethnopsychologies. (p. 150)

These scripts of how certain emotions arise and are lived implies a knowledge of causality: "(e.g., rejection of a marriage proposal may lead to disappointment or even anger) or our beliefs about the links between emotions and physiological states (e.g., fluttering signals attraction)" (Pavlenko, 2008b: 198).

Pavlenko (2008a, 2008b) focuses on emotion concepts as prototypical scripts in order to escape from the universalist/relativist debate about basic emotions, as this says nothing about emotions per se but only about their conceptualisation. A comparison of two different emotion concepts in language A and language B does not imply that that speakers of these languages will feel different when experiencing the emotion, only that they will have "different vantage points from which to evaluate and interpret their own and others' emotional experiences" (Pavlenko, 2008a: 150).

The different vantage points of multilinguals have been linked to differences in socialisation resulting in distinct linguistic repertoires in the different languages. Koven (1998) compared stories of the same personal experience told by Portuguese-French bilinguals, children of Portuguese immigrants in France, in their L1s and L2s. She found that participants used different lexical and morphosyntactic resources and registers in their two languages; they also perceived themselves differently and were differently described by the listeners. Participants said they felt different in French and Portuguese, related to people differently and had a different perspective on the world. They felt less sophisticated in their Portuguese, which came from their rural parents and relatives, than in their French, which was the language of peer socialisation in their urban setting.

Koven (2006) focused on the affective displays of Linda, the bilingual daughter of Portuguese migrants, in French and Portuguese. She was found to perform the voices of quoted characters in more forceful, marked styles in French than in Portuguese (p. 84). Both Linda and listeners perceived her as enacting a different kind of emotion in both languages: "She is perceived in French not just as angrier in the here and now, but as an angrier person. On the other hand, in Portuguese she comes across as someone who uses less profanity, restrains herself, and is thus a more 'calm, reserved person'" (p. 84).

Koven concluded that the different sociolinguistic and biographical contexts in which Linda had learned and spoken her two languages are critical to understanding the role of bilingualism in her affective experience (p. 86). Ożańska-Ponikwia's (2013) study on Polish-English bilinguals showed that immersion and socialization in the L2 influenced perception and expression of emotions in both Polish L1 and English L2.

To conclude this brief overview, the bulk of study on emotion is situated within psychology, ranging from more neuropsychological to more social constructivist and cultural psychological approaches. I can understand the attraction of the neurological approach, but I feel that its limitations are still too great. Neurology can do little more than point to which brain areas light up under the scanner when particular emotions occur. Not only is there huge intra- and inter-individual variation, it has also appeared to be almost impossible to link specific emotions in a one-to-one relationship with electro-physiological processes taking place in the brain. In other words, the lack of isomorphism between our emotions (as we experience them) and what can be observed as brain activity can be viewed as the lack of an interface that can do just that (van Praag, 2008: 162–163). I also feel that neuropsychological researchers consider emotions from a *"pars pro toto"* perspective, while I think that emotions can best be studied as *"totus prius partibus"* (Gestalt) (cf. Averill, 1982). It is important to leave a place for a self, which is sharply divergent from the physical brain and body.

Several psychological journals focus explicitly on emotion (*Emotion and Cognition, Emotion Review*). No such journal exists within applied linguistics. Not surprisingly, the study of emotion within the broad field of Applied Linguistics, language teaching research and cognitive linguistics is much more limited. Although emotions play a crucial part in foreign language learning, researchers have typically focused on the emotions that drive the acquisition of the LX (i.e. motivation, FLA) and on the effect that the learning, or use, of an LX has on the sense of self of the learner (much of this research has been published in social psychological journals). The topic of communication of emotion in an LX has generated relatively little attention in interlanguage pragmatic research but in recent years it has attracted the attention of a growing number of researchers with interdisciplinary orientations, as will be demonstrated in the following chapters.

2
Epistemological and Methodological Perspectives in SLA and Multilingualism Research

The domain of communication of emotion in an LX is situated on the crossroads of various disciplines within social sciences. The main sources of concepts and methods are sociolinguistics, sociopragmatics, intercultural pragmatics, cognitive linguistics, didactics, language pedagogy, social psychology, cognitive psychology and cultural psychology.

Interdisciplinary research on communication of emotion in an LX requires a general broadening of the theoretical, epistemological and methodological horizons (Dewaele, 2005c, 2011c, 2012, 2013a, b, c; Griffiths, 2008; Ogarkova and Borgeaud, 2009; Ogarkova, Borgeaud and Scherer, 2009; Segalowitz, 2001; Williams et al., 2004; Wu and Thierry, 2012). The field does not only need more breadth, but also more depth and detail. The broadening implies that findings in specific subfields should be communicated to the wider applied linguistics community through presentations at international conferences and publications in journals with a wide focus. Applied linguists need to be aware of developments in contiguous areas that might benefit their own research. An awareness of the psychological research on individual differences and on post-modernist case studies of LX learners, for example, may help to get rid of the monolithic view of the prototypical faceless LX learner, whose identity often disappears in crude group averages.

Nobody will deny that every language learner is unique, but shares – to varying degrees – interacting psychological traits, social, cultural and biographical characteristics that can be linked to individual differences in the development, production and perception of an LX (Dewaele, 2005c, 2008c).

Any claim about the effect of particular variables in LX acquisition is dependent on the population used for the research. Foreign language learners on which studies are based are typically young adults enrolled at the universities where the researchers work. They may therefore not be representative of the general population of LX users in terms of ethnic or linguistic background, age, ability and so on.

The emic-etic distinction in SLA and multilingualism research

This epistemological opposition was introduced by Pike (1954) in ethnographical research. Reflecting on the origin of the opposition between emic and etic, he wrote:

> I coined the term EMIC (in Pike, 1954) from the linguistic term PHONEMIC, to apply to contrastive items of nonphonological material rather than to just phonological data [...] Any theory which we can live by must be able to grant that insiders to a system (such as the native speakers of a language) may call or treat several items or concepts as the same even though outside analysts may notice differences between them. This EMIC SAMENESS in the face of ETIC DIVERGENCE. (Pike, 1993: 16–18)

This insight emerged from his own experience as a language user and later as a trained phonetician:

> It was with astonishment, years ago, that I learned that the two p-sounds of the word paper are different in my own dialect of English – the first is aspirated (pronounced with a tiny puff of breath following it), but the second is unaspirated. The sameness was for me emic (phonemic); I had not observed the etic difference until I had studied some phonetics. On the other hand, with the concept "house", I had no difficulty in calling a bog house and a little house by the same term.[...] The variability within sameness may be easier for the insider to recognise in relation to nonphonological items and behavior than it is within phonology. (Pike 1993: 18–19)

Etic analyses and interpretations are thus based on the use of carefully defined and relatively stable concepts from the analytic language of the social sciences (Pike, 1954). This makes them useful for comparative research across languages, situations and cultures. Emic analyses, on the other hand, incorporate the participants' perspectives and interpretations of behaviour, events and situations using the descriptive language of the participants (Pike, 1954).

In a letter to Arthur Van Essen, Pike wrote:

> The term emic, of the subtitle, and its partner etic, (...) builds on an interest in unwritten languages spoken in Latin America, Africa, and Asia, bringing together some of the mental struggles we might face in an attempt to integrate scholarly disciplines, rather than isolating them. It builds on normal human experience as an ultimate starting point for the development of postulates of science (personal communication).

A debate has been raging in the SLA literature on these ontological and epistemological questions (Firth and Wagner, 2007; Gregg, 2006). Current research in foreign language teaching and SLA varies widely in terms of preference for emic or etic perspectives, or combinations of both.

More than a decade ago, Williams and Burden (1999: 194) deplored the fact that "comparatively little work has been carried out from a truly constructivist perspective that begins with the actual thoughts and feelings of the participants".

In a similar vein, Firth and Wagner (2007) complain that methodologies and theories within SLA reflect an imbalance between cognitive and mentalist orientations, and social and contextual orientations to language. They plead for an enhanced awareness of the contextual and interactional dimensions of language use and an increased emic sensitivity toward fundamental concepts. It is not entirely clear whether Firth and Wagner (2007) want the balance to shift completely. Previous defences of emic perspectives in SLA, like Watson-Gegeo (1988), stated that emic and etic analyses were complimentary: "a carefully done emic analysis precedes and forms the basis for etic extensions that allow for cross-cultural or cross-setting comparisons" (pp. 581–582).

A stronger focus on the emic perspective is characteristic of the Conversation Analysis (CA) paradigm and the post-modernist study of L2 socialisation. CA researchers are interested in an "emic reality" (Ten Have, 2007: 37). In order to uncover "the procedural infrastructure of situated action" (p. 37) they carry out an inductive search for patterns of interaction in episodes of naturally occurring interactions. No attempt is made to generalize findings, as researchers have a committment to "elucidate the local logic" (p. 199). Given the uniqueness of participants, researchers are resistant to generalising findings (see below for more on this topic). This approach has been successfully applied to SLA (Mondada and Pekarek, 2004). Duff (2007) underlines the importance of this approach within current sociocultural approaches in SLA when the focus is on the impact of socialisation processes and the environment on an individual's psychology (see also Lantolf, 2007).

Most attitudinal research in SLA privileges a more etic perspective: opinions and attitudes of participants are heard but they are collected through research instruments designed and formulated by the researchers. The first aim in this type of research is to gain an insight into relationships between variables in particular settings, with the ultimate aim of comparing these patterns with studies carried out in different settings. While these researchers acknowledge the uniqueness of L2 learners, their aim is to explain variations in the data through statistical analysis using carefully defined categories: "there are probably as many factors that might account for individual differences in achievement in a second language as there are individuals. However, they may be grouped into one of the two classifications of cognitive or affective variables" (Gardner and MacIntyre, 1992: 212).

Ogarkova, Borgeaud and Scherer (2009: 343) reflect on the concern voiced by defenders of etic perspectives in emotion research on emic approaches in the social, behavioral and neurosciences. They defend an emic perspective, arguing that:

> language is an integral part of emotion research at large, be it in the form of language signs, that is, verbal labels conventionally used to designate emotion states in a natural language, or language-in-use, that is, propositional analyses, lay persons' verbal accounts of past or present emotional experiences, or various scaling instruments that employ language to access a participant's emotional state. (p. 343)

Ogarkova, Borgeaud and Scherer (2009) acknowledge that the use of verbal reports may have shortcomings, but is "the only available means to measure the subjective experience of an emotion, as it is our only access to the way an individual interprets and categorizes an emotion episode s/he experiences" (Scherer, 2005: 712).

In an overview of developing trends in the field of motivation research in SLA, I have reported a growing number of studies combining etic and emic approaches (Dewaele, 2009c).

Qualitative and quantitative approaches in SLA and multilingualism research

Dörnyei (2007) reflects on the advantages and limitations of quantitative and qualitative approaches in SLA. As a veteran quantitative researcher into attitudes and motivation in SLA, he defends the quantitative approach because it is "systematic, rigorous, focused, and tightly controlled, involving precise measurement and producing reliable and replicable data that is generalisable to other contexts" (p. 34). However, Dörnyei admits that the downside of quantitative methods is that "they average out responses across the whole observed group of participants, and by working with concepts of averages it is impossible to do justice to the subjective variety of an individual life" (p. 35). Quantitative methods have a rather limited general exploratory capacity because they cannot easily uncover reasons for particular patterns or the dynamics underlying a situation or phenomenon (p. 35). MacIntyre (2007: 572) concurs with this last point, observing that "The methods currently in use, based on correlation or analysis of variance, offer a snapshot of the processes under study. This snapshot has value, but the action necessarily is stopped when we take the picture".

Qualitative methods are most appropriate for exploring uncharted areas and trying to understand the bigger picture: "I have also experienced again and again how much richer data we can obtain in a well-conducted and analysed qualitative study than even in a large-scale questionnaire survey" (Dörnyei, 2007: 47). Indeed, qualitative methods broaden the repertoire of possible interpretations and permit longitudinal examination of dynamic phenomena. Dörnyei (2007) and MacIntyre (2007) both agree that the advantage of qualitative methodologies is the richness of the descriptions of dynamic processes in participants' own terms (i.e. the emic perspective).

However, qualitative research also suffers weaknesses, namely, the small sample size and idiosyncratic focus (with the danger of biased results because of the researcher's leanings). MacIntyre (2007) reports the difficulties of biases in reporting memories, and Dörnyei (2007: 41–42) flags the lack of methodological rigour, the complexity or narrowness of theories and the amount of work involved as other potential problems with qualitative research. None of these potential pitfalls of qualitative research deter Dörnyei and MacIntyre. Both agree on the benefits of multi-method approaches for the field of SLA to move forward.

Dörnyei notes that "although there is no shortage of convincing intellectual arguments to justify paradigm incompatibility, most researchers have actually stopped short of claiming the inevitability of this conflict and, particularly in the last decade, scholars have started to look for some sort of an interface between the two research traditions" (Dörnyei, 2007: 29).

MacIntyre argues that the best methods for studying the affective changes "will be a combination of quantitative and qualitative approaches" (MacIntyre, 2007: 573). He is thus in agreement with Ushioda, who argued earlier: "There is clearly scope for a more qualitative approach to the study of language learning motivation, to complement this long-standing quantitative tradition of research" (Ushioda, 2001: 95). Ushioda and Chen (2011) point out that a combination of quantitative and qualitative approaches allow a combination of, on the one hand "methodological rigour and systematicity in data-gathering and analysis, as well as comparability and replicability of data, and generalizability to wider populations" (p. 46), and on the other hand the exploration and understanding in a grounded way of human experience which is "unique and deeply personal and subjective" (p. 47).

That is not to say that all studies should have to be based on mixed-methods design.

Hesse-Biber and Leavy (2006) pointed out that in the case of mixed-methods approaches the sum is not always greater than its parts. Dörnyei (2007: 46) goes even further, wondering whether more harm than good can be done when researchers are not adequately trained in qualitative and quantitative methods.

Groups and individuals in SLA and multilingualism research

Historically, research in SLA seems to have focused more on groups than on individuals. This could be linked primarily to a purely practical fact, namely that teachers and researchers typically face groups of learners in their language classes, and involve them in their experiments. They typically test the effect of different teaching techniques on different groups. Study-abroad programmes have provided researchers with ready-made research designs: a sample of students performs tests or interviews allowing the researcher to calculate values for specific variables at "time 1", and a sub-sample leaves the home institution to study in the L2 environment, while the others continue their study at home. Both groups are tested again when they are reunited after a number of months ("time 2") and averages for both groups on the same tests and interviews are compared. The difference is then attributed to the "study-abroad" effect (Freed, 1995). There may be some methodological problems in such designs as it is assumed that the group that stays at home has no extra exposure to the target language outside the language classes. Yet many determined home-staying language learners may achieve similar levels of exposure to the target language through access to the media, Internet, films and satellite television. Moreover large cities have increasingly multilingual and multicultural populations, allowing the motivated language learner to practise his/her language skills with NSs. In other words, a language learner in a metropolitan city who is prepared to make an extra effort can come into contact with an LX without having to leave his/her home country. Researchers in study-abroad projects typically rely on empiricist quantitative analyses (but see also Kinginger, 2008, 2009). The resulting view of the learner is thus rather monolithic, namely that of an "average language learner" in a certain teaching/exposure condition. I am certainly not claiming that such an approach does not provide rich insights, only that by considering groups that may be heterogeneous in many other ways individual differences tend to be ironed out.

The second possible historical reason for privileging groups rather than individuals may be traced to the Chomskyan notion of the ideal NS: "Linguistic theory is concerned primarily with an ideal speaker-listener, in a completely homogeneous speech-community..." (Chomsky, 1965: 3). In that perspective, individual differences do not matter. The researcher is interested in what groups of participants have in common rather than in what makes each of them unique. Considering broad group averages is a way of constructing faceless average learners. The focus is not so much on traits shared by individuals, but rather on the unique characteristics and the effects of the experimental treatment. There is of course nothing wrong with testing teaching methods, and trying to understand how the acquisition process functions using large samples of learners. But there is a danger that in the quest for easy generalisations one loses sight of individual learners, with their unique cultural, linguistic, psychological, social and cognitive characteristics, who function within well-determined sociocultural contexts.

Leppänen and Kalaja (2002) warn specifically about the danger of stripping L2 learners of their agency:

> Endowed with a set of personal characteristics, such as motivation, viewed as stable in nature and measured by objective means, the learner is treated as a physical object operating under universal laws. Importantly, the learner is stripped of agency, or intentional actions, and experiences of his/her own, taking place in particular contexts and in relation to those of others. (Leppänen and Kalaja, 2002: 190)

Post-modernist researchers make an important contribution to the development of new insights in our field when they criticise the mainstream empiricist SLA approach and refuse to see learners as mere "bunches of variables" (Lantolf and Pavlenko, 2001). They reject the static and homogeneous character of categories such as gender, age, ethnicity and social class and focus instead on issues of personal identity and second language socialisation (Belz and Kinginger, 2002, 2003; Pavlenko, 2002c, 2005). They are less interested in the acquisition process within the classroom walls than in the usage of the new language knowledge outside school in authentic interactions with TL speakers. In other words, they focus on how a particular learner develops his/her understanding of a TL through participation in relevant social interaction, where issues of personal identity are at stake (Barcelos, Kalaja and Menezes, 2008; Belz and Kinginger, 2002; Kalaja and Barcelos, 2003; Kinginger, 2004a, 2008, 2009).

For example, Belz and Kinginger (2003) state in their study on address pronouns in French and German: "learning to use these forms and to understand their meaning is as much a function of language socialisation as of language acquisition" (p. 208).

The learner is not only an object of scientific curiosity, but also a crucial witness of her/his own learning process. Interviews with students after their study abroad (Evans, 1988; Kinginger, 2008, 2009; Regan, Howard and Lemée, 2009) highlight important differences in self-reported social behaviour of language students during their stay abroad. While some students use every opportunity to engage in conversations with NSs of the TL, others avoid contact outside their own linguistic community. This might account for the wide inter-individual variation in the amount of linguistic progress after such a stay abroad (cf. Kinginger and Blattner, 2008; Regan, 2004, 2005; Regan, Howard and Lemée, 2009; Towell and Dewaele, 2005) and in the amount of meta-pragmatic awareness the students gained through interactions with NSs of the (Kinginger and Farrell Whitworth, 2005). In other words, by carrying out detailed qualitative research on a limited number of participants, patterns can be uncovered that could help in the interpretation of quantitative research findings on larger population samples.

These arguments have clearly had an impact on traditionally quantitative researchers. MacIntyre (2007), for example, introduced the concept of volition, i.e. free will, acknowledging the fact that L2 learners and users are not just puppets on strings, and that their actions are rooted in their linguistic, social or psychological past, present and imagined future. He points out that to understand how motivational processes affect communicative behaviour, "one must study the moment in which they are applied" (p. 569). In other words, the process of exercising volition "provides a way to specify how motivational tendencies are enacted in the moment-to-moment choices we make, such as choosing to speak up or to remain quiet" (p. 569). A growing number of traditionally quantitative SLA researchers are taking an interest in learners' intentional actions, unique life experiences and the variable effects that these have on their attitudes and motivation.

One can see merit in the critical arguments discussed above without rejecting empirical quantitative research methodologies. Quite to the contrary, although I agree with post-modernist researchers that L2 learners and users are more than just bunches of variables, I still believe that rigorous quantitative analyses of these variables can help researchers to obtain a more complete picture. My own theoretical basis is variable-informed psychological research and quantitative sociolinguistics. However, these paradigms may miss some of the phenomena uncovered by post-modernists, hence the argument in favour of triangulation in SLA research:

> I argue that poststructuralist studies, which see L2 learning as a process of socialisation rather than creative construction or interlanguage development, provide new ways of framing the interaction between social contexts and learning processes, which can productively be combined with more linguistically and cognitively oriented interactionist approaches in SLA. (Pavlenko, 2002c: 291)

Indeed, there is growing acceptance within the SLA community that learners' feelings and reflections on their learning process, language use and changing identity offer valuable insights into aspects traditionally overlooked in SLA. It would be impossible for every study to combine the different approaches. Wierzbicka (2004) observes on this topic:

> I am not saying that every opinion of every bilingual person should be regarded as authoritative, or that testimonies of bilingual persons should replace all other methods of studying human emotions. Rather, I am saying that such testimonies need to be taken into account, and that they complement semantic (and other) objective approaches. (p. 95)

The need for interdisciplinarity in SLA and multilingualism research

The current lack of interdisciplinarity means that too few concepts and methodologies from neighbouring disciplines are properly understood or adopted by applied linguists. When concepts from contiguous research areas are introduced in SLA and multilingualism research, they are often viewed with suspicion or are plainly misunderstood. Certain common research techniques, such as statistics, have become more widely used, but applied linguists are often self-taught in these matters, and a great deal of the early research lacked methodological rigor or were based on small samples (cf. Norris and Ortega, 2000). The problem also exists within SLA and multilingualism research, as different subfields use various methodologies that belong to specific paradigms and provide evidence that might not be considered equally valid in other fields. Moreover, there is insufficient tolerance of, or interest in, other theories imported from other equally legitimate outside fields and schools. There is a natural belief among applied linguists in the superiority of the research methods from their own paradigm and a suspicion toward methods and objectives from other fields.

Public debates between applied linguists are healthy, but sometimes the general perspective is lost. For example, the debate on the primacy of sociolinguistic approaches versus psycholinguistic approaches (Firth and Wagner, 1997) obscured the fact that the individual learner, like the bilingual (cf. Grosjean, 1989, 1992; Cook, 2002, 2007), is more than the sum of his/her parts. Just as the movement of legs is insufficient to explain the phenomenon of walking, no single sociobiographical or psychological characteristic of the learner can account for the speed and "success" of the language learning process and of the actual speech production. Rubin (1975), who was instrumental in encouraging research into the "good language learner", has recently emphasised that there are different kinds of good language learners and researchers need to focus on the combinations of factors which lead to success (Rubin, 2008).

Foreign language learning is an extremely complex process and we need to abandon the dream of representing a learner's progress in a gentle upward line toward native-like status. It is equally unworkable to try to fit every learner in a single well-defined category and make simplistic predictions about her/his linguistic development. Dörnyei (2001) showed that highly motivated learners may be less motivated to carry out a task that they find boring. Moreover, a learner with a usually low level of motivation for learning foreign languages, like the fictional Gregorius Raimund, may suddenly fall in love with a text, a film, a song or a speaker of the L2, resulting in a shift in attitude and concomitant progress. The early realisation that interlanguage development is dynamic and non-linear (Larsen-Freeman and Long, 1991) has been better understood and substantiated in more recent research such as that by de Bot, Lowie and Verspoor (2007), Herdina and Jessner (2002), Jessner (2006, 2008), Larsen-Freeman's (1997) and Larsen-Freeman and Cameron's (2008) application of chaos theory to SLA and multilingualism. Subsystems of the interlanguage do not necessarily progress smoothly toward a target-like norm. They can display U-shaped progression patterns before reaching equilibrium points (Dewaele, 2007d). If the system displays non-native use for a prolonged period, it will labelled as being "fossilized" (Han, 2009), but random events or teacher intervention may push the system out of its equilibrium, either upward or downward.

Language learners or users are constantly bombarded by events that continuously shape and reshape their personality and identity, resulting in linguistic progress, stagnation or loss. It is an illusion to hope that all the independent variables can be fully controlled in applied linguistics studies. A multitude of potentially interacting situational, social, psychological, cognitive and neurobiological, but also cultural and ideological, factors determine – to a variable extent – the learning process, the production and the comprehension of the LX(s).

In sum, it is my strong belief that methodological and epistemological diversity can greatly benefit applied linguistic research.

The epistemological and methodological choices that I have made for the empirical study that I will present in the following chapters have been inspired by the limitations encountered in previous work in the area of emotion and SLA (Dewaele and Pavlenko, 2002, 2003). In these studies, we adopted a purely etic and quantitative approach to measuring inter-individual variation in the proportion of emotion words and lexical richness in corpora of semi-structured interviews and film retellings. The studies allowed us to establish links between independent and dependent variables, but they left us largely in the dark about the possible causes for the relationships. Why, for example, did less proficient L2 learners produce a significantly smaller proportion of emotion words compared to more proficient L2 learners? We also realised that it very difficult to gather linguistic traces of the emotions of the speakers. As Sapir (1921) pointed out about emotion in language (i.e. native language):

> Emotion, indeed, is proverbially inclined to speechlessness [...] On the whole, it must be admitted that ideation reigns supreme in language, that volition and emotion come in as distinctly secondary factors. [...] All this does not mean that volition and emotion are not expressed. They are, strictly speaking, never absent from normal speech, but their expression is not of a truly linguistic nature. (pp. 38–40)

We realised that to gain a better understanding of how L2 learners and users communicate emotions, we would have to ask them. We were also very much aware of the limitations of using data elicited through specific questions by relatively small numbers of participants sharing similar linguistic profiles. We thus decided to set up a web questionnaire (see the following chapter) combining closed and open questions, and I later decided to complement this with in-depth interviews covering the topics appearing in the web questionnaire. This perspective was thus emic, and would combine quantitative and more qualitative analyses. The statistical analyses would allow us to calculate group averages and measure the effect of independent variables on dependent variables for the several languages of the participants, and yet the feedback from the open questions and the interviews would also allow us to understand the unique complexity of a sample of multilinguals and the possible causes for the patterns observed in the data. We felt that such an emic, mixed-method research design would yield rich, good-quality data and that the analyses would have sufficient validity and reliability. The following chapter will show how our research questions determined the research design, and I will highlight some of the limitations of this approach.

3
Method, Research Question and Hypotheses

The Bilingualism and Emotion Questionnaire (BEQ)

The Bilingualism and Emotions Questionnaire (BEQ) (Dewaele and Pavlenko, 2001–2003) was put on a dedicated Birkbeck webpage and advertised through several listservs (Linguistlist, discussion lists on bilingualism) as well as through thousands of targeted emails to multilingual colleagues and their students in academic institutions, appeals in translators' magazines and informal contacts around the world. It has been included as an appendix in the present book. We do not know how many multilinguals were reached through these different methods; this makes the calculation of a response rate impossible but given the very large number of respondents, we assumed that we had a representative sample.

The first part of the questionnaire contained 13 questions relating to participants' gender, age, education level, ethnic group, occupation, languages known, dominant language(s), chronological order of language acquisition, context of acquisition, age of onset, frequency of use, typical interlocutors and self-rated proficiency scores for speaking, comprehending, reading and writing in the languages in question.

The second part of the questionnaire consisted of 13 closed-ended Likert-type questions on language choice for the expression of various emotions with various interlocutors; on code-switching behaviour in inner and articulated speech; on language choice for mental calculation; on language choice for expressing feelings in general, and more specifically anger; on the use and perception of swear-words; on attitudes toward the different languages and, finally, on communicative and foreign language anxiety in the different languages. The closed questions allowed the gathering of numerical data through the use of Likert scales and permitted further statistical analysis.

The last part of the BEQ presented nine open-ended questions which asked about: (1) the weight of the phrase "I love you" in the participants' respective languages, (2) their linguistic preferences for emotion terms and terms of endearment (3) the emotional significance of their languages, (4) the language used for a personal diary, (5) the preferred language to recall bad or difficult memories, (6) the language spoken at home and language in which they argue in; (7) feeling like a different person when using different languages, and (8) the ease or difficulty to talk about emotional topics in a second or third language. A final open question invited the participant to comment on the questionnaire itself. The data elicited through the open questions yielded a corpus of about 150,000 words. The questionnaire took about 15 minutes to complete by a bilingual, about 30 minutes for a pentalingual.

The BEQ remained online between 2001 and 2003. Participants had the option to remain anonymous but were asked to provide a letter or number code so that their feedback on the BEQ could be linked to scores on the Trait Emotional Intelligence Questionnaire (Petrides and Furnham, 2001), which participants were invited to fill out after finishing the BEQ. Concerning the use of information obtained through the BEQ, participants were given the choice between three options: 1) to be given a credit and cited by name, 2) the use of responses as quotes while maintaining their anonymity and 3) the use of responses without quoting them. Feedback from participants would therefore be preceded either by a letter code or by their first name. Nearly 1800 multilinguals filled out the web questionnaire. About 200 incomplete questionnaires were discarded. The final database contains the feedback of 1579 multilinguals (1114 females (71 percent) and 465 males (29 per cent). The participants spoke a total of 71 different L1s. Anglophone NSs represented the largest group (n = 433, 27 per cent), followed by NSs of Spanish (n = 165; 10 per cent), French (n = 159; 10 per cent), Chinese (i.e. Cantonese, Hakka and Mandarin) (n = 136; 9 per cent), German (n = 131; 8 per cent), Dutch (n = 96; 6 per cent) and Italian (n = 66; 4 per cent). The remaining 389 participants shared another 64 languages: Afrikaans, Albanian, Arabic, Armenian, Basque, Bengali, Boobe, Bosnian, Bulgarian, Cheyenne, French Creole, Croatian, Czech, Danish, Esperanto, Estonian, Faroese, Farsi, Frisian, Galician, Greek, Gujarati, Hebrew, Hindi, Hungarian, Ibo, Icelandic, Indonesian, Irish, Korean, Latvian, Lingala, Lithuanian, Luganda, Lugwara, Luxembourgish, Macedonian, Malay, Malinke, Marathi, Norwegian, Oriya, Polish, Portuguese, Punjabi, Romanian, Russian, Rwandan, Serbian, Serbo-Croatian, Sindhi, Slovak, Slovene, Sundanese, Tagalog, Taiwanese, Tamil, Turkish, Ukrainian, Vietnamese, Welsh, Wobe, Yiddish and Zulu.

English was the most frequently cited L2 (n = 723; 46 per cent), followed by French (n = 303; 19 per cent) and Spanish (n = 146; 9 per cent). English and French were the most frequent L3s (n = 328; 21 per cent and n = 323, 21 per cent respectively), followed by German (n = 194; 12 per cent) and Spanish (n = 124; 8 per cent). German was the most frequent L4 (n = 196; 12 per cent), followed by French (n = 163; 10 per cent), Spanish (n = 124; 8 per cent) and English (n = 68; 4 per cent). Spanish was the most frequent L5 (n = 81; 5 per cent), followed by German (n = 65; 4 per cent). Only ten participants (0.6 per cent) reported English as an L5).

Languages were labelled L1, L2, L3, L4 and L5 according to their order of acquisition. The participants consisted of 323 bilinguals (20 per cent), 376 trilinguals (24 per cent), 377 quadrilinguals (24 per cent), and 503 pentalinguals (32 per cent).

Two-thirds of participants were dominant in one language (n = 1045; 66.5 per cent) with the remaining third being dominant in two or more languages (n = 526; 33.3 per cent).

Participants were generally highly educated with 160 having a high school diploma (10 per cent), 539 a Bachelor's degree (34 per cent), 454 a Master's degree (29 per cent) and 421 a doctoral degree (27 per cent). Age ranged from 16 to 73 (Mean = 34.3; SD: 11.5).

A large majority of participants worked in language-related professions, including students at all levels, teachers at all levels in the education system, researchers and translators (n = 1242).

The BEQ web questionnaire allowed us to gather data efficiently from a very large sample of learners and long-time users of multiple languages from across the world and from a wide age range (cf. Wilson and Dewaele, 2010). The sampling strategy was not random, it could rather be described as convenience sampling on a relatively large scale. We are aware that access to the BEQ was limited to people with access to the Internet and to people with sufficient knowledge of English. It is thus fair to say that the study looked at multilingualism among English users, though not overwhelmingly native speakers of English ("only" 27 per cent had English as an L1, 46 per cent had English as an L2 and English represented 21 per cent of the L3s of participants). We agree that this relatively high proportion of English users somewhat limits the generalisability of our findings to other groups of multilingual speakers. Although our participants turned out to have a wide diversity of L1s, we wished we had obtained more response from certain language groups. For example, we had only small numbers of Arabic speakers, speakers of African languages and Japanese speakers, and only a few participants of former Soviet states.

Looking at the sociodemographic composition of the sample it is clear that there is an over-representation of highly educated, female, polyglot participants. This is not surprising; as Buchanan (2001) noted, self-selected participants who are motivated enough to complete an online questionnaire are likely to differ from a random sample of Internet users (see also Feldman Barrett, cited in Jaffe, 2005; Hewson et al., 2003).

Pavlenko (2004) suggests that the dominance of female respondents in the BEQ database is perhaps best explained by the topic itself, as it is quite possible that, as a group, women may be more comfortable discussing emotions, parenting and relationships. The high proportion of participants with very high levels of education is probably linked to the fact that the BEQ required a certain degree of self-confidence, an interest in the topic and a sufficient amount of meta-linguistic awareness of one's language practices. It is likely that participants had already read books and papers on the topics covered by the BEQ, and that they may have come across the BEQ while searching the Internet using keywords that figured in the BEQ.

Filling out questionnaires is a particular literacy skill that university students in social sciences acquire quickly. It implies an ability to condense complex experiences, feelings and beliefs on a five-point Likert scale. It also implies an understanding of the convention that the feedback is the best possible approximation of a multilayered and infinitely complex truth. For somebody who has never filled out such a questionnaire, it must seem a baffling exercise, comparable to one's first encounter with a dictionary.

The BEQ inquired about complex issues that required a certain understanding of how communication works, how particular languages are linked to specific discourse domains and speech acts and how inherently variable language choices, attitudes and emotion in various languages can be. In other words, only participants who had developed a certain level of metalinguistic and metapragmatic awareness about their experiences and feelings as multilinguals could engage in this exercise. One obviously does not need a PhD to reflect on one's experiences in multiple languages, and a good number of our participants had no higher education level than a high school certificate. Their responses were generally comparable to those with higher levels of education (Dewaele, 2004a, 2004b, 2006a). Participants with higher levels of education had the confidence to share their experience and their views with the researchers. Fewer participants with lower levels of education may have had that confidence. I tried to find multilinguals with lower levels of education who might be willing to fill out hard copies of the BEQ. Dr Benedetta Bassetti offered to collect data from bilingual Italians but her attempt at data collection was less than successful. I reproduce an email I received from her in order to illustrate the difficulties researchers can face in gathering data:

> I finally managed to get hold of a bunch of very uneducated Italian-English bilingual males, and tried to administer your questionnaire. Given the very low levels of literacy, I did it orally and recorded the answers. I thought this would be an intimate one-to-one interview, instead everybody around thought that this was a new game, so it became a sort of social event. I had to intervene a lot to clarify lots of things, so in the end I contaminated the data, but it's not my fault, they really didn't understand a lot of things. And after I ran the first one, the others thought this was just not good and ducked out. (...) The first problem was of course getting the message across, these people have a down-to-earth approach that is simply devastating. "This research is about language and emotions." "About what?" Language and – it's about how you express your emotions in Italian and in English, like, y'know, when you're in love, do you prefer to express this feeling in English or in Italian? You are THICK, of course if I'm in love with an Italian girl I say it in Italian, if I'm in love with an English I say it in English. OK (sigh!), yes, of course, but which one do you prefer, like, in which language do you feel more comfortable

> to express this emotion, or in which language is it more meaningful? – the informant didn't get this abstract idea, and the discussion shifted to whether he preferred an Italian or English girlfriend. The second problem was suspicion. Why do they want to know this? E' un professore dell'università di Londra, he's doing some research. Why does a professore want to know my opinion? Well you know, he has to do research to get his salary. He gets paid to do this?!?
>
> But apart from all this, there were some objective problems with the questionnaire (...) First of all, the terminology is well beyond their repertoire. "Emotional strength" was incomprehensible, I translated it into Italian, but "valore emotivo" didn't make any more sense either. Some questions were perceived as totally inappropriate for a man. Like, the first reaction to the question "If you keep a personal diary..." was: "I DON'T keep a diary, I'm not a poof!!!!!!" Finally, I would say that the level of abstraction was too high. At the question "if you had some unpleasant experiences in the past", he answered "I didn't have any unpleasant experiences", so I decided to change the question into a concrete image "for instance, if your mother dies, would it be easier to talk about this in English or in Italian?" He looked at me thoughtfully and thoroughly scratched his testicles for two minutes (Italian version of touching wood). (personal communication, 2003)

It is quite clear that these potential Italian participants would never have participated in the online questionnaire even if they had had Internet access and time to do so. They would probably have provided incomplete information if they had been forced to fill out the paper version of the questionnaire. It is important to keep in mind that research instruments such as questionnaires may look intimidating and even threatening to people who are not used to them. Their unwillingness to fill out these questionnaires may be linked to a fear of looking stupid in the eyes of the researcher. It is a good reminder that obtaining good data from a representative sample of the population is something applied linguists need to strive for, but that it can be difficult.

Validity and reliability

Flynn and Foley (2009) define the validity of a study as the extent to which "results genuinely test the claims of the study" (p. 32). Validity is strengthened when evidence from different tasks points in the same direction (p. 32). The authors also distinguish between internal and external validity. Internal validity "refers to factors internal to a study that may affect whether the data collection procedures are truly measuring what the study claims they measure (p. 32). External validity "refers to generalizability" (p. 32).

The authors define reliability as the true reflection of the targeted knowledge. It is thus "connected to consistency in data collection procedures and in scoring data" (Flynn and Foley, 2009: 31). They refer to Brown and Rodgers (2002), who noted that studies are reliable when other researchers can analyse the data and find the same patterns (internal reliability) or when they could replicate the study and obtain similar results (external reliability).

I would not claim that the validity and reliability of the data elicited by the BEQ were 100 per cent but I feel that they were more than adequate for the research questions under investigation.

The high proportion of highly educated female polyglots does not undermine the external validity, although it is acknowledged that the sample does not represent the general population. Regardless of gender, education level and material resources, all multilinguals focus on the same issues.

The data elicited through the closed and open questions of the questionnaire, and their combination with the interview data, have strengthened the overall validity of the research. Studies that have replicated research based on the BEQ, such as Powers' (2009) study on the emotional weight of *I love you* among 37 participants living in the Seattle area in the US (native speakers of English, Cantonese, Dutch, French, Fujianese, Indonesian, Korean, Mandarin Chinese, Marathi, Spanish, Tagalog and Vietnamese), revealed strikingly similar patterns in the data.

Formulation of questions

One problematic point was the understanding of the participants' understanding of the language labels (L1, L2...). Although the question clearly focused on the order of acquisition rather than the relative strength of the different languages, some participants used the latter criterion. The question regarding the age of onset of language acquisition allowed a check on the correct use of the language labels. In some questions, participants had to specify which language they were talking about, which allowed a further check to see whether labels had been used consistently. In the cases where they had not, the data were discarded. This was also in a way the advantage of having a large pool of participants: the temptation to keep potentially tainted data might be greater with a small dataset.

The formulation of certain questions could have been better. Although the problem did not show up when the BEQ was pilot tested with 100 Birkbeck students, the background question "Which ethnic group/community do you belong to or most identify with?" elicited too many unclassifiable comments like "Earthling, human being, white non-resident alien, Caucasian, Swiss, Parisian". In other words, it ranged from the much too general to the much too specific. Participants should have been presented with a list of options to pick from. As a result it became impossible to distinguish between English, Spanish or French speakers from different countries and continents.

Some questions about frequency of language use with interlocutors were kept deliberately general. This elicited the criticism from some participants (the last question invited open-ended comments) that it was not specific enough. Indeed, to the question "how frequently do you use your L1/L2/L3/L4/L5 with friends", some participants objected that they used their L2 almost never with some friends, but always with others.

The reason for choosing to be very general in formulating the questions was linked to questionnaire length. Introducing too detailed questions, could have discouraged potential participants from completing the questionnaire. Questionnaires are by nature incomplete as one is forced to find a fine balance between the number of topics covered and the amount of detail requested while keeping total length under control. Dörnyei (2003: 132) suggests a maximum length of about four pages and 30 minutes to complete. A pentalingual needed about 30 minutes to complete the BEQ.

As Aneta Pavlenko and I were preparing the BEQ, we also wondered whether to insert a question on the length of foreign language instruction. In the end we decided against it, despite the fact that it would have produced potentially valuable data. The reason is that ideally one would wish to have the total number of hours of study (cf. Muñoz, 2006). We were unsure however whether adult multilinguals could reliably remember how many hours of study they had had in a particular foreign language. Asking them the number of years of study might have been preferable, but it might have been too vague: a person who had enjoyed ten years of foreign language instruction at a rate of one hour a week would have had a hypothetical 300 hours of instruction. These 300 hours would typically be delivered over a two-year period in Belgium. The value in years would have been unreliable. We thus simply asked whether participants had had formal instruction in a language, whether that formal instruction had been combined with authentic use of the language outside the classroom or whether their acquisition had been entirely naturalistic. Here again we realised that we could have asked more precise information (immersion, study abroad, type of foreign language teaching) but decided against it because we considered this to be only one of the many independent variables in our research design.

Quality

Since the BEQ merely invited participants to report their linguistic experiences, it did not seek to test their language competence in any way. Given the huge diversity of languages, this would have been impossible anyway. We felt that it is unlikely that the fact that English had to be used affected the results. Obviously, participants needed to be sufficiently proficient in English to understand the questions. The question of the quality of the data obtained through the BEQ will probably depend on the researcher's epistemological stance. By offering participants closed questions with Likert scales we did impose our perspective, but through the open questions participants could freely express their experiences and opinions. We thus had to keep in mind that in reporting the data the reader had to be reminded that any values were based on self-report. This is a well-known problem among researchers who use questionnaires (Dörnyei, 2003). Some participants might "fake good", or exaggerate their proficiency or claims. The only defence against this argument is that our participants had nothing to gain from providing inaccurate information, and that the questions about language preferences did not have an obvious socially desirable answer. It is also hard to see the attraction of falsifying answers to an online questionnaire. Ping Li, Sepanski and Xiaowei Zhao (2006), cross-checked the participants' language history against their self-assessed proficiency and found this to be highly correlated.

On the whole, I feel that the potential benefits of the questionnaire and the research design, namely the possibility to collect data from adult multilinguals with a wide variety of language combinations, outweigh the disadvantages. The economic aspect is not to be underestimated either: gathering this amount of material from more than 1500 participants through the pen and paper method would have cost considerably more in money and researcher time. The web questionnaire allowed us to transfer the collected data straight into Excel files where they could be processed after some "cleaning up". I thus agree with Gosling et al., (2004) that the ability to collect data from large and diverse samples and motivated respondents and the ease and efficiency with which the data can be collected outweigh the methodological constraints (p. 102). I also think that having a self-selected sample of highly linguistically and pragmatically aware multilinguals may in fact have contributed to the quality of the information gathered. Wilson (2008) reported that self-selected participants were more likely to make an effort to provide complete and accurate feedback.

In-depth "multilingual lives" interview corpus

The second group of participants in the present study consisted of 20 fluent multilinguals (12 females, eight males) who filled out the BEQ before being interviewed by a research assistant, Dr Benedetta Bassetti, on the topics covered by the BEQ. The aim of these interviews, which were semi-structured, was to establish the direction of CS, something about which the BEQ did not inquire. The interviews were transcribed and amounted to 115,000 words (including the interviewer's questions and comments). This group of participants has a similar sociodemographic make-up to the participants in the BEQ. They lived in or around London. The youngest participant was 23, the oldest 65, with a mean age of 36 years. One participant had a high school degree, five a BA, three an MA and seven a PhD. There were five bilinguals, seven trilinguals, four quadrilinguals, three pentalinguals and one sextalingual. Participants were native speakers of German (n = 3), Italian (n = 3), Japanese (n = 3), Arabic (n = 2), English (n = 2), Greek (n = 2), Catalan (n = 1), French (n = 1), Kurdish (n = 1), Serbian (n = 1) and Taiwanese (n = 1).

Research question

The present study proposes investigating the following general research question:

> To what extent can inter-individual variation in self-perceived competence in the LX, frequency of use of the LX to communicate emotion, attitudes and perception of emotionality of the LX and foreign language anxiety be linked to background variables such as the history of the learning of the LX, the present use of the LX and the linguistic, social, educational and psychological profile of the multilingual?

Hypotheses

Hypothesis 1a: There will be a monotonic decline from L1 to L5 in self-perceived competence, frequency of language use, attitude and perception scores.
Hypothesis 1b: There will be a monotonic increase in communicative anxiety and foreign language anxiety (FLA) scores from L1 to L5.

Hypothesis 2: Participants who started learning an LX later in life will feel less proficient in that LX and less inclined to use that LX, attitudes and perceptions toward the LX will be weaker and levels of FLA will be higher, compared to participants who started learning the LX earlier.

Hypothesis 3: Participants who learned an LX only in a classroom will feel less proficient in that LX and less inclined to use that LX, attitudes and perceptions toward the LX will be weaker and levels of FLA will be higher, compared to participants who learned the LX naturalistically or through a combination of classroom instruction and authentic extra-curricular use.

Hypothesis 4: Frequent users of an LX will feel more proficient in that LX and more inclined to use that LX, attitudes and perceptions toward the LX will be stronger and levels of FLA will be lower, compared to participants who use the LX less frequently.

Hypothesis 5: Participants with higher levels of socialisation in an LX will feel more proficient in that LX and more inclined to use that LX, attitudes and perceptions toward the LX will be stronger and levels of FLA will be lower, compared to participants with lower levels of socialisation.

Hypothesis 6: Participants with larger networks of interlocutors in an LX will feel more proficient in that LX and more inclined to use that LX, attitudes and perceptions toward the LX will be stronger and levels of FLA will be lower, compared to participants with smaller networks of interlocutors.

Hypothesis 7: Participants knowing more languages will feel more proficient in all their languages and more inclined to use their LXs, attitudes and perceptions toward their LXs will be stronger and levels of FLA will be lower across their languages, compared to participants with fewer languages.

Hypothesis 8: Participants with higher levels of trait Emotional Intelligence will feel more proficient in that LX and more inclined to use that LX, attitudes and perceptions toward the LX will be stronger and levels of FLA will be lower, compared to participants with lower levels of trait Emotional Intelligence.

Hypothesis 9: Gender, age and level of education might affect the dependent variables, but no particular direction can be hypothesised.

4
The Independent Variables

Introduction

The present study rests on the assumption that basic emotions are neurologically based, originate through social interaction and that their expression is shaped by a wide variety of cultural, linguistic, situational and individual variables. The interaction of independent variables affecting the encoding and expression of emotion in a monolingual speaker is undoubtedly complex. Yet, the complexity of the interaction underlying the expression of emotion in a multilingual speaker is of a different order altogether. Multilinguals' trajectories of acquisition and use of their different languages are unique, resulting in rich and varied conceptual representations (Pavlenko, 2005, 2008a, 2008b, 2008c). In other words, multilinguals are even more likely than monolinguals to express emotion and perceive emotion in a unique way because of the variable influence of their different languages and cultures. The objective of the present chapter is to present a series of independent variables that might contribute to the funnel of effects affecting the expression of emotion in multilinguals' different languages, as well as their perception of their different languages and their anxiety in using them.

Chronology of acquisition (L1, L2, L3, L4, L5)

Introducing the variable

I have pointed out in the introduction that one way to label languages is by chronology of acquisition. Although the validity of this classification has sometimes been questioned, I have shown in Dewaele (2005d) that the chronology of language acquisition has a stronger effect on self-perceived competence among a subgroup of BEQ participants, namely the 473 pentalinguals, than communicative anxiety, the network of interlocutors, LX socialisation, age of onset of acquisition, context of acquisition and education level. The only independent variable to have a stronger effect on self-perceived competence was the reported frequency of use of the LX.

I concluded that the labels L2, L3, L4 are meaningful and certainly not arbitrary when dealing with self-perceived competence of adult LX users.

In a recent study (Dewaele, 2011a), I have investigated whether the labels "L1" and "L2" made any difference in self-reported use and perception of the L1 and L2 among a subgroup of 386 BEQ participants, namely those who reported to be most proficient in their L1 and L2 and used both languages constantly. A quantitative analysis showed that participants preferred using the L1 for the communication of their feelings, anger, swearing, for addressing their children, for mental calculation and for inner speech. They also perceived their L1 to be emotionally stronger than their L2 and reported lower levels of communicative anxiety in using their L1. In other words, the first language to have been acquired retained a superior status for these multilinguals despite the apparently equivalent status of both languages. It thus seems that the chronology of acquisition does affect the perception and use of multilinguals' languages, even when crucial factors such as frequency and proficiency are controlled for.

I did signal in the introduction that the use of the labels is more complicated for the minority of multilinguals in the database who acquired multiple languages simultaneously from birth. My daughter Livia, for example, was born in a trilingual environment, hearing French from me, Dutch from my wife and English everywhere outside the house. So French could be labelled "L1a", Dutch "L1b" and English "L1c". At the age of six months she started spending her afternoons with a Pakistani child-minder who used both English and Urdu with the children. She developed a limited passive competence in Urdu: she was able to fetch objects after being told so in Urdu, and built up a active vocabulary of about 50 words. She started losing her Urdu by the age of four, when she moved to an English-speaking nursery school (Dewaele, 2000) and stopped getting input in Urdu. The question now is whether Urdu was another (short-lived and now fully attrited) L1, or whether it was an early L2 (indeed she did not hear it from birth, although she did hear before the age of three – the threshold for the L1 according to McLaughlin, 1984). Now aged 13, she will start a first truly "foreign" language at school, Spanish. So there can be some discussion as to whether this is her L2 or her L3, or in fact her L5, as it is the fifth language she will encounter in her life.

Livia sounds like an NS in her three "first" languages, but English is clearly her dominant language, being the language of school, the language of numeracy and literacy and the language used for most social interactions. Despite occasional errors in French and Dutch, she uses these languages confidently, can read them and learns to write French at school. In other words, the label "L1" refers to a historical fact in an individual's life, the age of onset of acquisition, and it should not be confused with "level of competence", which is variable. Indeed language dominance can shift over relatively short periods, depending on the frequency of use of the different languages.

Operationalising the variable

Participants were asked the following question:

> "Which languages do you know and what order did you learn them in?"

Combined with the information on the age of onset of acquisition, we had clear data concerning the chronology of acquisition of the different languages. Simultaneous bilinguals (n = 223) and trilinguals (n = 28) assigned the label L1, L2, L3 as they saw fit.

Age of onset of Acquisition (AoA)

Introducing the variable

The topic of age effects in foreign language learning, and the possible existence of critical periods in the acquisition of various aspects of the foreign language, has been at the forefront of debates within the field of applied linguistics and beyond. The massive interest outside the academic community in research on age effects is linked to the question about the optimal age to introduce foreign language teaching into the school curriculum. Politicians, parents and educators worry that the introduction of foreign language teaching at the start of secondary education might be too late, as students might already be past the "critical period" (CP) and might therefore struggle to attain very high levels of proficiency in the foreign language (Lenneberg, 1967; Penfield and Roberts, 1959). The basic idea is that children lose the cerebral flexibility to learn languages from mere exposure to the language after puberty. Foreign language learning is still possible after puberty, but it will require "a conscious and laboured effort" (Lenneberg, 1967: 167). The debate has been raging ever since on the validity of the hypothesis, the definition of the term "critical period" and its possible causes and its effects. There has been a flourish of contributions and edited volumes on the topic recently (Abello-Contesse et al., 2006; Abrahamsson and Hyltenstam, 2008, 2009; Dewaele, 2009a; García Mayo and García Lecumberri, 2003; Llanes and Muñoz 2013; Muñoz, 2006, 2008a, 2008b; Singleton and Ryan, 2004). The common view that "younger is better" in learning a foreign language has led to the introduction of early foreign language teaching in many European countries. No such unanimity exists within the applied linguistics community. Critics have claimed that the idea of CP in SLA should be abandoned (Singleton and Ryan, 2004). Others have adopted a more nuanced position, pointing out that it is crucial to draw the correct implications from research findings (Scovel, 2006). The fact, for example, that it seems very hard for anyone acquiring an L2 after about the age of twelve to speak that L2 without a foreign accent does not automatically imply that foreign language instruction should be initiated in childhood (p. 43). He argues that exposure to a new language before puberty might be one of several factors that contribute to growing up into a successful LX user (pp. 43–44).

Critical overviews of the research on the Critical Period Hypothesis (CPH) can be found in DeKeyser and Larson-Hall (2005), Dewaele (2009a), Hyltenstam and Abrahamsson (2003), Larson-Hall (2008), and Muñoz (2008a, 2008b).

Researchers like Paradis (2004) have suggested that CP effects are caused by the decline of procedural memory for late L2 learners which forces these learners to rely on explicit learning instead:

> It is the acquisition of implicit competence that is affected by age both biologically (gradual loss of plasticity of the procedural memory for language after about age 5) and cognitively (greater reliance on conscious declarative memory for learning in general and, consequently, for learning a language from about age 7). (Paradis, 2004: 59)

Paradis (2004) points out that the upper age limit varies with respect to the component of the implicit language system that is being acquired through exposure to language interaction. This is, in chronological order, prosody, phonology, morphology and syntax (p. 59). Since the learning of vocabulary is subserved by declarative memory, it is not susceptible to the CP (p. 59).

Most researchers agree that in SLA there are age effects, or "general age factors" (Singleton, 2003), but they disagree on the existence of cut-off points (i.e. the term "critical"), the effect of confounding variables and the exact cause of the age effects. This age-related decline in FL abilities is gradual and varies according to individual aptitude and ability, as well as age of onset (Chandler, 2006). In other words, "a number of exogenous and endogenous variables may come into play that can affect the ultimate attainment of SL learners" (Birdsong, 2005).

DeKeyser and Larson-Hall (2005) defend the existence of a CP for SLA but they point out that this CP is not the only maturational effect to play a role: "individuals go through gradual physical and psychological changes of all kinds all through their life-span" (p. 103). These changes are superimposed on the CP phenomenon and further complicate the analysis (p. 103).

The seminal works on the CPH date from the 1980s. A low Age of onset of Acquisition (AoA) was found to be linked to higher scores on grammaticality judgement tasks (Johnson and Newport, 1989; DeKeyser, 2000). Having found a strong negative correlation between AoA and scores on the grammaticality judgement test, DeKeyser (2000) argued that this is a clear indication that "early age confers an absolute, not a statistical, advantage—that is, there may very well be no exceptions to the age effect. Somewhere between the ages of 6–7 and 16–17, everybody loses the mental equipment required for the implicit induction of the abstract patterns underlying a human language, and the critical period really deserves its name" (p. 518).

There has been a lively debate about what would be accepted as counter-evidence to the CPH (cf. Birdsong, 2005, 2007, 2009). Long (1990) stated that it would be enough "to produce learners who have demonstrably attained native-like proficiency despite having begun exposure well after the closure of the hypothetised [sic] sensitive periods" (p. 274). Following this line of reasoning, researchers (Birdsong, 2005, 2007, 2009) have indeed come up with cases of NNSs who scored at NS level on various linguistic tests.

It remains to be seen whether this is indeed sufficient evidence to reject the CPH, as a majority of participants remain below NS range. Can CPH research focus on these exceptional language learners, who are clearly outliers in statistical terms? Researchers have argued that a distribution of end-state performance, to be consistent with the CPH, should incorporate a point of inflection, which Birdsong (2007) describes as "an elbow", corresponding to the start of a decline in learning ability, i.e. the offset of the period of peak sensitivity. Birdsong (2007) proposes three basic patterns: first, a stretched L; second, an upside down mirror image of the stretched L, resembling a stretched "7"; and third a stretched "Z". The first pattern (A) shows an age-related decline ceasing at a point that coincides with the end of maturation. The second pattern (B) shows a flat portion where success is guaranteed, followed by a steady decline. The third pattern (C) begins with a period where individuals perform at a ceiling level, followed by a period of steady decline that ceases at the end of maturation, after which the age function becomes a flat line and no further age effects are seen. Birdsong points out that there is evidence in the literature (DeKeyser, 2000) about the left portion of pattern but that there is no evidence for the right segment of the stretched L, i.e. a flat function or floor effect, because later learners show a random array of scores or a continuous decline in performance with increasing AoA. Evidence has been found for pattern B where the left segment represents the "window of opportunity", with scores at a ceiling level, followed by an unbounded decline in ultimate attainment with advancing AoA. Dewaele (2009b) has reported a slight U-shaped pattern for AoA on a number of variables related to the communication of feelings, of inner speech and of self-perceived competence in the L2, L3 and L4 of adult bi- and multilinguals. This was explained by the fact that languages learnt later in life may in fact retain a higher level of activation than previous foreign languages.

Operationalising the variable

The question "At what age did start learning your L2/L3/L4/L5?" yielded a numerical value. In the present study, five groups have been created: those who were introduced to the L2 between birth and the age of two, between the ages of three and seven, between eight and 12, between 13 and 18 and those who started aged 19 or older. As can be seen in Table 1, the highest proportion of L2 and L3 learners started between ages eight and 12, while most L4 learners started between the ages of 13 and 18 and most L5 learners started at the age of 19 or above.

Table 1 Distribution of participants according to AoA (in %)

AoA	L2	L3	L4	L5
0–2	3	1	0	0
3–7	27	9	2	2
8–12	48	40	16	6
13–18	16	34	44	31
19+	6	17	37	61

Context of acquisition

Introducing the variable

The effect of authentic language use with NSs of the TL on the development of the interlanguage has been clearly demonstrated (for an overview, see Dewaele, 2007d). After their stay abroad or after prolonged contact with NSs, LX users approximate the NS norm. Both productive and receptive knowledge of the LX benefit from a stay abroad. Taguchi (2008) found a significant increase in the speed and accuracy of pragmatic comprehension in the TL after a stay abroad. The stay abroad has more variable effects on attitudes: some students come back with extremely positive attitudes toward the TL community, others come back loathing every speaker of the TL (see also Byram, 2009). The effect of extra-curricular authentic TL use has been found to stimulate the development of the interlanguage (Housen, Schoonjans, Janssens, Welcomme, Schoonheere & Pierrard, 2011). Housen (2002) looked at the English L2 of Italian primary school children (aged eight to ten) in four different contexts: one group of learners in foreign language classroom from a mainstream school in Bologna, three groups of learners in the European Schools of Varese (Italy), Brussels (Belgium) and Culham (UK) and one control group of English L1 speakers from the European School of Brussels. The amount of formal instruction was similar across the groups; only the amount of extra-curricular contact with the TL varied. The amount of contact with English outside the classroom was limited in Bologna and Brussels and much more frequent in Varese and Culham. Although ANOVAs failed to uncover an overall effect for context on verb type diversity, lexical richness, verb/noun ratios and global lexical mastery, post-hoc tests did show that the Culham group scored significantly higher than the two other learner groups, but remained significantly below the scores of the English L1 control group. This clearly demonstrates the beneficial effects of frequent interaction in the TL in addition to the formal instruction.

The amount of TL use within the LX classroom has also been found to be linked to students' levels of FLA (Frantzen and Magnan, 2005; Levine, 2003; von Wörde, 2003). Too little and too much LX use were both linked to higher levels of FLA. Students in LX-only classrooms commented that not understanding the LX caused anxiety (Frantzen and Magnan, 2005; von Wörde, 2003).

Operationalising the variable

The variable "context of acquisition" distinguishes between three types of contexts: 1) naturalistic context (i.e. no classroom contact, only naturalistic communication outside school), 2) mixed context (i.e. classroom contact + naturalistic contact) and 3) instructed context (i.e. formal classroom contact only). No further distinction was made between types of formal instruction, such as, for instance, "immersion classrooms", where the TL serves as the medium for teaching non-language subject matter and "non-immersion classrooms", where the TL is the instructional target. Similarly, the notion of "naturalistic context" as used here is a cover term for a wide range of ways in which a language can be learned without guidance from a particular teacher or programme, but developed gradually or spontaneously through interaction with speakers of the TL. Clearly, the variable "context of acquisition" cannot be easily disambiguated from the "context of use". One could argue that the instructed learner whose only contact with the TL was in the classroom would rarely be compelled to express anger in that language. This distinction between the three contexts of acquisition is obviously quite crude. More fine-grained categories could have been used for the instructed context to distinguish between "foreign language-classrooms", where the TL is the instructional target, and "immersion classrooms", where the TL primarily serves as the medium for teaching non-language subject matter. I observed in Dewaele (2005a) that learning and teaching practices at school have evolved considerably over the years, and still vary widely both geographically and socially, but they all share one aspect, namely that the learning happens within the confines of the classroom walls, in the presence of a teacher and classmates, and that an official programme has to be followed. The notion of "naturalistic context" refers to a wide range of ways in which one can learn a language naturalistically. What they all have in common is that the learning process is not intentionally guided by a particular teacher or programme, but developed gradually and spontaneously through interaction with speakers of the TL.

Table 2 presents the distribution of the participants according to context of acquisition for the L2, L3, L4 and L5. The most striking difference occurs between the L2 and the other languages: less than half of the participants

Table 2 Distribution of participants according to context of acquisition of the LX (in %)

Context of acquisition	L2	L3	L4	L5
Instructed	43	67	69	66
Mixed	43	26	22	21
Naturalistic	14	6	9	13

learned the L2 solely through formal instruction, while this rose to more than two-thirds of the participants for the L3, L4 and L5.

Frequency of language use

Introducing the variable

Languages that are used rarely are likely to have declining levels of activation until they become dormant (Green, 1986). Languages that are used regularly in a wide range of contexts will have higher levels of activation, and if these languages are still being acquired, the acquisition rate will increase. Research on immersion education and study abroad has shown that increased contact with the L2 typically boosts the acquisition of different areas of it, including sociolinguistic competence (Etienne and Sax, 2009; Mougeon, Nadasdi and Rehner, 2002, 2010; Regan, 2005), sociopragmatic competence (Belz and Kinginger, 2002) and grammatical competence (Howard, 2005). However, as Kinginger (2008) pointed out, study abroad may create the potential for rapid development in the LX, but it is insufficient in itself.

Yashima, Zenuk-Nishide and Shimizu (2004) showed that frequency and amount of L2 communication by Japanese students who participated in a study-abroad programme in the United States related to satisfaction with the experience of their stay, and satisfaction regarding their friendship with their hosts. A better perceived quality of human relationships with host family members was linked to more interest in intercultural communication and/or international affairs. This in turn motivated students to put more effort into learning the L2, which led to a further improvement in communicative skills and self-confidence. Practice in authentic communication in the TL country clearly boosts self-confidence: Matsuda and Gobel (2004) found that those of their Japanese students of English who had been overseas experienced significantly lower FLA in speaking. Baker and MacIntyre (2000) compared two groups of Anglophone learners of French in an immersion and a non-immersion programme. While both groups showed near identical levels of CA in English, those in the immersion programme suffered much less from FLA in French: "The increased contact with the language in the immersion program seems to give the students an opportunity to improve their ability to predict and confirm expectations (...), thereby increasing their perceived competence. This sets off a chain of behaviour in which the student feels less anxious about communicating and thus more competent" (p. 333).

Operationalising the variable

Participants were asked the following question:

Table 3 Distribution of participants according to frequency of use of the different languages (in %)

Frequency of use	L1	L2	L3	L4	L5
Yearly or less	0.9	10.8	35.9	50.9	52.5
Monthly	3.5	8.7	16.5	16.2	17.4
Weekly	11.7	16.1	19.9	15.1	14.6
Daily	19.7	24.2	14.2	8.8	9.1
All day	64.2	40.2	13.5	9.1	6.4

"How frequently do you use your languages?"

Possible answers on five-point Likert scale included 1) Yearly or less, 2) Monthly, 3) Weekly, 4) Daily and 5) All day.

Feedback revealed that the proportion of participants using a language all day decreases from 64.2 per cent for the L1 to 6.4 per cent for the L5. Inversely, the proportion of participants who use a language only on a yearly basis increases from 1 per cent in the L1 to more than half for the L5 (Table 3).

LX socialisation

Introducing the variable

Research into language socialisation in multilingual settings shows that the process of acquisition of new interpretative frameworks occurs at different times during the life time of multilingual speakers (Bayley and Schecter, 2003). The focus of the early research on L2 socialisation was on how children and adults immersed in an L2 culture, typically observed within the classroom, developed interactional competences enabling them to participate appropriately and effectively in their new environment (Kasper, 2009: 274). Kasper notes that recent L2 socialisation studies have been based in a broader and more complex context. There is also a growing acknowledgement that social contexts of learning are complex, dynamic and multilingual, and that people are concurrently negotiating and maintaining memberships and identities in different communities (Duff, 2003, 2007). Pavlenko (2004) focused on parent-child communication within multilingual families and considered the effects of L2 socialisation on language choice for the communication of emotion. While a majority of multilingual parents reported a preference for the L1 for emotional communication with their children, a minority of parents reported that as a result of the socialisation process their LX had acquired strong affective connotations.

Table 4 Distribution of participants according to degree of socialisation in the LX (in %)

LX socialisation	L2	L3	L4	L5
Very weak	51.2	78.5	85.4	88.3
Weak	25.9	10	8.0	7.2
Moderate	12.1	6.7	4.4	2.5
Strong	10.8	4.8	2.2	2.0

Operationalising the variable

The variable "socialisation in the LX" is a second-order variable based on the difference in the general frequency of use of the L1 and an LX (either the L2, L3, L4 or L5). The data were collected through the method shown in the previous section. The subtraction of the score for the LX from the score for the L1, gives a value that reflects the difference in frequency of use of the L1 and the LX. For example, if a participant indicated that she/he used the L1 "all day" (score 5) and the L2 "weekly" (score 3), the L2 socialisation score would be 2, indicating a "very weak" degree of socialisation in the L2. If, on the other hand, the L2 was used "all day" (score 5) and the L1 "weekly" (score 3), the L2 socialisation score would be –2, indicating a "moderate" degree of socialisation in the L2. The distribution across categories can be seen in Table 4. The category "very weak" socialisation represents over half the participants in the L2; this climbs to three-quarters of the participants for the L3, and an even higher proportion for the L4 and L5. Inversely, those in the categories "moderate" to "strong" socialisation represent about a fifth of the participants in the L2 and this drops to 10 per cent and below in the subsequent languages.

Network of interlocutors

Introducing the variable

Social networks play an important role in daily language choices as speakers adapt their choice to that of the members of a particular network.

Gal (1979) identified the social network as one of the three dominant factors influencing language choice in the Austrian town of Oberwart (the other two being the speaker's age and gender). She noticed that a language shift was taking place in the community from Hungarian to German. Those who mixed more with peasants spoke more Hungarian than German while those mixing predominantly in non-peasant networks were German-dominant.

Hamers (1994) showed that the development of bilingualism and retention of the native tongue in children of immigrants in French Canada are linked to family attitudes and the children's social networks. Children in environments that foster multiculturalism with denser and richer networks were found to learn the L2 more effectively while maintaining the L1. Similar findings emerged from Wiklund's (2002) study of the relationship between the social network characteristics of bilingual adolescents from immigrant backgrounds in an upper secondary school in Sweden and their language proficiency. Not just size of the L2 network, but also the quality of interpersonal relationships with host family and peers were found by Yashima, Zenuk-Nishide and Shimizu (2004) to be important predictors of willingness to communicate.

Operationalising the variable

The questionnaire contained one question on interlocutors, which was formulated as follows:

> "Who do you usually use the language with?"

Possible answers were (1) all, (2) colleagues, (3) friends, (4) family and (5) strangers.

The focus is thus on the type of interlocutor, rather than on the size of the social network in which a language would normally be used (which would have been a better, but more difficult, question to answer). Only two types of interlocutors can easily be translated into a numerical value: "all" refers to a maximal size of the network and the term "strangers" points to an absence of network, as it implies random encounters with unknown interlocutors. It turns out that very few participants use a particular language with everyone. Languages learned early in life are more likely to be used with family, whereas languages learned later are more likely to be used only with strangers (see Table 5). In-depth interviews with a subsample of 20 participants showed that the network of colleagues tends to be larger than that of friends, and the family network tends to be the smallest (Dewaele, 2007b). I therefore assigned these groups numerical values for respectively 2, 3, and 4 while remaining aware that these differences might be small.

Table 5 Distribution of participants according to the network of interlocutors in the different languages (in %)

Network of interlocutors	L1	L2	L3	L4	L5
Strangers	3	12	29	37	40
Colleagues	11	35	35	26	22
Friends	14	28	27	28	26
Family	66	21	9	8	11
All	6	5	1	.5	.5

Number of languages known

Introducing the variable

Studies with multilingual learners generally establish a positive association between bilingualism and additional foreign language achievement (Baetens Beardsmore, 2003; Baker, 2006; Bialystok, 2002; Cenoz, 2001; Cenoz and Hoffman, 2003; Cenoz and Jessner 2009; De Angelis, 2007), but several researchers have also pointed out that positive effects tend to emerge only in additive learning contexts. Cenoz (2003), for instance, emphasises that studies that involve bilingual subtractive learning environments do not show significant differences between bi/multilinguals and monolingual learners: "bilingualism has a positive effect on third language acquisition when L3 acquisition takes place in additive contexts and bilinguals have acquired literacy skills in both their languages" (p. 83).

Swain et al., (1990) claim that it is not bilingualism per se but bilingual literacy that has an impact on the acquisition of a new language. The researchers looked at children in an English/French bilingual immersion programme in Canada. Some of these children spoke a heritage language at home but did not have literacy skills in that language, while the heritage speakers who had also acquired literacy skills by attending heritage language programmes outperformed the first group in tests measuring their writing, reading, speaking and listening skills in French L3. The authors found that bilingualism has a positive effect on third language learning, but only when coupled with the acquisition of literacy skills. Bilinguals who are literate in their two languages do seem to have an advantage in additional language learning (Keshavarz and Astaneh, 2004).

Biliteracy is not the only factor facilitating foreign language achievement. Having a third language in the school curriculum can enhance achievement in the second language. Griessler (2001) compared German L1 students studying in three different Austrian schools. The first group of students went to an English immersion school, the second went to a school where English is part of the curriculum and French is also taught early on in the programme, while the third group attended a regular Austrian secondary school where English was the only foreign language taught. Unsurprisingly, the first group of students scored highest on all measures of English proficiency. The second group of students outperformed the third group and since the only difference between these two groups was the presence of French in the curriculum, Griessler concluded that French had boosted the second group's proficiency in English.

The knowledge of more languages has been linked to a capacity for grasping grammar faster in a new language by applying a wider variety of learning strategies (Kemp, 2007); a stronger inclination to pursue the study of foreign languages (Dewaele and Thirtle, 2009); more metapragmatic awareness (Kemp, 2007; Safont Jordà, 2005) and an increased linguistic awareness (Jessner, 1999,

2006), which is seen as an emergent property of multilingual proficiency and consists of metalinguistic awareness (Jessner, 1999, 2008) and cross-linguistic awareness (i.e. "the learner's tacit and explicit awareness of the links between their language systems and communicative ability" (Jessner, 2006: 30)).

An example of this metalinguistic thinking involving cross-linguistic consultation is presented by Jessner (1999) with reference to data from Italian/German bilingual learners of English as an L3. These learners were asked to think aloud while completing an English academic writing task and some of the remarks they made show unambiguously that multilinguals completed the task by thinking it through in three different languages.

Fouser (2001) considered metalinguistic awareness to explain the results of an introspective study of two English L1 learners of Korean L3 and L5. Both learners had advanced knowledge of Japanese, a language that is similar to Korean in syntax and morphology but dissimilar in phonology, as a non-native language. Fouser (2001) found that his learners were drawing extensively on their knowledge of Japanese, particularly in the area of syntax, morphology and the lexicon. The learners also showed a good understanding of their own learning processes and of the relationship between Korean and Japanese.

Multilinguals also seem to benefit from general cognitive advantages over monolinguals. The former have been found to outperform the latter on non-verbal control tasks (Bialystok and Martin, 2004; Bialystok and Shapero, 2005; Bialystok, Craik and Luk, 2012). More recent research has found that the effect extends to trilingual children (Poarch and Van Hell, 2012). The bilinguals' superior performance has been linked to extensive practice with two active languages, which constantly requires the activation of one language and the inhibition of the other language, and switching between the languages (Bialystok and Shapero, 2005). However, more recent research based on younger and elderly bilinguals with varied language and educational histories has failed to find such an effect in various executive functions tasks, while controlling for processing speed differences, hence the need to be careful in drawing general conclusions about the cognitive benefits of multilinguals (Meuter and Orr, 2011).

The positive effect of knowing more languages has been clearly confirmed in the area of affective factors. Lasagabaster (2005a) found that the knowledge of a second foreign language exerted a significant positive influence on attitudes towards English L3 among 1087 Basque undergraduates (who had either Basque or Spanish, or both as L1s). Dewaele (2007f) found that quadrilinguals and trilinguals reported lower levels of FLA in their L2 when compared to bilinguals. One possible explanation for this phenomenon is that trilinguals and quadrilinguals have become better communicators as a result of their multilingualism and that their self-confidence, as well as their self-perceived competence, has grown as a result. The effect did not extend to FLA levels in the L3, however, where trilinguals and quadrilinguals experienced similar levels of FLA. A more consistent effect of multilingualism on

CA/FLA emerged in Dewaele (2007f) and Dewaele, Petrides and Furnham (2008). Participants with a knowledge of more languages reported significantly lower levels of CA/FLA in some situations in the L1 and L2, and in more situations in the L3 and L4. The authors speculated that the relative weakness of the effect in the L1 and L2 is linked to the fact that regular use means that speakers are less likely to have to mobilise all their resources to produce the L1 or L2. However, when producing a language learnt later in life, in which one generally feels less proficient, one may feel like one is entering relatively uncharted linguistic waters. Knowing more languages may give the LX user a little bit more confidence in their ability to avoid linguistic icebergs (Dewaele, Petrides and Furnham, 2008).

The effect of the knowledge of more languages in additional language learning has recently been considered in the light of Gibson's (1979) theory of affordances, i.e. "the perceived opportunities for action provided for the observer by an environment" (Gibson, 1979, cited in Singleton and Aronin (2007: 84). They refer to a metaphor proposed by Heft (2001):

> An affordance is the perceived functional significance of an object, event, or place for an individual. For example, a firm, obstacle-free ground surface is perceivable as a surface on which one can walk. In contrast, a boggy surface or a surface cluttered with obstacles (e.g., a boulder field) is typically perceived as impeding walking. (Heft, 2001: 123, cited in Singleton and Aronin. (2007: 84)

Singleton and Aronin (2007) point out that multilingual language learners and users not only have larger overall linguistic repertoires, but also more of such potential affordances available to them than monolingual language users (p. 92).

This observation is linked to that of Ringbom (2007: 1), who observes that cross-linguistic and intralinguistic knowledge can be highly relevant when learning a new language. Just how relevant such prior linguistic knowledge is depends on the proximity of the target language (TL) and any languages known: "If you learn a language closely related to your L1, prior knowledge will be consistently useful, but if the languages are very distant, not much prior knowledge is relevant" (p. 1).

Berthele (2011) and Berthele and Lambelet (2009) explored the effect of previous linguistic knowledge on receptive multilingualism. The studies showed that multilinguals who are highly proficient in two languages that are closely related to unknown TLs are better at interlingual inferencing, possibly because of a higher level of "perceptive tolerance", compared to multilinguals who are proficient in two languages that are more distant from a lexical point of view. Perceptive tolerance is defined as the increased sensitivity to possible and potential correspondences between two or more related systems (Berthele and Lambelet, 2009).

Developing this idea about the effect of typological proximity and affordances, and the overall effect of multilingualism (and possible superior sociocognitive fitness), Dewaele (2010b) tried to determine the effect of the knowledge of more languages in general, and, more specifically, languages belonging to the same language family as the TL (in this case French L2, L3 or L4), on self-perceived communicative competence and CA in that language. Both affordances and – to a lesser degree multilingualism – were found to have a significant effect on the dependent variables. Affordances had the strongest effect on French L2 and L3, for which participants reported medium to advanced levels of proficiency, but it had no effect on French L4, for which participants reported extremely low levels of proficiency. A possible explanation for this difference between L2/L3 and L4 is that the former is able to combine intralinguistic reflection with linguistic knowledge of other Romance languages, to compensate for gaps in the knowledge of French. However, if the level of French is too low, the basis is too weak to benefit from a transfer of linguistic knowledge from other Romance languages. It was concluded that affordances could thus be seen as a crutch for some learners, providing extra support for those with one functioning leg, but less useful for those without legs.

Recently researchers have investigated whether it is multilingualism per se or rather the specific experience of learning a new language that leads to increased metacommunicative awareness (Le Pichon et al., 2009a, 2010). The researchers suggest that children with previous language learning experience are more expert than bilingual children (who have not yet learned an LX through classroom instruction) in understanding, treating and solving a communication problem in an extreme exolingual situation, i.e. a situation of communication in which the interlocutors did not share the same languages. A comparison of monolingual and multilingual children failed to show significant average differences in the strategy used (2010). However, children with previous language learning experience were found to possess an enhanced strategic competence as the result of a superior monitoring and control of the situation. The authors speculate that the learning of a new language in a formal context is accompanied by reflections on the learning process itself, something that would not necessarily occur with simultaneous bilinguals. The researchers point out that groups of multilingual children used in previous research may be far less homogeneous than is generally assumed, and this may hide important intra-group differences.

Language dominance

Introducing the variable

Language dominance refers to a multilingual's perception of which is his/her strongest language overall. There are three broad possibilities: if the L1 is perceived as the dominant language, it suggests that ulterior language learning and use has not affected the status of the L1; a second possibility is that the L1 shares dominance with one or several languages acquired later in life; a final possibility is that the L1 is no longer the dominant language but that some language(s) acquired later has become the dominant language. It is possible that in the latter case the L1 may be attriting.

Language dominance is a key factor influencing language choice(s) in parental talk (Pavlenko 2004: 186), or the perceived emotionality of the phrase "I love you" (Dewaele 2008: 1771).

Dewaele (2004 c) found that multilinguals who reported shared dominance in their L1 and some LX scored a little lower on self-reported proficiency in the L1. They also tended to give lower scores on perceived usefulness, colourfulness, richness, poetic and emotional character of their L1. These patterns were more striking among the participants who did no longer include the L1 among their dominant languages. They reported significantly lower proficiency levels in the L1 and lower levels of use of the L1. Some clearly felt that their L1 had attrited, others reported more subtle problems when using their L1 such as the fact that the language no longer allowed them to project a contemporary image of self. This was the case of Eric, a participant in BEQ database, whose language dominance had shifted from German L1 to English L2:

> When speaking German I feel either immature or unprofessional to a certain extent. I feel like my German has been frozen at the age of 18. When speaking German I feel as if I should be expressing myself more maturely though I'm not sure exactly in what way. I feel less confident when using German than English now never having had to function professionally completely in German.

Dewaele and van Oudenhoven (2009) and Dewaele and Stavans (2012) reported that a shift in language dominance from the L1 to an LX had a significant negative effect on Emotional Stability: L1-dominant participants scored significantly higher than the LX-dominant participants.

Operationalising the variable

The feedback on the BEQ question "Which do you consider to be your dominant language(s)?" was coded as follows: 1) dominance in the L1, 2) dominance in the L1 and one or more languages acquired later in life, 3) dominance one or more languages acquired later in life (i.e. no longer the L1). Half of the participants reported dominance in the L1 (n = 784), a third reported dominance in their L1 and some LX (n = 516), and a tenth of participants felt they had become dominant in an LX (n = 156). The effect of this variable will only be considered in Chapter 10.

Trait emotional intelligence

Introducing the variable

Trait theorists argue that personality has a joint biological and environmental basis but is also influenced by culture, in the sense that behaviours are expressed according to local norms (Eysenck and Eysenck, 1985). Personality traits tend to be stable over the life span, as has been found in several longitudinal studies (Caspi and Roberts, 1999). This stability can be affected by trauma, brain damage or very consistent exposure to stimuli. Brackett et al., (2004) and Petrides and Furnham (2003) distinguished between two types of Emotional Intelligence (EI): ability EI and trait EI. The former type concerns actual cognitive abilities and must be measured through maximum performance tests, similar to those used in IQ assessments. However, the development of such tests in the area of EI has proven very difficult because the realm of emotional experience is inherently subjective (Robinson and Clore, 2002) and thus not amenable to truly objective scoring procedures. The conceptual differences between ability EI and trait EI are summarised in Petrides, Furnham and Frederickson (2004).

These differences are directly reflected in empirical findings, which reveal very low, often non-significant, correlations between measures of trait EI and ability EI, thereby supporting an explicit distinction between the two constructs (Warwick and Nettelbeck, 2004).

The latter type, also labelled "trait emotional self-efficacy", essentially views the construct as a personality trait encompassing a constellation of emotion-related dispositions and self-perceptions. Trait EI (TEI) is measured via self-report questionnaires and is located at the lower levels of personality hierarchies (Petrides and Furnham, 2001). Personality traits are hierarchically organised with a small number of broad, orthogonal dimensions (ranging between three and six, depending on the theorist) at the apex and a larger number of more specific traits further down the hierarchy (Matthews, Deary and Whiteman, 2003). Trait EI is narrower than the higher order personality dimensions and correlates with several of them; hence, it is conceptualised as a lower order trait (see also Petrides, Pita and Kokkinaki, 2007).

This operationalisation is consistent not only with the mainstream theories of personality but also with the bulk of the available evidence from multiple studies in different domains. Thus, trait EI has consistently shown near-zero correlations with IQ tests (Petrides, Frederickson, and Furnham, 2004), as expected given the general independence of personality and cognitive ability, and consistently high correlations with the basic personality dimensions (Tett, Fox and Wang, 2005), as expected given its status as a lower order personality construct (Petrides and Furnham, 2001). Based on analyses of over 36 independent datasets using many different instruments, Petrides and Furnham estimate that the variance overlap between trait EI and the Big Five personality dimensions is in the order of 70 per cent. In the light of this evidence, Petrides, Furnham and Mavroveli (2007) have argued that models that view the EI construct as anything other than a personality trait are problematic. The construct of trait EI, then, lies wholly outside the domain of cognitive ability and concerns exclusively emotion-related self-perceptions, rather than actual abilities, competences or skills.

Operationalising the variable

Participants who had finished completing the BEQ were invited to fill out the Trait Emotional Intelligence Questionnaire–Short Form (TEIQue-SF; Petrides and Furnham, 2006). A total of 454 participants completed both questionnaires.

The TEIQue-SF is based on the long form of the TEIQue and comprises 30 items, responded to on a seven-point Likert scale. Two items from each of the 15 subscales (adaptability, emotion expression, emotion perception, emotion regulation, empathy, relationships, social competence, etc.) of the TEIQue were selected for inclusion, based primarily on their correlations with the corresponding total subscale scores. Scores on the questionnaire ranged from 83 to 198, with a mean of 157.5 (SD = 20.5) and were slightly negatively skewed. Three groups were created: those whose score was more than one standard deviation below the mean were labelled "Low trait EI" (n = 70), those whose score was more than one standard deviation above the mean were labelled "High trait EI" (n = 58) while the remaining participants whose score was situated within one standard deviation around the mean were labelled "Medium trait EI" (n = 326).

A t-test for equality of means revealed that females scored significantly higher than males, $t\ (462) = 2.93$, $p < .01$, although the effect size of this difference was small ($\eta^2 = .02$; mean females = 159.2, mean males = 152.8). A one-way ANOVA with level of education as the independent variable showed a significant effect on trait EI scores, $F\ (3, 460) = 3.82$, $p < .01$, although the effect size was again small ($\eta^2 = .02$). A Scheffé post hoc analysis showed that participants with A-levels (high-school) scored significantly lower than their peers with postgraduate degrees (MA or PhD, $p < .05$). Finally, there was a positive correlation between trait EI and age, $r\ (461) = .093$, $p < .05$, with older participants tending to have higher trait EI scores. The internal consistency of the TEIQue-SF was very satisfactory (Cronbach's alpha = .79, N = 425). Hitherto, the TEIQue-SF has been translated into 15 languages and used in many studies around the world (Chamorro-Premuzic, Bennett and Furnham, 2007).

Gender, age and education level

Introducing the variables

Studies on sex and gender differences have focused on encoding, decoding and representing emotion. Women have been found to identify emotions in facial expression more quickly than men (Hampson, van Anders and Mullin, 2006) and to react faster to lexical emotion (Grunwald et al., 1999). The type of emotion (positive or negative) also had an effect, with women responding more quickly to negative emotions (Hampson, van Anders and Mullin, 2006). Barrett et al., (2000) studied gender differences in the complexity and differentiation of people's representations of emotional experience. They noted that the empirical status of gender differences in emotion remains unresolved.

Women consistently describe themselves as more emotionally intense than men when emotionality is defined as a global disposition largely independent of the social context (Barrett et al., 2000). However, the differences are less clear cut when emotionality is defined as the experience of a specific emotion in a specific social context. Barrett et al., (1998) asked participants to provide global, retrospective descriptions of their emotional characteristics at an initial session, and then to provide momentary emotion ratings as well as details about the social context in which they experienced their emotions over a one-week period. A comparison between the male and female participants showed significant differences in the global self-descriptions but not in the averaged momentary ratings of emotion. The authors also found that the gender of the interaction partner elicited gender differences in emotionality; participants experienced and expressed more emotion when in opposite-gender dyads (p. 555).

Barrett reports that only half of the studies on this topic report gender differences in fear or anxiety, anger, depression or sadness. These differences are "typically in the stereotypic direction" (Barrett et al., 2000: 1027). Some researchers suggest that there are gender differences in emotional experience, primarily linked to differential socialisation experiences, while others suggest that differences are inconsistent and exist mainly for emotional expressions (p. 1027).

Some researchers have also focused on gender differences in emotion recognition in a second language. Dromey, Silveira and Sandor (2005), for example, found that their female participants scored better in tasks of recognition of affective prosody in English as an L2.

Table 6 Cross-tabulation of gender and age of participants

Age group	Female	Male	Total
Teenagers	62	20	82
Twenty+	417	141	558
Thirty+	348	138	486
Forty+	174	74	248
Fifty+	85	59	144
Sixty+	25	28	53
Seventy+	0	2	2
TOTAL	1111	462	1573

Williams, Burden and Lanvers (2002) found that in their survey of 11–13-year-old pupils in the south-west of England there was a higher level of motivation for studying French among girls than boys, and that boys in particular were more highly motivated to learn German than French.

Operationalising the variable

Participants were requested to tick the box indicating their gender and to provide their age. Table 6 presents a cross-tabulation of gender and age data after the participants were grouped in seven age groups. For the statistical analyses, the two participants over the age of 70 were added to the sixty+ group.

Information about education level was obtained through a closed question inviting the participant to tick his/her level of education. Options were: A-level (secondary education), Bachelors (BA), Masters (MA), Doctorate (PhD).

5
Results: Self-perceived Competence in Oral and Written Language

The concept of self-perceived competence

Self-perceived competence is a person's evaluation of their ability to communicate (McCroskey and McCroskey, 1988). It is a judgement that reflects a sum of various aspects of the L2, including perceived competence in grammar, phonology, lexis, syntax and, especially, pragmatics among experienced LX users. It is a holistic judgement covering all types of communication. It is probably also influenced by past traumas or successes in the LX, as well as recent experiences in intercultural communication. Although it does not reflect the communication of emotion per se, I feel that it includes the ability to communicate emotion. It is hard to imagine someone claiming to be maximally competent in an LX if she/he was not able to communicate emotion in it. Communicative competence includes so-called "strategic competence", i.e., the ability to compensate for breakdowns in communication and the capacity to enhance the effectiveness of communication (Canale, 1983: 11).

Self-report measures were shown to correlate highly with linguistic measures of proficiency. Mettewie (2004) correlated self-reported oral proficiency scores for Dutch and French with an objective measure of language proficiency (based on results for grammar tests, reading and listening comprehension exercises) among 338 pupils in Brussels. She found highly significant positive relationships between the measures ($r = .83$ for Dutch and $r = .76$ for French, all $p < .0001$), which led her to conclude that self-reports provide valid measures to researchers (p. 238). MacIntyre, Noels and Clément (1997) looked at perceived competence in French L2 as a function of actual competence and language anxiety in a sample of 37 adult Anglophone students. They completed scales of language anxiety and a "can-do" test, which assessed their self-perceptions of competence in 26 French tasks. They then performed each of those tasks. Scores for perceived L2 competence and actual L2 competence were found to be strongly intercorrelated. It thus seems that measures of perception of proficiency are acceptable indicators of actual proficiency. Although some personality types tend to overestimate their proficiency slightly (MacIntyre et al., 1997), this is compensated for by the fact that an equal number tend to underestimate their proficiency slightly. Self-perceived measures have the added advantage of being easy to collect, enabling researchers to consider larger sample sizes than in research based on production data.

A crucial difference between performance in a dominant language (typically the L1) and a weaker language is that in the former case participants do not have to worry about language processing (production and reception), which is largely automatic, and can therefore focus on the content of the interaction (cf. Paradis, 2004). However, LX users will typically rely more on controlled processing, involving searches for words, expressions, grammar rules, pragmatic rules, idioms and metaphors. This will involve a considerable demand on working memory and will limit the amount of attention LX users can pay to content and to observation of the interlocutor. In this juggling act, LX users are much likely to stumble at some point, and feel generally less sure-footed as a result. The other challenge facing LX users in reporting emotional experiences is that of potentially incomplete conceptual representations of emotion words and scripts, as well as of metaphors and other figures of speech that play a crucial role in emotional communication between native speakers (Gibbs, Leggitt and Turner, 2002). Gibbs et al., (2002) suggest that speakers use metaphors to convey a variety of subtle meanings, which may not always have been consciously intended at the time of production. By resorting to metaphors, native speakers can describe their emotional experiences in more detail and with more nuance than would be possible using terms from the literal emotion lexicon.

Operationalising the variable

The data was obtained through the following question:

> "On the scale from 1 (least proficient) to 5 (fully fluent) how do you rate yourself in speaking, understanding, reading, writing in all of the languages in question?"

Possible answers on a five-point Likert scale were: minimal = 1, low = 2, medium = 3, high = 4 and maximal = 5.

Information was collected for the L1, L2, L3, L4 and L5. The dependent variables are thus the numerical values reflecting self-perceived competence in four language skills.

Cronbach alpha analyses revealed very high internal consistency reliability for oral and written skills in the different languages: L1 (alpha = .92), L2 (alpha = .94), L3 (alpha = .93), L4 (alpha = .93) and L5 (alpha = .93).

A series of one-sample Kolmogorov-Smirnov tests revealed that the values for self-perceived competence in the four skills in up to five languages are not normally distributed (Kolmogorov-Smirnov Z values vary between 3.8

and 20.1, all $p < .0001$). As a consequence, Kruskal-Wallis tests were used as non-parametric equivalents to one-way ANOVAs, and Wilcoxon Signed Ranks Tests and Mann-Whitney tests were used instead of t-tests.

As the statistical analyses focus on the pentalinguals only, it is important to point out that their profiles did not differ from that of the database as a whole. Mean age was 36.8 (SD = 11.5). The mean score on the Trait Emotional Intelligence questionnaire was 155.8 (SD = 11.5). Of the 486 pentalinguals who provided data for all variables, 69 per cent were women (n = 336), 7 percent had a high school degree (n = 34), a quarter had a BA (n = 117), a third had a MA (n = 156) and a third had a PhD (n = 179). English was the most frequently used L1 (n = 109), followed by Dutch (n = 58), German (n = 58), French (n = 46), Spanish (n = 30).

The most frequent L2 was English (n = 166) and French (n = 116). The same distribution existed for the most frequent L3s: English (n = 148) and French (n = 106). German was the most frequent L4 (n = 106), followed by French (n = 105). Spanish was the most frequent L5 (n = 85) followed by German (n = 66), Italian (n = 65).

Hypothesis 1a: Monotonic decline in self-perceived competence from L1 to L5

Since repeated measures tests delete participants for whom data may be missing in a particular column, only the pentalinguals who filled out scores for all the different skills in all the different languages were included in the analysis.

The Friedman's ANOVA tests for related samples revealed a highly significant effect (Table 7). Participants felt much more competent in their L1 compared to languages that had been learned later in life (L2, L3, L4, L5). This effect was strongest for oral skills and – very marginally – weaker for written skills (See Figure 1).

Most participants who mentioned levels of competence in their various languages conformed to the quantitative pattern, namely higher levels of

Table 7 The effect of chronology of acquisition on self-perceived competence from L1 to L5 (χ^2)

Variable	N	df	χ^2	p
Speaking	466	4	995.2	***
Comprehending	468	4	947.1	***
Reading	456	4	844.1	***
Writing	436	4	899.1	***

***$p < .0001$

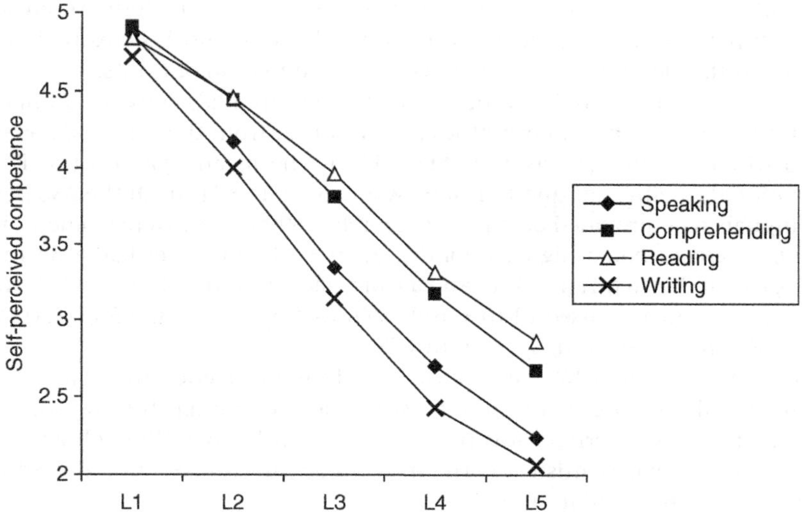

Figure 1 Mean values for self-perceived competence from L1 to L5

self-perceived competence in languages acquired earlier in life:

Stefanie (German L1, English L2, Spanish L3, French L4, Irish L5):

> Stefanie: In a way it is easier to express myself exactly in L1 German.

One particular group of participants goes against this general trend, namely L1 attriters, like a participant who wished to remain anonymous, SO (Taiwanese L1, Mandarin Chinese L2, English L3, Spanish L4), who rarely uses her L1, and feels more proficient in Spanish, which she learnt at the age of 16:

> SO: I think it's easier for me to express in Spanish or sometimes English because Spanish has been my dominant language for at least last 15 years. Taiwanese and Mandarin Chinese are rarely used. Although I may use them if the circumstances require. I'm not sure.

Hypothesis 2: The effect of Age of onset of Acquisition in the LX on self-perceived competence in oral and written skills in the LX

A series of Kruskal-Wallis tests revealed highly significant effects of AoA on self-perceived competence in the L2, L3 and L4, with significant effects on comprehension and reading in the L5 (Table 8).

Participants who started learning an LX earlier in life feel generally more competent in that LX than later starters. The mean values for self-perceived competence descend quite linearly across AoA groups in the L2, with a slight

Table 8 The effect of AoA in the LX on self-perceived competence in oral and written skills (χ^2)

Competence	L2	L3	L4	L5
Speaking	103***	54***	13**	7
Comprehending	96***	63***	18***	13**
Reading	65***	54***	18***	9*
Writing	98***	67***	15**	5

*** p < .0001, ** p < .001, * p < .05

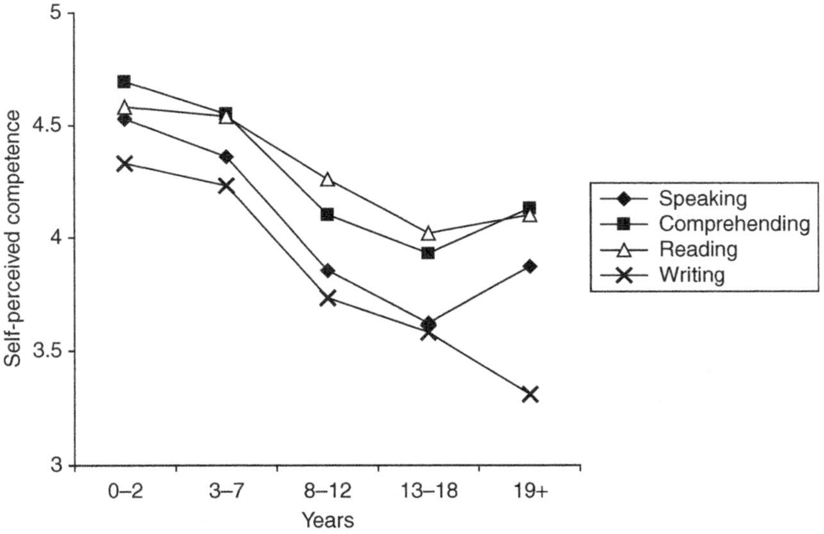

Figure 2 Mean values for self-perceived competence in oral and written skills in the L2 according to AoA

resurgence for the 19+ group for speaking, comprehension and reading, but not writing (Figure 2).

Testimonies like the one from Elisabeth (English L1, German L2, French L3, Korean L4), who started learning German at the age of 15, are quite frequent in the database. She links her perceived deficit in German to her late AoA. She sees this deficit as something permanent that no amount of authentic interactions in German will overcome:

> Elisabeth: I'm always more comfortable communicating in English. I think I started with German too late to really ever feel satisfied with my communicative competence even though I've lived in Germany for 5 years.

Some participants point out that AoA is only one of the factors that determined their proficiency in an LX. Iris (German L1, Italian L2, English L3) explains that after moving from Germany to Italy when she was 12, her parents started speaking Italian to her, which became her dominant language over a two-to-three-year period:

> Iris: I never spoke Italian until I was twelve (and in Germany I was really good at school) then we moved from Germany to Italy and I learned Italian and my parents started to speak Italian to me (they spoke German in Germany to me) and Italian became in maybe just two or three years my main language.

One participant, Monika (German L1, English L2, Dutch L3, French L4) wondered whether her early exposure to English might have played a role in her rapid development once she returned there as a teenager:

> Monika: My parents moved to the US (Illinois) for two years when I was six weeks old, they spoke German to each other but English with their environment so I was exposed to bilingual surroundings for two years. Then we moved back to Germany and a monolingual environment and I only started to "learn" English when I entered school. My foreign language acquisition proceeded normally – I did well but not spectacularly. When I was fifteen I went on a six-week trip to the US staying with friends of my parents in different parts of the country and speaking nothing but English. That was as if a dam had burst – I came back completely fluent.

Hypothesis 3: The effect of context of acquisition of the LX on self-perceived competence in oral and written skills in the LX

The Kruskal-Wallis tests revealed that acquisition context had a highly significant effect overall on self-perceived competence in oral and written skills in the different languages (Table 9). A closer look at the mean values

Table 9 The effect of context of acquisition of the LX on self-perceived competence in oral and written skills (χ^2)

Competence	L2	L3	L4	L5
Speaking	207***	146***	88***	33***
Comprehending	223***	153***	72***	36***
Reading	136***	75***	42***	17***
Writing	129***	50***	40***	13**

*** p < .0001, ** p < .001, * p < .05

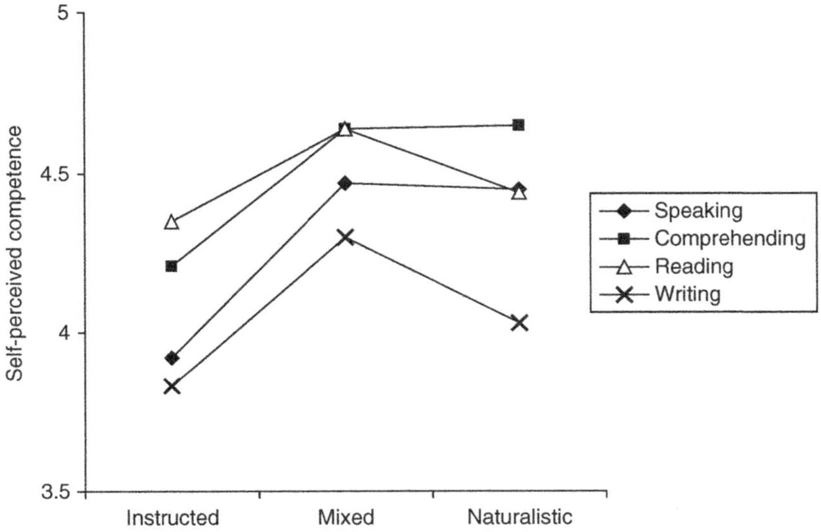

Figure 3 Mean values for self-perceived competence in oral and written skills in the L2 according to context of acquisition

for the three groups in the L2 shows that the instructed learners feel less competent than mixed and naturalistic learners (Figure 3). The difference between mixed and naturalistic learners is minimal for speaking and comprehension, but the latter have slightly lower scores for written language, which may be linked to the fact that mastering written skills outside the classroom is more difficult than acquiring oral skills.

A number of participants like SW (German L1, English L2, French L3) reported that they did not like an LX at school and that they only started to become more proficient in it once they encountered it later in life. In SW's case, the foreign language even became the "language of the heart":

> SW: I've always hated English at school until I discovered it by myself (...) I would consider English as my "language of the heart" – I feel a strong attraction (not only the language but also landscapes and people with Celtic background).

Hypothesis 4: The effect of general frequency of use of the LX on self-perceived competence in oral and written skills in the LX

The Kruskal-Wallis tests reveal that frequency of use of an LX has highly significant effects (all $p < .0001$) on self-perceived competence in the different languages (Table 10). Unsurprisingly, the more frequently a language is used, the more proficient one feels in that language.

Figure 4 shows that the relationship between frequency of use of the L2 and self-perceived competence is almost linear. Moreover, the relationship is very similar for the four language skills.

Carolyn (English L1, French L2, Spanish L3, Arabic L4) remembers a time where she felt reasonably proficient in Arabic. However, she no longer uses the language and, as a result, no longer feels proficient in it:

> Carolyn: Although I am not speaking Arabic now, when I lived in the Middle East, I frequently used phrases such as "praise to God", "God willing", "God give you the strength" etc. that I could not imagine myself saying in English.

Table 10 The effect of general frequency of use of the LX on self-perceived competence in oral and written skills (χ^2)

Competence	L2	L3	L4	L5
Speaking	483***	431***	247***	134***
Comprehending	364***	375***	195***	133***
Reading	337***	291***	154***	107***
Writing	455***	379***	201***	129***

*** p < .0001, ** p < .001, * p < .05

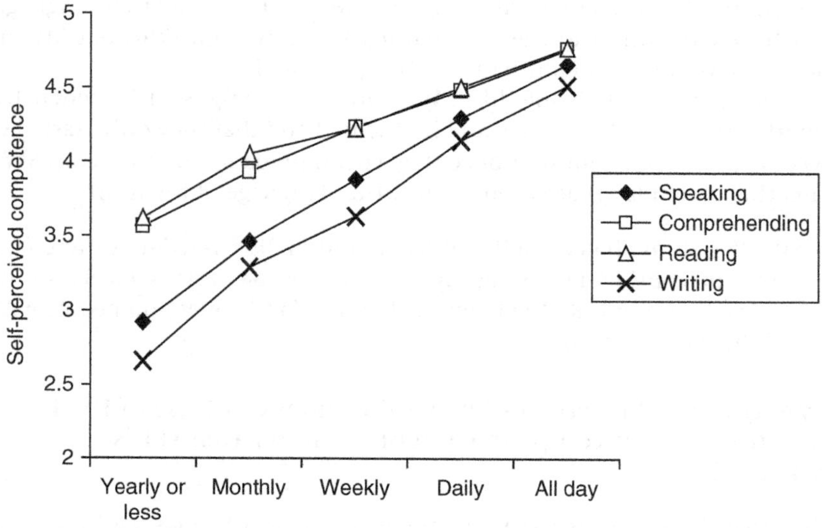

Figure 4 Mean values for self-perceived competence in the L2 according to frequency of use of the L2

Hypothesis 5: The effect of degree of socialisation in the LX on self-perceived competence in oral and written skills in the LX

The Kruskal-Wallis analyses show a highly significant effect (all $p < .0001$) for socialisation in the L2, L3, L4 and L5 on self-perceived communicative competence in these languages (Table 11).

Higher levels of socialisation are linked to higher levels of self-perceived competence in the different languages. Figure 5 shows the mean values for the L2. The biggest difference appears to be between participants with minimal levels of socialisation in the L2 ("very weak socialisation") and the group with a "weak socialisation" in the L2. Self-perceived competence values rise only slightly across the groups with higher levels of socialisation in the L2.

Table 11 The effect of degree of socialisation in the LX on self-perceived competence in oral and written skills (χ^2)

Competence	L2	L3	L4	L5
Speaking	300***	239***	108***	59***
Comprehending	244***	196***	103***	63***
Reading	208***	180***	69***	52***
Writing	282***	203***	99***	51***

*** $p < .0001$, ** $p < .001$, * $p < .05$

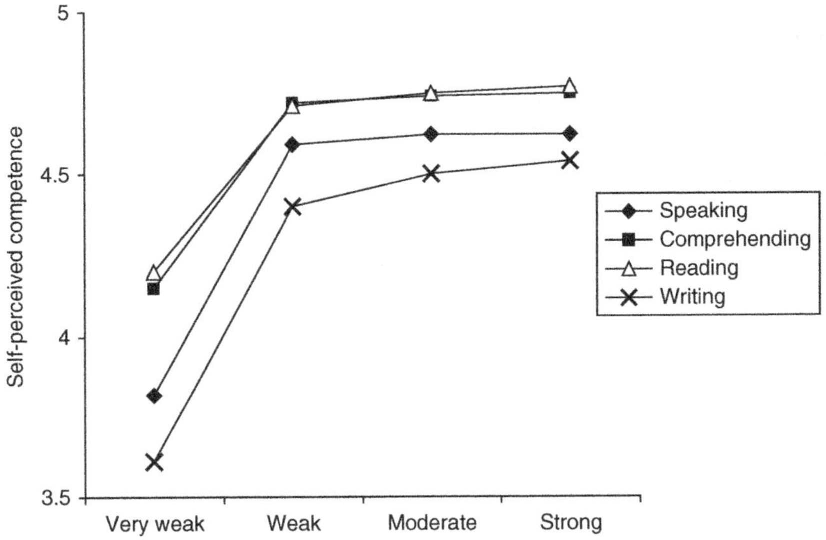

Figure 5 Mean values for self-perceived competence in the L2 according to level of socialisation in the L2

One participant, Bruce (English L1, Chinese L2, French L3), works as a publishing consultant in China, is married to a Chinese speaker and feels highly socialised and highly competent in his oral L2 Mandarin Chinese:

> Bruce: Chinese is more intimate, more real. For the last 20+ years everything important to me emotionally happened in Chinese. Conversations were in Chinese and I "experienced" them in Chinese.

He does report some "bumps" in his socialisation process, specifically linked to cultural practices:

> Bruce: I was considered rude and insufficiently "respectful" of my father-in-law.

Despite his strong socialisation in Chinese, he still prefers English for writing and for psychological analysis:

> Bruce: Even though I think and speak daily in Chinese (rarely speak in English) it is harder to write Chinese than English (by its nature and because of my education in it having been so late). I think in terms of psychology and tend to "analyze" myself and others. Chinese is a very poetic and rich language but many concepts from modern social science – Freud's theories, concepts of racism etc. – are not familiar to many Chinese and when they are mentioned in daily language sound "weird" and "translated".

Hypothesis 6: The effect of network of interlocutors in the LX on self-perceived competence in oral and written skills in the LX

A series of Kruskal-Wallis analyses show that the network of interlocutors has a highly significant effect on self-perceived competence in the L2, L3 and L4. It has a significant effect only on writing in the L5 (Table 12).

Table 12 The effect of network of interlocutors in the LX on self-perceived competence in oral and written skills (χ^2)

Competence	L2	L3	L4	L5
Speaking	87***	137***	85***	3
Comprehending	68***	85***	66***	5
Reading	50***	74***	54***	7
Writing	62***	110***	67***	10*

*** $p < .0001$, * $p < .05$

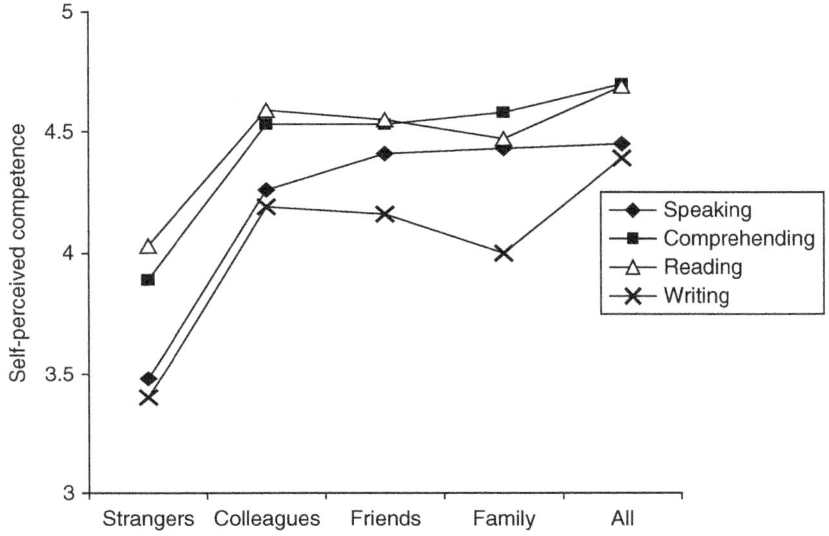

Figure 6 Mean values for self-perceived competence in the L2 according to network of interlocutors

Unsurprisingly, scores for self-perceived competence in the L2 are the lowest if that language is only used with strangers and highest if the L2 is used with everybody (Figure 6).

Elisabeth (German L1, English L2, French L3, Japanese L4, Spanish L5, dominant in German and English) feels equally competent in German and English, which she acquired when she was ten years old and which she now teaches at university. She reports using English with friends, colleagues, students but not with members of her family and German friends:

> Elisabeth: I use English with almost EVERYBODY (i.e. all categories except family because they either do not speak English or don't speak it well enough to make it appropriate (they all live in Germany). I also don't use it with German friends and of course I don't speak English in Germany unless I'm speaking to people who speak English too (duh!). I use German with everybody who speaks German with me in any and all contexts that would make it appropriate: professional, personal, public, private.

CW (English L1, French L2, Arabic L3, German L4, Finnish L5) links the frequency of her use of her foreign languages with particular interlocutors, contrary to her L1, which she uses with the widest number of interlocutors:

CW: Most comfortable with English and use it regularly. However French is a shared language with my brothers (not parents) as we all went to immersion schools. Finnish is also a family language (my grandparents) with strong emotional connotations simply because it's a way to connect with my mother's side of the family after my parents' divorce.

Sue (English L1, German L2, French L3) reports on the difficulty of her son in using English (one of his L1s) outside his usual network of interlocutors, namely with the English teacher at school:

Sue: A child learns English from birth (as the only language spoken to him by both parents) and German simultaneously through outside influences. He is then put into an English beginners class (at school) at the age of 10 and fails lamentably. He can read Harry Potter in English with very little problem. He had been able to speak English very well but seems to be losing his command of the language although speaking English at home.

Hypothesis 7: The effect of knowing more languages on self-perceived competence in oral and written skills in the LX

The Kruskal-Wallis analyses reveal the highly significant effect of the number of languages known on self-perceived competence in these various languages (Table 13). Values for self-perceived competence increase gradually from bilinguals to trilinguals, and continue to rise from quadrilinguals to pentalinguals (Figure 7).

Hypothesis 8: The effect of Trait Emotional Intelligence on self-perceived competence in oral and written skills in the LX

A series of Kruskal-Wallis analyses showed no significant effect of TEI on self-perceived competence in oral and written skills in any language (Table 14).

Table 13 The effect of knowing more languages on self-perceived competence in oral and written skills (χ^2)

Competence	L2	L3	L4
Speaking	72***	43***	16***
Comprehending	91***	62***	22***
Reading	83***	56***	27***
Writing	50***	32***	10*

*** $p < .0001$, ** $p < .001$, * $p < .05$

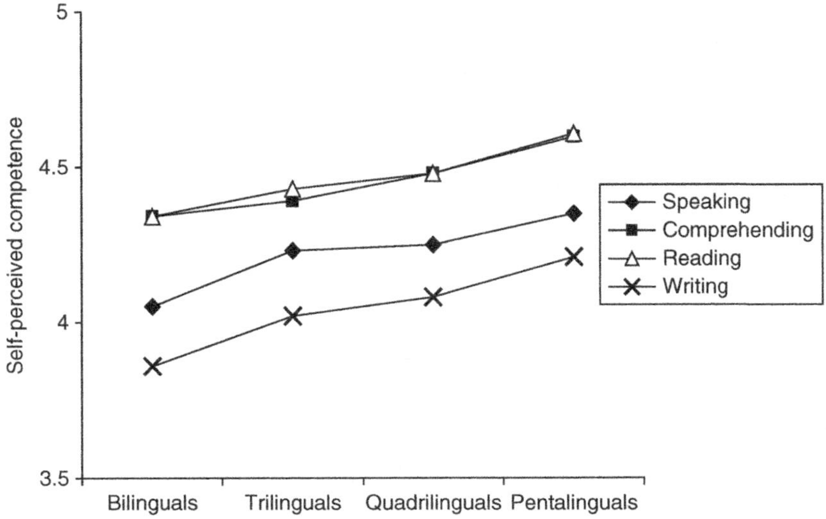

Figure 7 Mean values for self-perceived competence in oral and written skills in the L2 according to the knowledge of more languages

Table 14 The effect of TEI on self-perceived competence in oral and written skills (χ^2)

Competence	L2	L3	L4	L5
Speaking	1	1	3	1
Comprehending	1	1	3	1
Reading	0	0	1	1
Writing	0	1	3	0

all $p > .05$

Hypothesis 9: The effect of gender, age and level of education on self-perceived competence in oral and written skills in the LX

Gender

A series of Mann-Whitney tests revealed significant differences in self-perceived competence between female and male participants in the L2, L3 and L5 (Table 15). The difference for speaking was significant for the L2, L3 and L5. The only significant difference between female and male participants for comprehension appeared in the L2. The differences between both sexes for self-perceived reading skills were significant in the L2, L3 and L5. The only significant difference in self-perceived writing skills between the sexes occurred in the L5. The pattern is similar across skills and languages: when there is a difference, female participants score higher than male participants (see Figure 8 for the mean values for the L2).

Table 15 Differences in self-perceived competence between female and male participants

Competence		L2	L3	L4	L5
Speaking	Mann-Whitney U	234426	140464	72610	20857
	Z	−2.7*	2.4*	1.4	2.3*
Comprehending	Mann-Whitney U	232606	143650	75035	22151
	Z	−2.9*	1.6	0.7	1.5
Reading	Mann-Whitney U	235422	141634	70585	19987
	Z	−2.2*	2.0*	1.5	2.7*
Writing	Mann-Whitney U	235270	144174	70594	20035
	Z	−1.8	1.2	−0.7	2.0*

* $p < .05$

Age

A series of Kruskal-Wallis tests reveal systematic age differences in self-perceived competence in the L2 and more scattered effects in the L4 and L5 (Table 16). Teenagers feel most competent, mean values tend to decrease across the twenty+ and thirty+ age groups, before bouncing back in the following ones (with the exception of speaking and comprehension in the oldest age group which shows a sudden decline) (Figure 9).

Education

A series of Kruskal-Wallis analyses show a highly significant and systematic effect of education level on self-perceived competence in skills in the L2 (Table 17). A more limited effect was also found in the L3 and L4, but none in the L5. A look at the scores for the L2 reveals that the age effect is not linear: participants with A-level education score higher than participants with a BA, after which scores bounce up again for participants with an MA and participants with a PhD score highest (Figure 10).

Summing up

All the hypotheses were confirmed, with the exception of hypothesis 8 on the effect of Trait Emotional Intelligence on self-perceived competence. The comments by participants generally confirmed the statistical patterns but also added important nuances.

Languages acquired later in life were given systematically lower scores for self-perceived competence than languages acquired early. The scores of pentalinguals are thus highest for the L1 and lowest for the L5. The only exception to this pattern is the group of participants who rarely use a language acquired early in life and who could be potential "attriters" for that language (Schmid, 2009). The linear decrease in mean self-perceived competence scores can also be altered by individuals who felt highly proficient in a language they acquired later in life because they married a speaker of that language or moved to a region where that language was used.

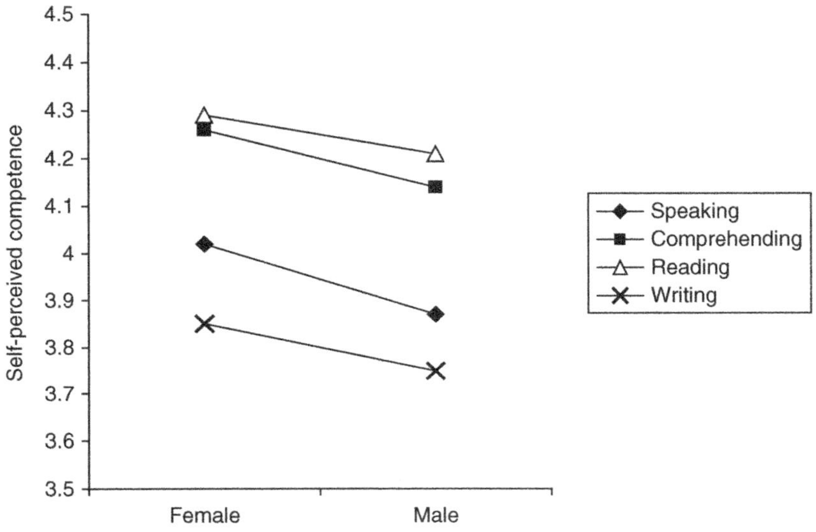

Figure 8 Differences in self-perceived competence between female and male participants in the L2

Table 16 The effect of age on self-perceived competence in oral and written skills (χ^2)

Competence	L2	L3	L4	L5
Speaking	22**	2	9	9
Comprehending	35***	3	13*	14*
Reading	37***	9	14*	19**
Writing	13*	6	2	2

*** p < .0001, ** p < .001, * p < .05

The two independent variables dealing with "history of learning a language" turned out to have significant effects on self-perceived competence from the L2 to the L5. Younger starters felt more proficient in speaking, comprehending, reading and writing their various languages (the effect was less pronounced for the L5). Also, participants who had learnt a language both within and outside the classroom felt significantly more proficient in that language than participants who had learnt a language only through formal instruction. This does suggest that when a language is perceived as an actual communication tool during the learning period, and not as some abstract linguistic system that needs to be mastered because it is part of the school curriculum, the chances are that learners/users will feel more competent in it.

The three independent variables reflecting the current use of the LX: frequency of general use, socialisation and network of interlocutors also turned out to have a highly significant effect across languages. Unsurprisingly,

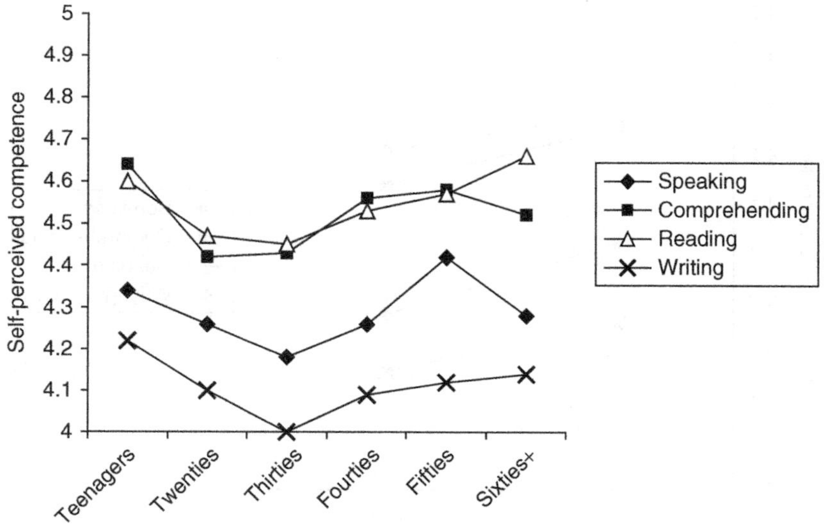

Figure 9 The effect of age on self-perceived competence in the L2

Table 17 The effect of education level on self-perceived competence in oral and written skills (χ^2)

Competence	L2	L3	L4	L5
Speaking	50***	1	3	1
Comprehending	64***	1	6	2
Reading	81***	10*	7*	6
Writing	36***	7*	1	6

*** $p < .0001$, ** $p < .001$, * $p < .05$

frequent use, strong socialisation and a wide network of interlocutors were linked to higher scores of self-perceived competence. The comments from participants underlined how dynamic their self-perceived competence is: geographical and cultural displacement, and changes of partner or of colleagues alter the fragile equilibrium between their languages. One participant reported how her son struggled to use his L1 outside his usual family network, namely with the teacher in a foreign language class. While he clearly had all the implicit knowledge to enable him to function as a literate native speaker in his L1, he lacked any explicit knowledge, and was probably baffled to be told to learn grammar rules he did not know existed, in a language he spoke fluently.

The participants' linguistic profile, i.e. the number of languages they had acquired, also had a significant effect on their self-perceived competence in their different languages. The knowledge of more languages was linked to higher self-perceived competence scores across all their languages. This

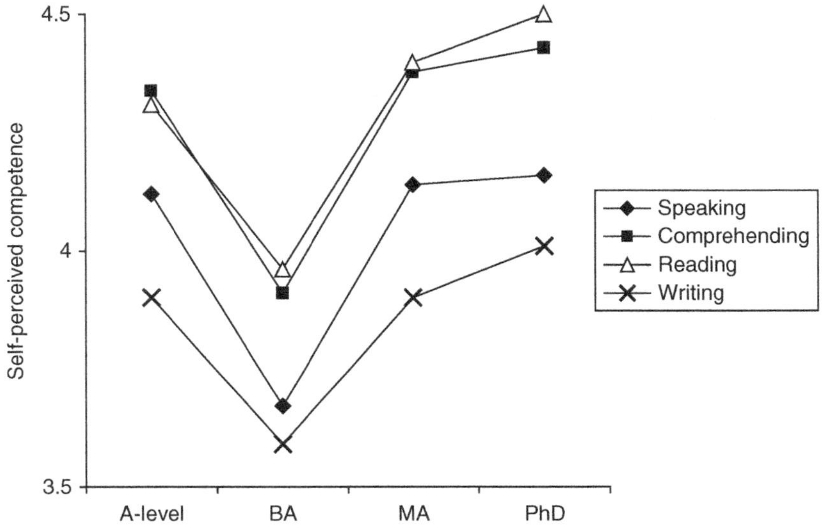

Figure 10 The effect of education level on self-perceived competence in the L2

confirms earlier findings with different samples (Dewaele, 2007f) and with a subsample of the BEQ (Dewaele, 2007a; Dewaele, Petrides and Furnham, 2008).

Trait Emotional Intelligence turned out to have no effect on self-perceived competence.

The effects that were uncovered for gender, age and education level are a trifle harder to interpret. First, female participants felt more competent than male participants in their L2, L3 and L5, but not in the L4. This finding seems to confirm the findings of Aida (1994) and Gu (2002) that female students outperformed male students in foreign language classes. Second, the effects for age were most significant in the L2, where participants in their twenties and thirties scored lower than the younger and older age cohorts. A similar, but weakened pattern emerged in the L4 and L5, but no effect was found in the L3. Third, education level also had the strongest effect in the L2. Just as for age, the effect was not linear: participants with a BA scored lower than their peers with lower and higher levels of education. Level of education had a more scattered effect in the L3 and L4, but not the L5. One possible interpretation for this surprising pattern is that contrary to participants with only a high school education, participants with a BA may have been in more systematic contact with highly proficient and highly educated multilinguals, which made them more aware of the distance they still had to cover in order to reach such high levels of proficiency and education. High-school leavers on the other hand, might not have had to confront their linguistic and educational limitations in the same way, and were thus less likely to perceive their competence as being rather low.

6
Results: Communicating Feelings (in general)

Communicating feelings in different languages

Communicating feelings in an LX is challenging if they have to be channelled through narrow and partial linguistic translations. In some cases the particular feeling or emotion may even be untranslatable (Farrell, 2006; Panayiotou, 2004a, 2004b, 2006; Shweder, 2008; Wierzbicka and Harkins, 2001). Emotions are expressed very differently in Asian and Western cultures (Besemeres, 2004; Markus and Kitayama, 1991, 1994). An excellent illustration of this can be found in the study of Veronica Zhengdao Ye (2004), a Chinese scholar who emigrated to Australia in the 1990s. During her first years, Ye struggled with the easy use of terms of endearment and affectionate gestures in Australian public life. She tried to avoid overt expression of her feelings:

> I remain fundamentally Chinese deep inside. My sense of self is Chinese. And I feel most at home when I can express myself, especially my feelings and emotions, in the Chinese way – subtle, implicit and without words. (Ye, 2004: 139–140)

Ye portrays her feelings as very personal and not to be shared in public. Having to talk about her feelings makes her feel "stripped and vulnerable" (2004: 140). She is acutely aware that the difference between Chinese and English expressions of emotion is so great that there is a constant danger of misinterpretation and misunderstanding, placing stress on cross-cultural relationships. She is still amazed at the ease with which Australians use "honeyed words", such as saying "I love you" on the phone or when parting. She understands now that these expressions are pleasantries for social purposes (p. 140).

> We do not place so much emphasis on verbal expressions of love and affection, because they can evaporate quickly. For a Chinese, love and affection are embodied in care and concern, in doing what we believe are good things for the other party. (p. 140)

She and her parents have never said *I love you* to one another. She recalls leaving them for the first time to go to Australia:

> At the airport, we fought back our tears and urged each other repeatedly to take care; we wore the biggest smiles to wave good-bye to each other, to soothe each others' worries. Just like any other Chinese parting between those who love each other – there were no hugs and no "I love you". Yet I have never doubted my parents' profound love for me. (p. 141)

Interestingly, after a two-year separation from her parents, Ye decides to give them "a long and tight embrace" (p. 142).

Operationalising the variable

The present chapter focuses on the self-reported likelihood of language choice for expression of feelings in four different situations.

The data was obtained thought the following question:

> "What language do you express your deepest feelings in?"

Possible answers on a five-point Likert scale were: never = 1, maybe = 2, probably = 3, certainly = 4 and without any doubt = 5.

The situations included expressing feelings directed to oneself, to friends, to partners or family members and expressing feelings in letters or emails.

Information was collected for the L1, L2, L3, L4 and L5. The dependent variables are thus the numerical values reflecting the likelihood of choosing a language for the expression of feelings in four situations.

Cronbach alpha analyses revealed that internal consistency reliability was extremely high for the four items linked to language choice for feelings in the different languages: L1 (alpha = .88), L2 (alpha = .91), L3 (alpha = .92), L4 (alpha = .92) and L5 (alpha = .90).

A series of one-sample Kolmogorov-Smirnov tests revealed that the values for frequency of language choice for expression of feelings in the four situations in up to five languages are not normally distributed (Kolmogorov-Smirnov Z values vary between 7.4 and 13.9, all $p < .0001$). As a consequence, Kruskal-Wallis tests were used as non-parametric equivalents to one-way ANOVAs, and Wilcoxon Signed Ranks Tests and Mann-Whitney tests were used instead of t-tests.

Hypothesis 1a: Monotonic decline in likelihood of language choice for expressing feelings from L1 to L5

The Friedman's ANOVA tests for related samples showed a highly significant effect: participants were much more likely to express their feelings in languages acquired first (Table 18). Mean values for the likelihood of language

Table 18 The effect of chronology of acquisition on likelihood of choice of language for expressing feelings from L1 to L5 (χ^2)

	N	Df	χ^2	p
Alone	369	4	778.5	***
Letters	356	4	680.6	***
Friends	358	4	688.8	***
Parents	335	4	737.8	***

*** $p < .0001$

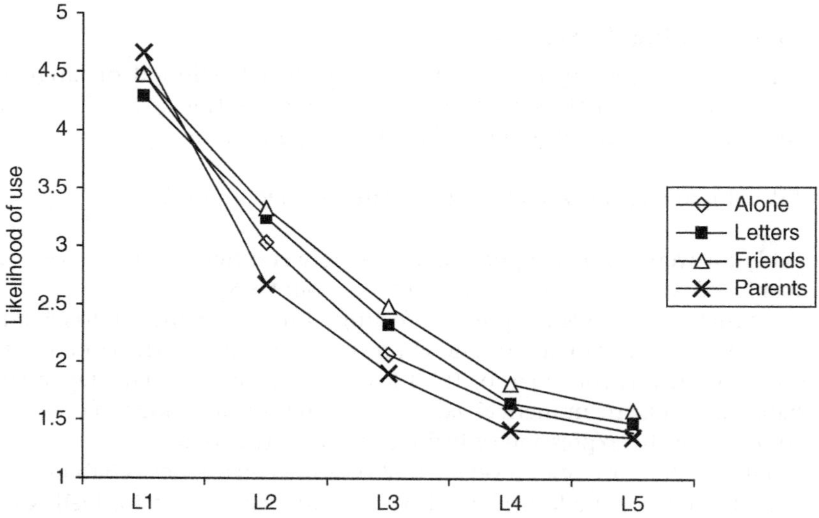

Figure 11 Mean values for likelihood to express feelings in the L1, L2, L3, L4 and L5

choice for expressing feelings in the five contexts are presented in Figure 11. It shows that multilinguals indicated that they would use their L1 somewhere between *certainly* and *without any doubt* to express feelings (the mean values range between 4.3 and 4.7 for the different situations). The L2 would be used, on average, *probably* (with scores ranging between 2.7 and 3.3). The L3 would be used, on average, between *maybe* and *probably* (score range 1.9–2.5). The L4 and L5 would be used, on average, between *never* or *maybe* (score range 1.4–1.8; and 1.4–1.6 respectively).

The preference for the L1 to express feelings was confirmed by the feedback to the open questions in the BEQ. Jokin explains that his preference for his L1 Basque is not linked to linguistic difficulty in expressing feelings in his L2 Spanish, but rather the stronger emotional resonance of Basque. Jokin (Basque L1, Spanish L2, English L3, French L4, Welsh L5) explains:

Jokin: I prefer Basque because it is the language in which I can express my deepest feelings better. It is not that I can't express myself as accurately in say Spanish, but the words do not carry the same emotional weight.

Ryoko (Japanese L1, English L2) offers a nice illustration of Grosjean's Complementarity Principle, namely that one language is more suited to certain topics and activities. Talking about her preferred language for writing, she juxtaposes English – which she teaches – for academic texts with Japanese, which seems to emerge spontaneously when she writes about her feelings:

Ryoko: I choose the language I feel like using for that day or even on the same day I switch languages following my urge. In other words, either of them appears in my mind naturally and that's the language I'll use to write. I feel that whenever I write in English, my thoughts become clearer than in Japanese. This is why I prefer writing papers (academic) in English. On the other hand, I tend to enjoy the vagueness and the poetic/artistic way Japanese comes out when you make sentences. It is in no way clear like English. If I write about my emotions Japanese sounds much suitable to my feelings than English.

Some participants do report a general preference for the L1 but add that for some situations or topics they might switch to an LX:

MA (Spanish L1, English L2): Most of the time I would use my native language. However there are certain expressions or words in English that are more useful and rich to express my feelings and emotions than in Spanish. I would choose one language or the other depending on the situation.

MA further explains that her preference to express feelings in her Spanish L1 does not imply that the L2 has less emotional resonance but because of the ease with which she can use her L1:

MA: both languages have an emotional significance for me. If I use my native language more than English it is because I feel more linguistically competent in Spanish than in English, especially to express your most intimate feelings.

A similar point is made by Arfon (Welsh L1, English L2). Although he reports that he is equally proficient in his L1 and L2, and is married to an L2 speaker, he still prefers his L1 to express his feelings to her:

Arfon: Welsh is my "heart" language and is most certainly more appropriate as the language of my emotions. The emotional significance of

English has been more complex – I've been on the "receiving end" in that my wife's first language is English. She now speaks Welsh fluently but still expresses her love for me in English – "I love you". However I express my feelings for her in Welsh.

Ricardo (Spanish L1, English L2, German L3, French L4, Italian L5) feels most sure-footed expressing feelings in his L1, but he might add some L2:

Ricardo: It's sometimes difficult enough to express my negative feelings in my mother tongue so it's always more difficult to use any other language to do so. On the other hand, when positive feelings are to be expressed it's sometimes easier to use some L2, the most accurate one being always Spanish.

Marco (Italian L1, English L2, German L3, French L4, Dutch L5) links his language choice to the type of emotion experienced:

Marco: I would use different languages according to the subject that I deal with. Italian for what happened during the day for example. English for general feelings, German for love emotions. Or deepest and perhaps harshest statements.

Alfredo (Portuguese L1, English L2, Spanish L3, Japanese L4) ponders why he seems to recall highly emotional events in his L2 despite the fact that they happened in his L1:

Alfredo: I tend to recall in English specific difficult memories which I know occurred in Portuguese. In one case, for example, my father and I both spoke in Portuguese; in my memory he speaks Portuguese and I speak English (...) I think I speak English (....) because I have had many occasions to tell this particular story in English (i.e. to friends in Western Canada where we tend to share our feelings lots) (...).

The L1 can also be the dispreferred choice to express feelings because of infrequent use and partial attrition. Gertrud (German L1, English L2, French L3, Spanish L4, Italian L5) a teacher of French who has been living in the UK for many years reports:

Gertrud: English is the language in which I can express my emotions most directly. French the language I enjoy playing about with. German is the language from which I probably feel most distant (apart from Spanish and Italian which I do not speak well enough to make any difference).

Asked by an interviewer whether he can express feelings with the same ease in his different languages, Chris (German L1, English L2, French L3,

Spanish L4), who has been living in the UK for a year, explains that strong emotion can completely block his speech production in his English L2:

B: Can you express the same?
C: Certainly not.
B: So why not?
C: Because the situations you have to react very rapidly and you don't have the vocabulary and it's not ready often.
B: In English?
C: Yeah in English ... yeah so ... your feelings may prevent you from saying anything because you are too emotional.
B: OK, so when you're emotional you don't control your languages?
C: Yeah yeah yeah you're more ... you're blocked.

Hypothesis 2: The effect of Age of onset of acquisition of the LX on likelihood of choice of the LX to express feelings

The Kruskal-Wallis tests shows that the effect of AoA on language choice for the expression of feelings is highly significant for the L2, and still significant for the L3, but it fails to reach significance in any situation in the L4 and L5. Participants who started learning their L2 and L3 early are thus more likely to use that language to express feelings. This pattern is significant across the four situations for the L2 and the L3 (Table 19). Mean values for the L2 are presented in Figure 12.

Some participants report that the expression of feelings is not part of their L1 culture but that having grown up in a foreign environment they learned to express their feelings from a young age in their LX. This is the case for Jennifer (Chinese L1, Burmese L2, English L3, Spanish L4, Japanese L5, dominant in English), who is more at ease in expressing feelings in her L3 rather than her L1:

Jennifer: My parents and siblings are not verbally affectionate. We support each other and show our love for one another through actions

Table 19 The effect of AoA of the LX on likelihood of choice of the LX to express feelings (χ^2)

Feelings	L2	L3	L4	L5
Alone	30***	17**	2	2
Letters	35***	26***	6	2
Friends	24***	14*	4	2
Parents	30***	8*	5	3

*** $p < .0001$, ** $p < .001$, * $p < .05$

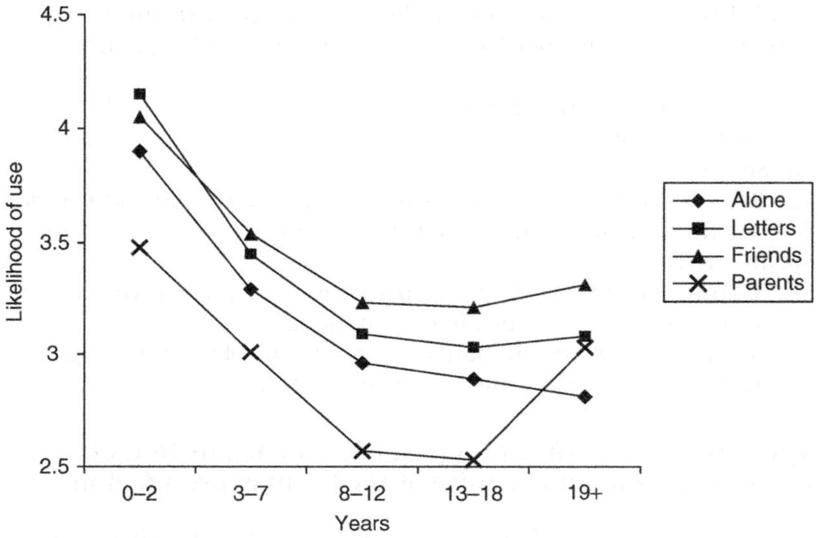

Figure 12 The effect of AoA on frequency of use of the L2 to express feelings

rather than words. Therefore I am not used to expressing my emotions in Chinese (L1). I was brought up in the U.S. where culturally expressing emotions verbally is acceptable and commonly practiced.

Barbara (German L1, English L2, French L3, married to an English speaker) presents the opposite, but complementary view, namely that emotional speech in English, which she learnt from the age of five, does not "feel" the same as emotional speech in German:

Barbara: The German words have a different significance for me because they have much more of a physical connection – something like a physical feeling when you think or say something? Like I tell off my kids and if I do it in German I get involved but if I do it in English it's a purely rational disciplinary thing. Expressing emotions in English to my English friends often feels as if I'm only pretending to have these emotions.

Hypothesis 3: The effect of context of acquisition of the LX on likelihood of choice of the LX to express feelings

The Kruskal-Wallis tests reveal that context of acquisition has a highly significant effect ($p < .0001$) on the likelihood of language choice for the expression of feelings across all languages (Table 20). A closer inspection of the mean values for the different languages shows that instructed learners are less likely to use the LX to express feelings in compared to mixed and naturalistic learners (Figure 13). The difference between the two latter groups is very limited.

Instructed learners like Pierre (French L1, Dutch L2, English L3, German L4) point out that emotional words learned in a classroom remain emotionally flat:

> Pierre: I do not feel the emotional load of words in foreign languages. I've only learned them in an "instructed" environment.

Table 20 The effect of context of acquisition of the LX on likelihood of choice of the LX to express feelings (χ^2)

Feelings	L2	L3	L4	L5
Alone	78***	70***	65***	34***
Letters	55***	48***	57***	32***
Friends	67***	90***	94***	44***
Parents	97***	68***	65***	27***

*** $p < .0001$

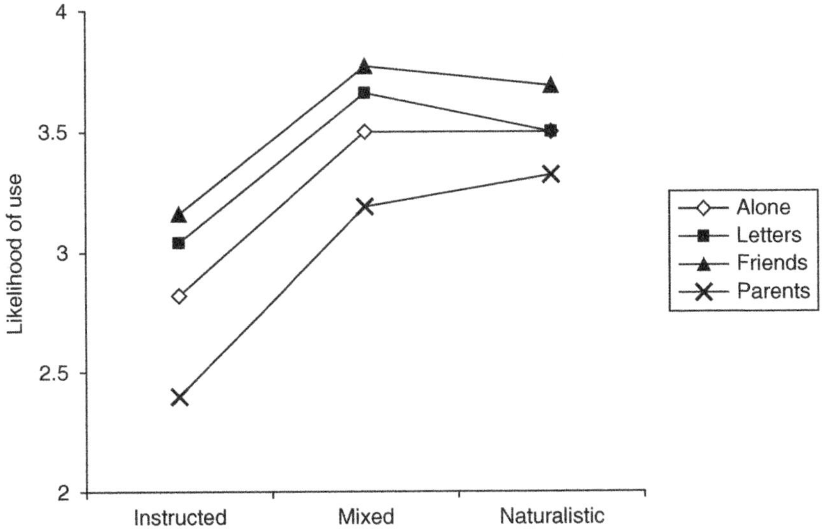

Figure 13 Mean values for likelihood of use of the L2 to express feelings according to context of acquisition of the L2

Ines (German L1, Italian L2, English L3, French L4, Spanish L5) reports that a language learned at school or only used at work was rarely used to express emotions:

> Ines: There is almost no difference regarding emotional topics with my first and second language. In my third language it is more difficult because I always used the English language either at school or at work and there have not been many possibilities to speak about emotional topics.

MP (English and Greek L1s, French L2, Albanian L3) makes a similar observation; only prolonged exposure to English and strong socialisation into that language reduced the effect of the formal context of acquisition. She reports:

> I was born in Greece and spent my formative years there. I remember a point at the age of 16 when I came to live in England with my parents. Although I've always gone to an English school I found it very difficult to find the words to express emotions in English (...).

Hypothesis 4: The effect of frequency of general use of the LX on likelihood of choice of the LX to express feelings

The Kruskal-Wallis tests show highly significant effects (all $p < .0001$) of the frequency of use of an LX on the likelihood of choice of that language to express feelings (Table 21). Here again, a higher general frequency of use is linked to an increased likelihood of using that language to express feelings.

An analysis of the means for the L2 (Figure 14) shows a modest increase in the likelihood of use of the L2 to express feelings for participants who use theirs less than weekly. A sharp increase can be observed among those who use the L2 daily, with those using it all day scoring still higher.

When two languages are mastered to the same level and used constantly, other factors determine the choice of a particular language to express

Table 21 The effect of frequency of general use of the LX on likelihood of language choice of the LX to express feelings (χ^2)

Feelings	L2	L3	L4	L5
Alone	327***	267***	210***	132***
Letters	334***	311***	172***	113***
Friends	400***	335***	199***	124***
Parents	303***	269***	178***	70***

*** $p < .0001$

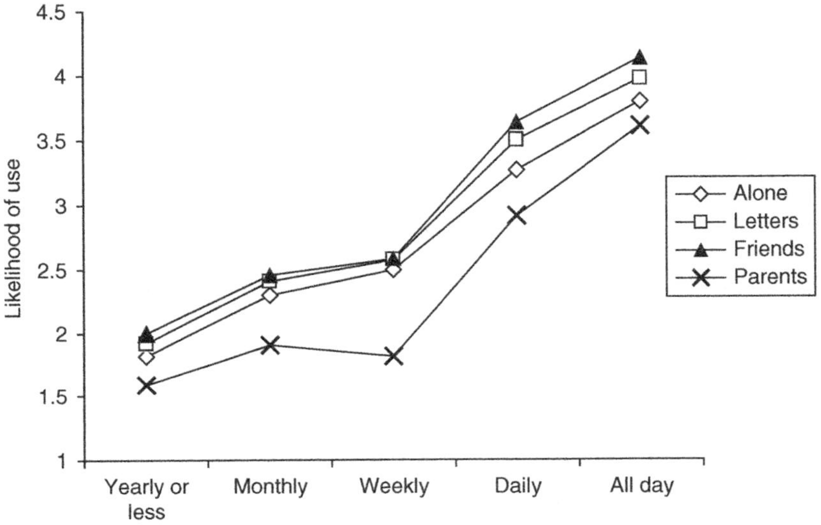

Figure 14 Mean values for likelihood of L2 use to express feelings according to frequency of general use of the L2

feelings or tell jokes. VV (English and Estonian L1s) explains that his choice is determined by the level of proficiency of his interlocutor and by the more general context, to which he can accommodate or from which he can diverge:

> VV: The social context of the countries my languages are associated with means that there are other variables besides language, but my linguistic personalities are certainly also different. I believe I'm a better joker in English. However I also feel interestingly that I change with the linguistic level I judge my interlocutor to have: my brother's Estonian is not as strong as mine and so I am slightly more constrained in the language and linguistic playfulness I use with him compared with native Estonian speakers. I also adapt to the linguistic surroundings. In Estonia, I believe I speak more quietly and probably in a more restrained manner though I often feel the need to rebel against that muted feeling that living in an Estonian cultural context might threaten to quell some of my best qualities: cheerfulness and talkativeness.

Participants report that infrequent use of a language and the resulting drop in proficiency can impede its use for the expression of emotions. For instance, DF (English L1, Afrikaans L2 learned at the age of five) observed that emotion talk is more difficult in Afrikaans, which she spoke fluently as child:

> DF: I don't have the opportunity to speak it frequently and struggle to "access" old vocabulary and learn new vocabulary.

Hypothesis 5: The effect of degree of socialisation in the LX on likelihood of choice of the LX to express feelings

The Kruskal-Wallis analyses show a highly significant effect (all $p < .0001$) of socialisation in the L2, L3, L4 and L5 on the likelihood of language choice to express feelings (Table 22).

Higher levels of socialisation in a language are linked to a higher likelihood to use that language to express feelings. Figure 15 shows the mean values for the L2. The biggest difference appears, again, to be situated between participants with minimal levels of socialisation in the L2 ("very weak socialisation") and the group with a "weak socialisation" in it. The likelihood to use the L2 to express feelings increases steadily across the groups with higher levels of socialisation in it.

RD (English L1, French L2, Japanese L3) has been living with a Japanese partner in Japan for the last six years, and they communicate in Japanese. His constant exposure to Japanese allowed him to notice important linguistic and cultural differences between the communication of emotions in English and Japanese:

> RD: I've come to believe that most Japanese people refrain from discussing their emotions with other people (of course there are exceptions). It seems to be considered selfish or ungentlemanly to discuss your emotions unless you are pleased or happy about something. Even then comments are restricted to a minimum. Feelings of irritation, frustration, anger, fear or sorrow can be communicated verbally or non-verbally but they appear to be more commonly communicated without words.

Table 22 The effect of degree of socialisation in the LX on likelihood of choice of the LX to express feelings (χ^2)

Feelings	L2	L3	L4	L5
Alone	262***	200***	125***	84***
Letters	227***	195***	69***	70***
Friends	288***	213***	84***	66***
Parents	271***	255***	121***	58***

*** $p < .0001$

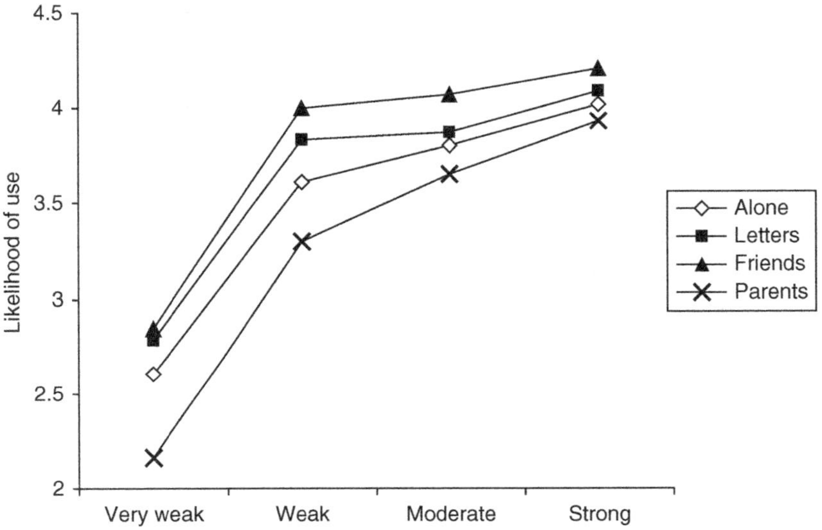

Figure 15 Mean values for likelihood of use of the L2 according to level of socialisation in the L2

Johanna (English L1, French L2, Italian L3, Spanish L4) reflects on the emotional power of her English L1 and Italian L2. She conforms to the general pattern in reporting a stronger resonance of English, and wonders which language would be more suited to talk about feelings in therapy. Despite the power of English, she reports that after strong socialisation in her L2, she is more likely to express her anger in that language:

Johanna: Probably easier in Italian if I want to keep my cool. Things that I find particularly upsetting are more likely to bring me to tears in English. I've wondered sometimes what it would be like to go to an Italian therapist and I think that if I were to need therapy, I would look for an American practicing in Italy. Not that it would be easier in English – probably the opposite – but I think in that kind of situation you want to be sure you're understood on all levels and that your personal traits aren't written off as cultural ones or vice-versa. And also because I think speaking in English would have a deeper effect in the long run. I'm more likely to express anger in Italian though. Mainly because I've only really learned how to in the last few years and since I've spent my young adulthood here. I've gotten more practice raging at the government or the landlord in my adopted language. I still end up feeling ridiculous when I get worked up about things in English.

Cristina (Catalan L1, Spanish L2, English L3, Italian L4, German L5) has been living in the UK for 17 years. She reports that although she still prefers Catalan to express very strong emotions, English words get activated too. She also feels that as a result of her socialisation in English, her Catalan reflects a former self:

> Cristina: English is now what is more readily available when I'm speaking, the first word that comes to my mind is English, and even when I'm talking to myself, kind of you know inner speech, I don't necessarily think it's Catalan (...) because I've been here for so long (...) and although my Catalan hasn't got an accent, actually my resources in Catalan are very limited, especially to express the experience of my last 15–17 years, which is a different self, a different person than what I was before. When I use Catalan, I can feel that I'm attached to almost the person that I was before, 'cos my language hasn't developed and it hasn't developed with my personality.

Very strong socialisation in the L2 can lead to a strong general preference for the L2 and could be the indirect cause of attrition of the L1. This is the case of MH's mother:

> MH: My mother was born and bred in Greece with Greek parents. English was a language she was taught in school. She emigrated at around the age of 35 and has been living in England for the last 15 years. She now finds it extremely difficult to express herself in Greek and interestingly she also finds it more difficult to relate to Greek people.

Hypothesis 6: The effect of network of interlocutors in the LX on likelihood of choice of the LX to express feelings

The Kruskal-Wallis analyses revealed a highly significant effect of the network of interlocutors on the likelihood of choice of the L2, L3 and L4 to express feelings in. In the L5 the effect was only significant for expressing feelings alone (Table 23). Values for likelihood of choice of the L2 increase with more familiar interlocutors (Figure 16).

Table 23 The effect of network of interlocutors in the LX on likelihood of choice of the LX to express feelings (χ^2)

Feelings	L2	L3	L4	L5
Alone	92***	99***	73***	14**
Letters	69***	109***	49***	6
Friends	89***	143***	73***	5
Parents	158***	168***	90***	4

*** p < .0001, ** p < .001, * p < .05

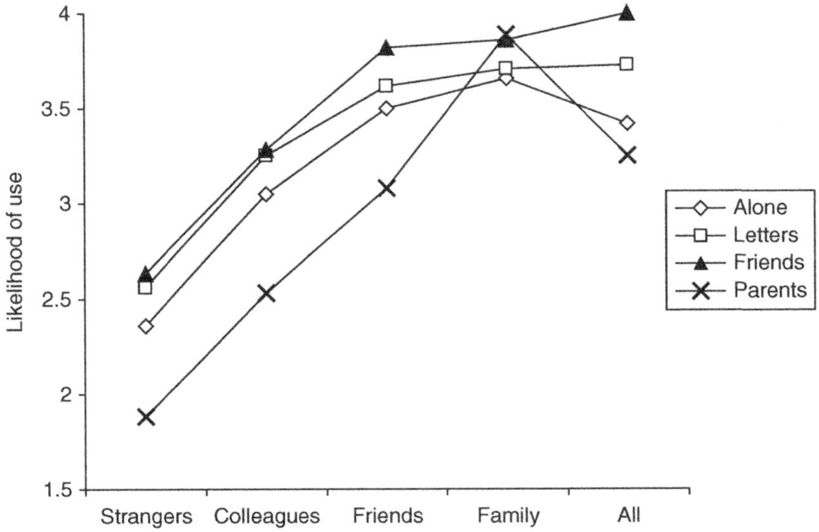

Figure 16 Mean values for likelihood of use of the L2 to express feelings according to network of interlocutors

Hypothesis 7: The effect of total language knowledge on likelihood of choice of the LX to express feelings

The Kruskal-Wallis analyses reveal a significant effect of total language knowledge on the likelihood of choice of the L2 and L3 to express feelings in, with the exception of feelings expressed to parents (Table 24). Values for the likelihood of choice of the L2 increase gradually from bilinguals to quadrilinguals and then tend to level off for the pentalinguals (Figure 17).

Alfredo (Portuguese L1, English L2, Spanish L3, Japanese L4), a Brazilian who is lecturer at a Japanese university, shows an acute awareness of which feelings can be discussed in which cultural context. He knows that his Japanese friends expect him to behave differently from them, but he refrains from engaging on "taboo topics", in his case, the death of his brother because of HIV:

> Alfredo: when the subject of HIV comes up for example I recognize that some of my Japanese friends – in an intimate situation – may not be comfortable hearing about my brother's death so I fight the impulse to mention it even though I know they expect me to do and say unexpected things. Also I wouldn't mention it either in English or Japanese. In Canada or Brazil I wouldn't hesitate.

Table 24 The effect of total language knowledge on likelihood of choice of the LX to express feelings (χ^2)

Feelings	L2	L3	L4
Alone	10*	10*	3
Letters	12*	13*	5
Friends	11*	21***	3
Parents	2	7	3

*** p < .0001, ** p < .001, * p < .05

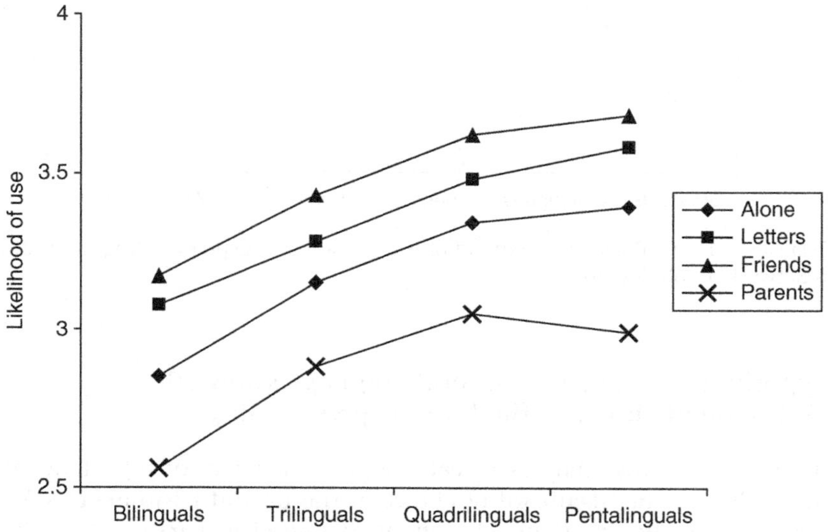

Figure 17 Mean values for likelihood of choice of the L2 to express feelings in according to total language knowledge

Some participants like IE (Japanese L1, English L2) report using a unique private "interlanguage" to communicate their feelings with their partner:

> IE: I have developed with my wife an interlanguage between English and Japanese in which prefixes and suffixes commonly used in Japanese indicative of affection (e.g., -pi cho-) are attached to root words in English (as well as Japanese words not normally used in this way).

Hypothesis 8: The effect of Trait Emotional Intelligence on likelihood of choice of the LX to express feelings

A series of Kruskal-Wallis analyses show no significant effect of TEI on the likelihood of language choice to express feelings in any language (Table 25).

Table 25 The effect of TEI on likelihood of choice of the LX to express feelings (χ^2)

Feelings	L2	L3	L4	L5
Alone	2	3	3	1
Letters	5	0	0	3
Friends	2	2	3	3
Parents	0	3	0	1

all $p > .05$

Hypothesis 9: The effect of gender, age and level of education on likelihood of choice of the LX to express feelings

Gender

A series of Mann-Whitney tests revealed significant differences in the likelihood of language choice to express feelings in the L2 but no effect emerged for the other languages (Table 26). Female participants were more likely to choose the L2 to express feelings than male participants (Figure 18).

Age

A series of Kruskal-Wallis tests reveal no age differences in the likelihood of choice of the L2, L3, L4 and L5 to express feelings (Table 27).

Education

A series of Kruskal-Wallis analyses showed no effect of education level on the likelihood of choice of the L2, L4 and L5 to express feelings. A significant effect was found in the L3, where higher levels of education corresponded to a stronger likelihood of choice of the L3 to express feelings when alone, in letters and to friends (Table 28).

Table 26 Differences in likelihood of language choice to express feelings between female and male participants in the LX

		L2	L3	L4	L5
Alone	Mann-Whitney	158461	106251	50131.5	15704
	Z	–3.7***	–0.5	–1.2	–0.5
Letters	Mann-Whitney	156377	104777	47694	14715
	Z	–2.8*	–0.1	–1.0	–0.3
Friends	Mann-Whitney	163627	103446	103446	103446
	Z	–2.6*	–0.2	–0.2	–0.2
Parents	Mann-Whitney	146787	91948	43637	12675
	Z	–3.1*	–0.4	–0.6	–1.0

* $p < .05$

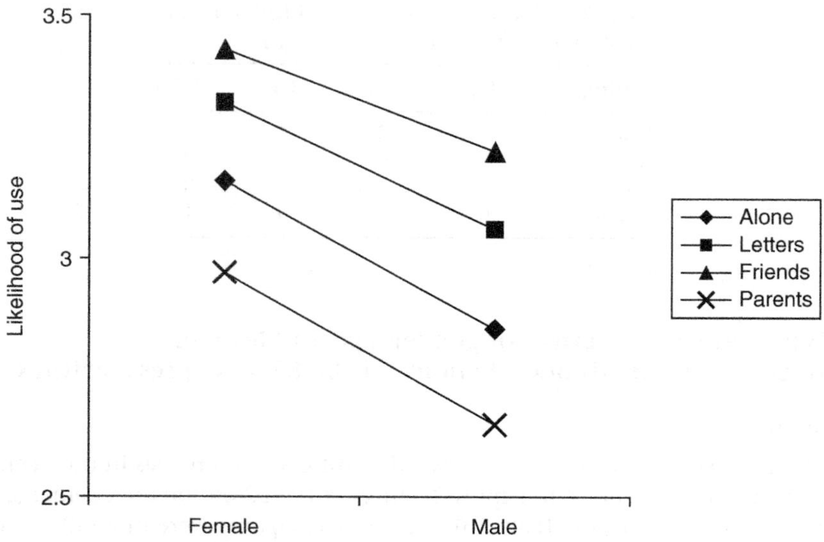

Figure 18 Differences in likelihood of L2 choice to express feelings between female and male participants

Table 27 The effect of age on likelihood of choice of the LX to express feelings (χ^2)

Feelings	**L2**	**L3**	**L4**	**L5**
Alone	3	5	4	4
Letters	6	6	3	2
Friends	3	9	5	6
Parents	1	6	3	6

all $p > .05$

Table 28 The effect of education level on likelihood of choice of the LX to express feelings (χ^2)

Feelings	**L2**	**L3**	**L4**	**L5**
Alone	7	10*	3	1
Letters	4	9*	2	1
Friends	3	2	2	1
Parents	7	13*	1	2

* $p < .05$

Summing up

Most hypotheses were confirmed, with the exception of hypothesis 8 on the effect of Trait Emotional Intelligence on self-perceived competence, and parts of hypothesis 9.

Languages acquired later in life were less likely to be chosen to express feelings than languages acquired early. Pentalinguals are thus most likely to express their feelings in the L1 and least likely to do so in the L5. Many participants explained that their preference was guided by what Grosjean (2008) calls the Complementarity Principle: some languages are used to communicate about non-emotional topics; others are used exclusively within the family and preferred for expressing feelings in. Participants who felt equally proficient in two or more languages explained that their choice of language to express feelings was decided on the grounds of the perceived emotional resonance of the language. This corresponds with the findings reported in Dewaele (2011b) based on a subsample of the BEQ consisting of participants who reported maximal competence in their L1 and L2 but typically preferred the L1 for expressing feelings in.

A number of participants rejected the categorical distinction between one language or another, and explained that they inserted bits of different languages to express feelings, or would choose one language over another according to the type of feeling. Here some participants also preferred an LX for expressing feelings in because they had married a speaker of that language or moved to a region where that language was used.

The "history of learning" variables had significant effects on the likelihood of choice of the LX to express feelings. Younger starters were more likely to use their L2 and L3 to express their feelings (not their L4 or L5). Also, participants who had learnt a language (L2, L3, L4 or L5) only through formal instruction were less likely to use that language to express feelings in compared to mixed or naturalistic learners. This does suggest that when a language is acquired early enough and is used as an actual communication tool during social interactions outside the classroom, it will take on the emotional resonance usually associated with the L1. If the learning of that language has started later, and has been confined to the relatively emotion-free classroom, the chances are that learners/users will be less inclined to express their feelings in that language.

The three independent variables reflecting current use of the LX (frequency of general use, socialisation and network of interlocutors), also turned out to have a highly significant effect across languages. Participants who used an LX frequently, were strongly socialised in the language and used it with a wide network of interlocutors were more likely to use that language to express feelings in. However, in some cases a language that was used with very few interlocutors could be the preferred language for expressing feelings in, typically if the interlocutors were family members or partners.

Some participants also reported that after moving to a new country, they lost their old network of interlocutors and felt unable to express culture-specific emotions in the new environment. This inability to communicate their feelings resulted in an acute sense of loss. Others regretted the fact that after spending a very long time abroad, their new emotional selves could not be fully expressed in their L1.

The participants' linguistic profiles, i.e. the number of languages mastered, also had a significant effect on the likelihood to use an LX to express feelings in. The knowledge of more languages was linked to higher likelihood to use the L2 and L3 to express feelings in (but not the L4 nor L5). Some participants also reported creating their own "blended" language to express feelings in. Highly multilingual participants were often proud of their unique multicultural personality. They also displayed a profound understanding of variations in cultural norms as to what emotional topics were considered appropriate for conversations with friends. The story of the death of a brother because of HIV would thus be told very differently according to the nationality and cultural background of the interlocutors.

Trait Emotional Intelligence had no effect on the likelihood to use an LX to express feelings in.

The effects of gender, age and education level on the likelihood to use an LX to express feelings in are scattered and relatively limited. First, female participants were more likely than male participants to use their L2 (but no other language) to express feelings in. Second, there were no effects for age. Third, education level only had an effect in the L3. Participants with higher levels of education were more likely to use the L3 to express feelings in certain situations.

7
Results: Communicating Anger and Swearing

Expressing anger and swearing in different languages

I referred earlier to the studies by Rintell (1984) and Graham et al., (2001), who discovered that LX users find it hard to judge the degree of emotional intensity of speech in English L2. Accuracy in identifying and rating the intensity of different emotions was found to be linked to linguistic/cultural background and partly to language proficiency. Learners from Asian or Arabic backgrounds experienced greater difficulty in identifying and rating the emotions on audiotape than European learners.

Possible reasons for the difficulties L2 learners encounter in dealing with anger and rudeness were explored in Toya and Kodis (1996). The authors considered the use of swearwords and the pragmatic use of rudeness in English in a small sample of NSs of Japanese with advanced English proficiency. They point to the specific difficulty that their learners face, i.e. having to "master two different norms of expressing emotions, especially Western and Oriental norms" (p. 280). The researchers used oral discourse completion tests and introspective interviews. Participants were presented with five situations in which anger was expected and were asked (1) how they would feel in each situation, (2) how they would or would not express their emotions verbally and/or non-verbally and finally (3) why they would or would not express themselves in those ways. The results demonstrated that frequency of use of rude expressions was linked to the length of stay in English-speaking countries and the confidence of the LX users. A control group of NSs of English were found to be more expressive than the LX users, although the difference in reactions was smaller than expected. The authors suggest that the lower degree of expressiveness in the L2 could be linked to the more restricted input to which the learners had been exposed (there is little display of anger in the foreign language classroom), and the fact that learners have little confidence in using angry words: "The acquisition of rude language appeared to be an extremely sensitive issue because of the possible danger and misunderstanding involved in using such expressions, of which NNSs were well aware" (p. 293).

Mugford (2008) argues that everyday communicative realities such as rudeness, disrespect and impoliteness should not be neglected in the English as a Foreign Language (EFL) classroom because impoliteness is likely to be experienced by LX users in the TL context or when interacting with other LX users.

Dewaele (2004c) analysed individual differences in the use of colloquial words (including swearwords) in a cross-sectional corpus of advanced oral French IL of Dutch L1 speakers and in a corpus of advanced French L2 by British students. One of the striking findings was that the frequency of contact with the TL and proficiency levels in the TL were positively correlated with proportions of colloquial words. Dewaele and Pavlenko (2002) came to similar conclusions concerning the effects of the frequency of contact and proficiency levels in the TL on the use of emotion words in IL corpora of advanced oral French IL of Dutch L1 speakers and advanced oral English IL of Russian L1 speakers. Higher proportions of colloquial and emotion words in the L2 could therefore be indicative of higher levels of L2 socialisation.

The comprehension and self-reported use of L2 swearwords has been linked to gender. Register (1996) found that male university-level English as a Second Language ESL learners in the USA comprehended more taboo terms than female students and reported that they would use them more frequently.

Swearing in different languages

Van Lancker and Cummings (1999: 99) observe that "in periods of anger, frustration, and other intense emotional situations, limbic structures are activated and limbic vocalizations may be facilitated". These outbursts are quite different in nature from speech routines or habituated verbal production. I have argued that this distinction is potentially important for multilinguals as speech routines in a particular language are the result of a speaker's conscious decision to use that language, while unplanned limbic vocalisations may escape the speaker's conscious control and be uttered in a different language than that used in the rest of the interaction (Dewaele, 2004a: 86). Swearwords are multifunctional, pragmatic units that assume, in addition to the expression of emotional attitudes, various discourse functions (Dewaele, 2004b, 2011b; Jay, 2000, 2009). Drescher (2000) points out that swearwords can contribute to the coordination of discourse among interlocutors, the organisation of the interaction and the structuring of verbal exchange, and that they can fulfil the function of discourse markers. Swearwords are also powerful markers of in-group membership and they establish boundaries and social norms for language use (Drescher, 2000; Stenstrom, 1995, 1999).

The literature on multilingual swearing is spread across various disciplines, with researchers using a wide range of methods to gather data. I will focus on the pragmatic approach (Jay, 2000; Jay and Janschewitz, 2008), the cognitive psychological approach (Harris et al., 2003, 2006) and my own applied linguistic approach (Dewaele, 2004a, 2004b, 2005, 2011b, 2011d).

Jay and Janschewitz (2008) point out that "The main purpose of swearing is to express emotions, especially anger and frustration. Swear words are well suited to express emotion as their primary meanings are connotative" (p. 267). The emotional impact of swearing is highly variable, and is linked to an individual's "experience with a culture and its language conventions" (p. 267). The authors investigated how 68 NSs of American English and 53 NNSs, all students at the University of California, Los Angeles, rated the offensiveness and likelihood of hypothetical scenarios involving taboo words. The authors found that appropriateness of swearing is highly contextually variable, dependent on the speaker-listener relationship in terms of status, social-physical context, i.e. in a public or private location, and particular word used. Female native speakers were found to provide higher offensiveness rating than male NSs, but no significant gender difference emerged among the NNSs (p. 283). The researchers found no effect for the level of English experience (NS versus NNS) on offensiveness or likelihood ratings, which they explain by the fact that the NNSs had spent an average of 11 years in the US, were highly fluent in English and quite used to swearing in the university context. A closer analysis of the NNS group revealed that early learners of English (before the age of 12) differed significantly from late learners (aged 12 and above) on offensiveness judgements, the latter providing a higher average offensiveness rating (p. 283).

The difficulties that foreign language users encounter in expressing feelings increase manifold when the feeling in question is anger. Indeed, anger, cursing and swearing involve a certain amount of loss of control over one's emotions, and may very well include a similar lack of control over linguistic resources, which makes it all the more challenging in the foreign language.

Before focusing on the foreign language aspect, we may just wonder why we curse. Jay and Janschewitz (2007) advance the following hypothesis:

> We curse to express our emotions and convey our emotions to other people. Taboo words communicate emotional information more effectively than non-taboo words. *Fuck you!* tells you immediately that I am frustrated or angry and permits me to vent my anger at the same time. There is no other way to say fuck you and convey the same level of contempt in polite language. Taboo words occupy a pivotal space on a continuum of emotional communication that ranges from physical expressions of emotion such as screaming, biting, or hitting, to abstract, symbolic expressions like sarcastic irony (e.g., *Mom, like I love you so much*). Cursing is

> unique in this respect; it allows us to express a strong emotional state in symbolic form without getting physical. (p. 215)

What makes it particularly difficult for foreign language users is getting the grading of taboo words for a given referent right. Not only are taboo words with the same referent not emotionally equivalent, they are not equally likely to be chosen in a given context with specific interlocutors. Jay and Janschewitz (2007) talk of "shades of gray". They point out, for example, that "references to the male genitalia, penis, pecker, dick, cock, wiener, dong, have the same referent but the level of offensiveness or arousal differs across the set" (p. 219).

Operationalising the variable

The present chapter considers self-reported choice of language for the expression of anger in five different situations and the habitual language choice for swearing.

The two questions were formulated as follows:

1) "If you are angry, how frequently do you typically use a language to express your anger?"
2) "If you swear in general, what language do you typically swear in?"

Possible answers on a five-point Likert scale included: never = 1, rarely = 2, sometimes = 3, frequently = 4 and constantly = 5.

The situations included anger directed at oneself, at friends, at family and at strangers, and anger expressed in letters or emails.

Information was collected for the L1, L2, L3, L4 and L5. The dependent variables are thus the numerical values reflecting the frequency of habitual language choice for the expression of anger in five situations.

Cronbach alpha analyses revealed that internal consistency reliability was extremely high for the five-item language choice for anger and swearing scales in the L1 (alpha = .87), L2 (alpha = .88), L3 (alpha = .89), L4 (alpha = .91) and L5 (alpha = .90).

A series of one-sample Kolmogorov-Smirnov tests revealed that the values for frequency of language choice for expression of anger in the five situations in up to five languages are not normally distributed (Kolmogorov-Smirnov Z values vary between 6.3 and 13.2, all $p < .0001$). The distribution of participants across five frequency categories (ranging from "never use this language" to "use this language all the time") are strongly skewed toward the positive end of the continuum for the L1, and are strongly skewed toward the negative end of the continuum for the L3, L4 and L4. The distribution for the L2 comes closest to a normal distribution but the Kolmogorov-Smirnov Z values are still significant. As a consequence, Kruskal-Wallis tests were used as non-parametric equivalents to one-way ANOVAs, and Wilcoxon Signed Ranks Tests and Mann-Whitney tests were used instead of t-tests.

Hypothesis 1a: Monotonic decline in language choice for expressing anger and swearing from L1 to L5

Friedman's ANOVA tests for related samples confirm that the frequency of use of a language to express anger decreases highly significantly from the L1 to the L5 in the different situations (see Table 29). Mean values for language choice for expressing anger in the five contexts and swearing are presented in Figure 19. This shows that multilinguals use the L1, on average, *frequently*

Table 29 The effect of chronology of acquisition on language choice for expressing anger and swearing from L1 to L5 (χ^2)

	N	df	χ^2	p
Alone	409	4	852.2	***
Letters	382	4	673.1	***
Friends	388	4	735.8	***
Parents	375	4	863.1	***
Strangers	381	4	587.7	***
Swearing	368	4	709.9	***

*** $p < .0001$

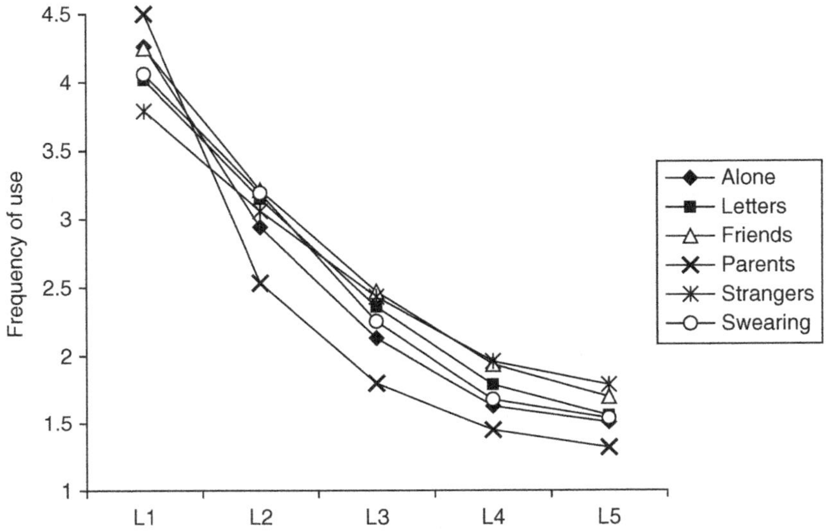

Figure 19 Mean values for language choice for expressing anger and swearing in the L1, L2, L3, L4 and L5

to express anger (the mean values range between 3.8 and 4.2 for the different situations). The L2 is used, on average, *sometimes* (with scores ranging between 2.5 and 3.2). The L3 is used, on average, between *rarely* and *sometimes* (scores ranging from 1.8 to 2.4). The L4 and L5 are, on average, *never* or *rarely* used (score range 1.4–2.0; and 1.3–1.8 respectively).

The respondents' comments reflect the patterns presented in Figure 19. Most participants report a preference for the L1 for expressing anger. A typical comment is that of Didi (Sundanase L1, Bahasa Indonesia L2, English L3):

> Didi: L1 is usually more significant to use when I get angry as I feel the effect is strongest even though the object of the anger does not know at all the language, e.g., I swear to somebody near Birkbeck College in 1997 using Sundanase while the person is English (it is also safer for me to do this).

Leah (English L1, Spanish L2) also has preferred languages according to the discourse domain and her emotional state:

> Leah: English is my anger and "counselling" language. If I really need to get mad or give advice English is my language of choice. If I need to explain technical things have neutral conversation etc.... Spanish will do just as well. English is definitely my emotional language.

KTH (English L1, French L2, Spanish L3, shared dominance in the L1 and L2) notes that she is perfectly capable of expressing emotions in her L1 and L2 but that for the expression of anger her L1 feels more appropriate:

> KTH: I feel as though I can convey my emotions better in English. To me "I'm mad" is really intense. Yet when I say "Je suis fâchée" in French, I know that I am mad but it feels different. (...) I think this all comes from the fact that I learned to be angry (...) first in English and then in French. For me English is more appropriate for my anger. French I am able to use for other emotions: sadness and extreme joy for example.

Other participants like ALG (English L1, Spanish L2) opt for the L1 to express anger because of its perceived seriousness:

> ALG: I see English as my stronger "more serious" language in terms of expressing anger or "serious matters". (...) However Spanish is more valuable to me when expressing endearment or feelings of love or affection.

The stronger perceived emotional weight of swearing in the L1 has the opposite effect on some participants, like Maria (Spanish L1, English L2), namely an inability to use L1 swearwords with L1 interlocutors:

Maria: I never swear in Spanish. I simply cannot. The words are too heavy and are truly a taboo for me.

The following participant, Johan (Afrikaans L1, English L2, Dutch L3, Zulu L4), reports that angry reproaches in the L2 do not seem to have the same perlocutionary effect as similar reproaches in the L1:

Johan: Critique in English (...) is usually not taken personally at all. In Afrikaans for example I would ponder on it more and take it more personally if applicable. E.g., "You are late!" – I'll think "Oh what the heck traffic". "Jy is laat!" – I'll think "I may seem tardy..."

SG (Greek L1, English L2, French L3, Italian L4) reports that she may discuss emotions in her foreign languages but that for extreme emotions the L1 is the preferred channel of communication:

SG: From experience when being in a romantic or friendly relationship using other languages I try to use the language of my partner/friend trying to express feeling in his/her language. Nevertheless for strongest emotions – anger, extreme annoyment (sic), passion, lust – my first instinct is L1 as it comes more naturally.

Barbara (German L1, English L2, Latin L3, French L4) also uses her partner's L1 to express emotions because of his lower proficiency in her L1. Although she is able to express anger in her L2, she reverts to her L1 when the anger boils over:

Barbara: In our relationship we use English for two reasons. My English is far better than his German and although his German is quite good by now he can always PREFER not to understand. We also argue in English which feels really really fake to me and I feel so helpless when there is anger building up inside me and I just can't express it. It feels so sterile arguing in English like I'm not actually getting rid of any of the emotional pressure and I sometimes just burst out in German to let off some steam. That's quite a bizarre situation then but it helps and sometimes makes both of us laugh.

The same participant also wonders whether she might overuse swearwords in her L2 when arguing in that language to make up for the lack of emotional resonance:

Barbara: And it's tempting to try and make up for what I perceive as lack of oomph in my expression of i.e. anger by the use of swearwords since they sound great but don't have any emotional consequence for me but that doesn't usually go down too well with my surroundings.

Some English swearwords have become "lingua franca" borrowings in many languages. As they still retain their foreign character, they may have a more limited emotional resonance and are therefore judged by Ilana (Russian L1, Hebrew L2, English L3) to be socially more acceptable:

> Ilana: The reason I swear in English more often than in other languages is because lovely English words such as "fuck" or "shit" are perfectly understandable by speakers of any language.

The interview with Piero (Italian L1, English L2, who has been living in the UK for ten years but still feels dominant in Italian) revealed that his language choice for expressing anger depends on the language spoken by his interlocutor. He thus uses English with English-speaking interlocutors and Italian with Italian speakers. When asked about his language choice for anger when being alone he answers:

> P: Alone? it's a mixture.
> B: Ah ah?
> P: It's a mixture [laughs].
> B: So?
> P: It's a bit of both, I can say 60–40, 60 per cent Italian, 40 per cent English.

The interviewer then asks him what language he would use with bilinguals who have the same language combination as him:

> P: With bilinguals? A bit of both, mixture, it's a mixture, and tend more and more and more in Italian but I put some English words, phrases as well.

Hypothesis 2: The effect of Age of onset of learning on frequency of use of the LX to express anger in the LX.

The Kruskal-Wallis tests show that the effect of AoA on language choice for the expression of anger is quite robust across all situations for the L2. It remains significant for four out of six situations in the L3, three out of six for the L4 and only one in the L5 (Table 30). The general pattern is that a lower age of onset of learning corresponds with a higher frequency of use of the language to express anger. The decline is almost linear in the first three AoA groups for the L2 (Figure 20), after which it remains unchanged or even rises slightly for the oldest AoA group.

Table 30 The effect of AoA on frequency of use of the LX to express anger and to swear (χ^2)

Anger	L2	L3	L4	L5
Alone	22***	11*	6	3
Letters	29***	18**	11*	1
Friends	37***	11*	9*	5
Parents	42***	7	14*	6
Strangers	16**	22***	5	6
Swearing	26***	7	3	10*

*** p < .0001, ** p < .001, * p < .05

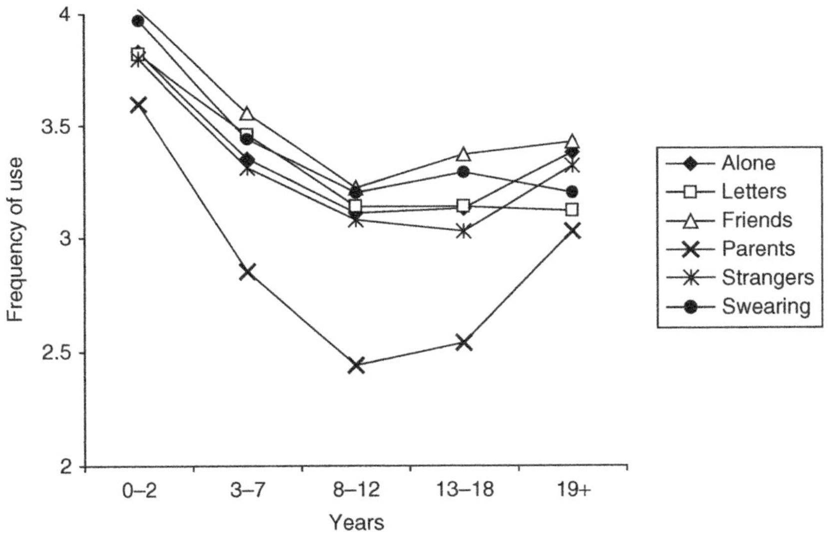

Figure 20 Mean values for frequency of use of the L2 to express anger according to AoA

Johanna (Dutch L1, Swiss German L2, High German L3, French L4, Italian L5) started learning Italian aged eight, after moving to Italy. Although she prefers Dutch or High German to express anger, she's comfortable expressing emotions in Italian:

> Johanna: I went to school my first years in Italy and was not able to speak a word of Italian on my first school day. But today (and ever since I mastered the language) I really love Italian and feel comfortable and "at home" when speaking it.

Hypothesis 3: The effect of context of acquisition on frequency of use of an LX to express anger in the LX

The Kruskal-Wallis tests reveal that acquisition context had a highly significant effect overall ($p < .0001$) on the self-reported language choice for the expression of anger (Table 31) in the different languages across situations. An inspection of the mean values for the different languages shows that instructed learners use the language less frequently for expressing anger and swearing, compared to mixed and naturalistic learners (Figure 21).

Table 31 The effect of context of acquisition on frequency of use of the LX to express anger (χ^2)

Anger	**L2**	**L3**	**L4**	**L5**
Alone	83***	70***	75***	32***
Letters	57***	46***	48***	29***
Friends	71***	86***	78***	33***
Parents	103***	48***	71***	36***
Strangers	39***	52***	47***	24***
Swearing	83***	76***	58***	37***

*** $p < .0001$

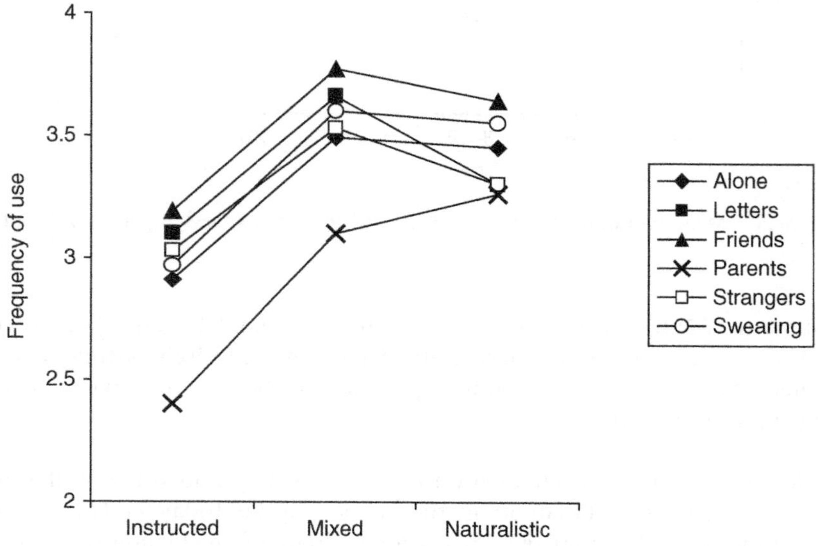

Figure 21 Mean values for frequency of use of the L2 to express anger according to context of acquisition

A number of instructed language learners point out that anger repertoires in the TL were not part of the curriculum, hence their difficulties in expressing anger or irritation in authentic communication in the TL. PS (Catalan L1, Spanish L2, English L3) and instructed learner of English explained that getting angry in English was very difficult for him: "I wasn't taught anger at school." In a similar vein, Bart (Dutch L1, French L2, English L3 and an instructed user of French) explains how he has occasionally struggled to find the appropriate "angry" tone in his French L2:

> Bart: in school we learn how to use French in a polite and friendly way but when I am calling to the Customer Service of a French company to complain about something and want to sound a bit more severe irritated angry ... then it is difficult to find that severe irritated angry tone because you are concentrating on French grammar and vocabulary... I wouldn't have to do that in Dutch.

The participants' responses show that naturalistic and mixed learners are able to make comparisons between anger scripts in their different languages, and are able to describe culture-specific aspects of anger and swearing in their languages. Participants who learned a language in a classroom context were less likely to make comments such as the following one by Sandra (German L1, Italian L2) about the untranslatability of anger scripts and swearing from the L1 into the L2:

> Sandra: Swearing in Italian means talking about God, Maria etc., in an obscene way which in German doesn't mean a thing. The other way round in German you might use animals' names to insult a person in Italian it wouldn't mean anything.

Andrew (English L1, French L2, Spanish L3) learned Spanish at school and picked up some colloquial expressions during a school trip to Spain. He explains to the interviewer that he incorporated the Spanish equivalent of "fuck" into his general swearing repertoire:

> Andrew: Yeah, I forgot, I swear in Spanish.
> B: You swear in Spanish, OK, so can you explain me why? [laughs]
> A: I don't know! (...) I learnt Spanish at school, so it's not it's not a language I have particularly deep emotional associations with, I never really get out with any Spanish, I don't have any close Spanish friends, I'm not interested in Spanish cinema, but since my trip to Spain when I was 16 I've always used the word "joder" to swear if I fall over, I would often rather than say "fuck" for example I would say "joder". I don't know why it stuck.
> B: You never lived there?

A: Never lived there, it's only I like that word.
B: OK.
A: And and it just, it is stuck.
B: OK, but no other words?
A: No other words no.
B: Only that one. OK, so which other languages do you use for swearing?
A: French and English.
B: Both of them?
A: Yeah.
B: Any preferences?
A: Err, I like swearing in all languages!
B: OK [laughs].
A: [laughs] Don't know why, but I don't use Spanish for anything except for swearing.

Hypothesis 4: The effect of general frequency of use on frequency of use of the LX to express anger in the LX

The Kruskal-Wallis tests show highly significant effects (all $p < .0001$) of frequency of use of an LX on the frequency of use of that language to express anger to various interlocutors (Table 32). A higher general frequency of use is significantly linked to an increased frequency of use of that language to express anger.

An analysis of the means for the L2 (Figure 22) shows a similar pattern to that observed for the communication of feelings in general. A modest increase in the frequency of use of the L2 to express anger for participants who use their L2 less than weekly is followed by a sharp increase among those who use the L2 daily or all day.

Michelle (Taiwanese L1, Mandarin L2, English L3) has lived in the UK for 17 years and feels very fluent in English, which she uses all the time. She reports that despite the fact that Chinese sociocultural norms forbid

Table 32 The effect of general frequency of use on frequency of use of the LX to express anger (χ^2)

Anger	L2	L3	L4	L5
Alone	341***	303***	211***	121***
Letters	395***	340***	207***	118***
Friends	482***	375***	240***	120***
Parents	303***	246***	235***	96***
Strangers	334***	251***	171***	78***
Swearing	286***	240***	145***	96***

*** $p < .0001$

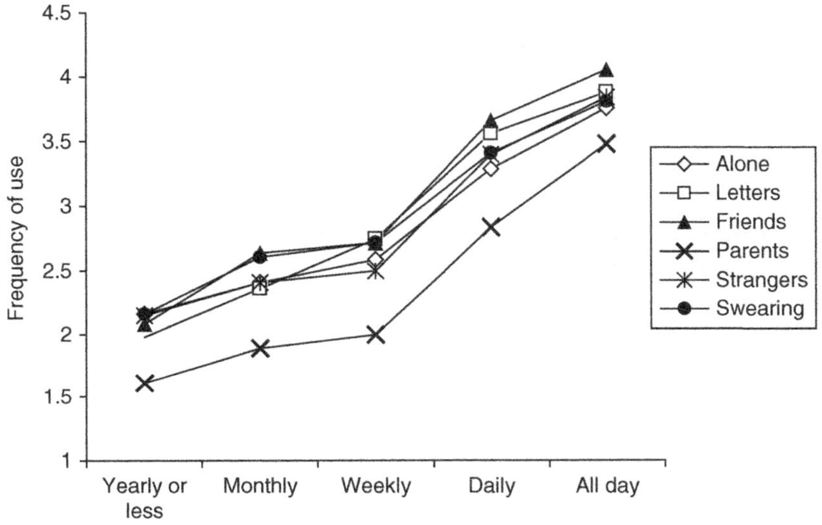

Figure 22 Mean values for frequency of use of the L2 to express anger according to general frequency of use of the L2

her from swearing, she does use mild English swearwords with her Chinese friends in London:

B: Do use ever use Chinese with your husband?
Mi: No! not even I swear or, because I don't swear in Chinese you see.
B: I see yeah.
Mi: It's not because I'm good, it's just because education, you see ehm it's different, ehm, English swearing is different from Chinese swearing. English swearing is quite common to even, you know, whatever you educated whatever you are, you do it, but in Chinese you really, most educated people don't swear.
B: So do feel something is missing when you speak Chinese, because you can't swear?
Mi: Ah ah! I haven't thought about that!
B: [laughs]
Mi: Maybe, yes, maybe, no. It's funny, you do get by isn't it without swearing, you still get by, but I just think that even now I swear, I swear when I'm with my friends, Chinese friends, you have to say "oh shoot" or "sugar" or whatever, and you know and then you say that in English, so...
B: While you speak in Chinese?
Mi: Yeah.
B: While you speak in Chinese you swear in English?

Mi: Yeah.
B: Or while you speak in English?
Mi: While I speak in Chinese, both. I never, I still swear because again I think it's a habit, because that reaction just come out, so it's a bit like you have to ask yourself what do I do before I knew English swearing, ehm, how do I survive?

Hypothesis 5: The effect of degree of socialisation in the LX on frequency of use of the LX to express anger

A series of Kruskal-Wallis tests show that socialisation in an LX has a highly significant effect overall ($p < .0001$) on the self-reported choice of the LX for the expression of anger (Table 33).

Strong socialisation in the L2 is linked to a more frequent choice of that language for the expression of anger. Similar patterns emerged for strong socialisation in the L3, L4 and L5 (Figure 23). The strongest increase is again situated between participants with minimal levels of socialisation in the L2 ("very weak socialisation") and the group with a "weak socialisation" in the L2. The frequency of use of the L2 to express anger continues to increase across the groups with higher levels of socialisation in the L2.

Participants with moderate levels of socialisation in the LX report feeling comfortable communicating anger in both languages. Marigold (French L1, English L2, German L3, Italian L4, Norwegian L5) reports using her L1 and L2 equally to express emotions:

Marigold: I discuss emotions with family and friends in both languages and express my feelings (positive or negative) to myself or others in both.

Some multilinguals, like HV (German L1, English L2, Spanish L3, French L4) apply principles of economy in their repertoire of anger, using short strong swearwords from the L2 within an L1 script for anger:

Table 33 The effect of degree of socialisation in the LX on frequency of use of the LX to express anger (χ^2)

Anger	L2	L3	L4	L5
Alone	296***	230***	123***	64***
Letters	246***	175***	98***	48***
Friends	345***	227***	108***	51***
Parents	279***	211***	159***	62***
Strangers	241***	157***	80***	38***
Swearing	195***	163***	82***	57***

*** $p < .0001$

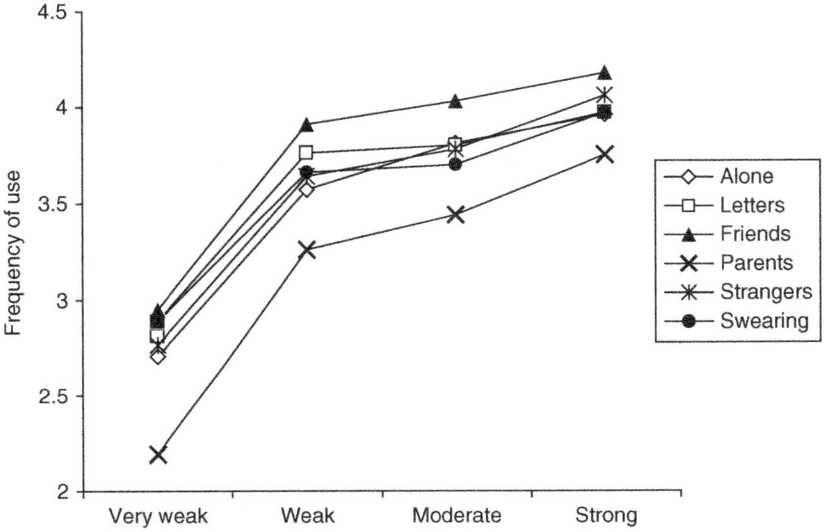

Figure 23 Mean values for frequency of use of the L2 to express anger according to level of socialisation in the L2

> HV: It's [English] the language I swear in too! Most appropriate to use for short outbursts ("damn!" versus German "verdammt" – a mouthful compared to the former one; does not lend itself well to one-vowel outbursts. See also "shit" "fuck" "darn" "blast" etc.). German therefore to be used for well-expressed anger.

Another participant, ML (Portuguese L1, French L2, English L3, Greek L4, Dutch L5) wrote that language choice for the expression of anger is solely dictated by the languages known by the interlocutor:

> ML: I express my anger and deepest feelings in the language that the person I'm talking to will understand better.

Several participants report a gradual shift in language choice for the expression of anger after a prolonged and intense use of that language with partners. In the case of KM (English L1, French L2, German L3, Chinese L4, Italian L5), the preferred language for arguments with her partner has shifted back from her L2 to the L1 (i.e. her dominant language) because it is less of an effort for her and because her partner has gained proficiency in her L1:

> KM: Initially we argued in French but as his English improved I find myself arguing more and more in English; it feels like I'm no longer "making the effort" but just expressing my anger.

Bruce (English L1, Chinese L2, French L3 and living in China) has completely adopted the language of his host country to express anger in:

> Bruce: Definitely argue in Chinese! I have had several native speakers of Chinese as girlfriends/lovers/spouse and some of them spoke English quite fluently. But when you argue English goes by the wayside. Three reasons I think: 1) A native Chinese speaker would prefer to revert to her first language when arguing because arguing in English would put her at a disadvantage with me a native English speaker; 2) Even though I learned Chinese as an adult my ability to express myself in "extreme" situations – under threat in great anger – is quite strong; 3) To me Chinese is like "Black English" in America. It may not be a "high-class" or "academic" language in the eyes of westerners but it is bloody good for expressing feelings.

The formulation of our question about expressing anger may in fact have been confusing for Japanese L1 or LX users, as more frequent use and exposure to Japanese would lead to a realisation that some emotions are best expressed non-verbally. This is confirmed by Kumiko (Japanese L1, English L2) who stated:

> Kumiko: It is easier to scold someone in English because the expressions are more direct. In Japanese scolding may be done through distance-creating acts rather than verbal scolding.

The effect of strong socialisation in English has an effect on linguistic choices for expressing angry emotions among Japanese who returned to Japan. Ryoko (Japanese L1, English L2) explains that she is more likely to express her anger in English:

> Ryoko: I tend to use English when I am angry, Japanese when I'm hurt or sad, both when I am happy or excited (...). My other bilingual friends who are all returnees like me said the same thing about using English when they're angry. I guess I like the sound of the swearing words since I heard it so many times during my stay in the US. This swearing doesn't happen so often in Japan. It's a cultural difference.

Other Asian participants reported that they in fact do appeal to English to escape the social taboo on the open expression of anger in their native languages.

Quipinia (Cantonese L1, English L2) reports that "my family kind of suppress the expression of emotion at home, therefore I feel a lot easier to use another language to express the feelings and the different personality inside me". She recalls an incident in which she burst out into English at her parents who know English but with whom she usually speaks Cantonese:

> Quipinia: But I remember one time when they were arguing with me and I was soooooooooo angry that I shouted out "IT'S UNFAIR!!!!" I guess it's regarded quite impolite if I shouted at my parents (you know Chinese Traditional family) but at that point I feel that I had to express my anger and let myself just do it in another language; perhaps I feel I'm another person if I say that in English.

Deborah's comments (English L1, French L2, German L3, Finnish L4, Italian L5 and currently living in Finland) suggest that some of her languages simply lend themselves more easily to emotion talk. Her Italian L5 seemed to offer her a wider emotional range than her Finnish L4 despite the fact that she was socialised in both languages. She does report swearing in both languages:

> Deborah: I currently only use English and Finnish. When I was living in Italy and speaking Italian everyday, I found it quite easy to talk about emotional topics in Italian, sometimes even with relative strangers like the lady I bought my milk from and the mothers whose children played with mine in the park. I also learned to swear quite fluently in Italian (and learned to drive a car in Italian so that even today when driving I sometimes swear in Italian at Finnish drivers). I have never found it easy to speak in Finnish about how I feel.

This does not stop Deborah from using Finnish swearwords; however, she cites emotional as well as pragmatic reasons for doing so:

> Deborah: I tend to swear slightly more often in Finnish than in English because Finnish has a trilled "r" that I find emotionally very satisfying. Also swearing in English to a Finn is sometimes counterproductive because they find it comic.

These comments suggest that the LX can become the preferred language for anger expression, once emotion scripts have been acquired in the process of socialisation.

We have already seen a participant, Michelle, for whom it is more acceptable to swear in English, the language in which she lives and works, rather than in Chinese where swearing is a sign of lack of education. Other participants argue that swearwords in an LX are not as bad and more fun than in the L1, while others feel that cultural constraints prohibit the use of swearwords in the L1. One participant, Tomomi (Japanese L1, English L2, Italian L3, Spanish L4, married to an Italian, dominant in Japanese and living in the UK for four years), extends this personal prohibition to all languages.

She mentions the sociocultural constraints weighing on the use of Japanese swearwords in Japan. She claims that she does not swear in any language:

B: Do you swear?
T: I don't.
B: No, never, in any language?
T: No, in Japanese we don't really have swearword, and English swearword I don't like it, especially you know with the kids, they can get so easily, so I don't have this habit to use swearword so I don't.
B: Have you learnt any Italian swearwords?
T: I know it because you know some people around me say that, but I don't, I don't use any.

Miho (Japanese L1, English L2, Thai L3, German L4, dominant in L1 and L2) also mentions the fact that girls are not supposed to use swearwords in Japan. She reports never swearing in Japanese, but has no problem using English swearwords:

B: So what's the difference in the use of swearwords between Japanese and English? Is the Japanese equivalent very strong?
M: Um... it's it's a native thing.
B: OK.
M: Yeah, so... I don't use that much.
B: OK.
M: Unless I was fighting... so I think it's very strong.
B: Do you use swearwords in English?
M: Yeah.
B: You do. Do you use swearwords in Japanese?
M: No
B: No. Why?
M: Um... never used it
B: Is it you or is everybody else?
M: I don't think girls use swearwords in Japanese.
B: I see, OK, but you use them in English?
M: Yeah.
B: Ah ah, do you have a problem with that?
M: No.
B: Ah ah, it comes naturally?
M: Yes, it's OK.

Other participants report that swearing is taboo in their L1 culture, but they might use mild swearwords in English. This is the case of Layla (Arabic L1, English L2) who feels dominant in both languages and has lived for five years in English-speaking countries.

L: Speaking of swearing, (....) I never swear in Arabic, never never at all, because I know exactly what it means, because it's my language anyway, and how offensive it would be to swear, but in English because it's not my native language, sometimes I use some swearwords, but I don't really aware I'm not really aware of how immense those words are. One of the words that sometimes I use is "bloody", "bloody rude" you know, this is the only swearword I use.

B: The only one? I see.

L: Yeah. Sometimes I use another one, you want to know what, you want to hear what kind of words I use?

B: Yes

L: Sometimes I say "shit".

B: OK, right

L: But it's just because I know many, many of my friends they keep using it, and I'm not really aware of how immense and strong this word, because it's not my native language so I feel like, I feel much more confident in swearing in English than Arabic

B: But if you're speaking Arabic and you are in a situation where you would normally use the swearword in English, what do you say in Arabic?

L: I don't, I don't because it's just, I was raised up in, my family never swear, never sweared never at all, and I never got used to it, and basically it's part of my, not only how I was raised, it's also part of my beliefs that I don't like to swear because I think it's uncivilized, it's uncivilized way of speaking, and I feel that I can use any, although sometimes you really really feel you'd like to do it, but I don't in Arabic, I never never say any swearword in Arabic, I never really honestly.

Finally, Jean (French L1, English L2), who arrived in the UK from France a year ago, declares that he prefers swearing in French, but he reports that one English swearword has recently been included in his repertoire:

J: Actually, it is French most of the time but since one year now I started to swear in English from ehm spontaneously.

B: OK.

J: But just, just "fuck".

B: OK.

J: It's just the word "fuck", sorry I give you these details but...

B: No no no, OK.

J: It's just the word "fuck" comes naturally, spontaneously, but this is recent, I mean this is just last year, before this it was always in French.

Hypothesis 6: The effect of network of interlocutors on frequency of use of the LX to express anger in the LX

The Kruskal-Wallis analyses show a highly significant effect of the network of interlocutors on frequency of choice of the L2, L3 and L4 to express anger in and to swear. The effect was only significant for expressing anger to friends in the L5 (Table 34). Values for the frequency of use of the L2 to express anger increase with more familiar interlocutors (Figure 24).

Mustafa (Kurdish and Turkish L1, German L2, French L3, Arabic L4 and English L5) has lived in the UK for 12 years and feels dominant in both

Table 34 The effect of network of interlocutors in the LX on likelihood of choice of the LX to express anger (χ^2)

Anger	L2	L3	L4	L5
Alone	88***	84***	82***	5
Letters	61***	81***	69***	4
Friends	86***	147***	92***	11*
Parents	180***	167***	126***	6
Strangers	26***	40***	21***	3
Swearing	66***	83***	59***	7

*** $p < .0001$, ** $p < .001$, * $p < .05$

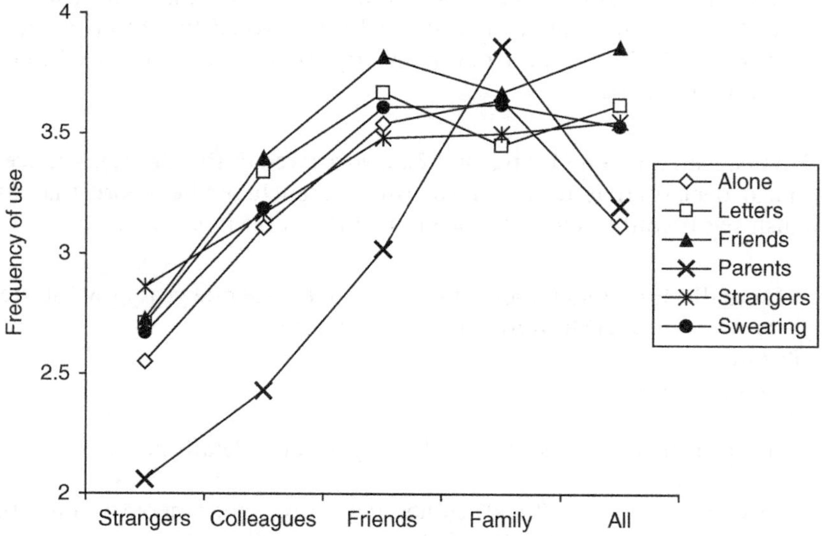

Figure 24 Mean values for frequency of use of the L2 to express anger and swear according to network of interlocutors

Turkish and English, which he uses with various interlocutors on a daily basis:

B: When you're angry, do you prefer to express your anger in one of your languages, and which one?
Mu: Um ... well, Turkish and English and Kurdish.
B: Turkish and English and Kurdish, OK, so in which language do you prefer to swear?
Mu: Turkish and English.
B: OK, how do you choose in which language to swear?
Mu: To swear? Um, you know if I am kind of, it's difficult because this is all about social life you know, and when I am too much involved you know, immersed in English, then I swear in English, because I have permanently been living with English friends outside Turkish Kurdish community in England, and Turkish as well sometimes of course you know is the language like my mother tongue and it's difficult to escape from it and that's how I yeah that's how I feel really swearing is always kind of in these two languages Turkish and English.
B: OK.
Mu: But not Kurdish.
B: Not Kurdish, why?
Mu: Because there aren't many swearwords in Kurdish, and there are extremely rude and undignified kind of expressions, it's kind of cultural, so even in Kurdish there aren't many swearwords that I can use, they are usually Turkish.

Hypothesis 7: The effect of total language knowledge on frequency of choice to express anger in the LX

The Kruskal-Wallis analyses reveal a significant effect of total language knowledge on the frequency of choice of the L3 to express anger in all situations, but the effect was significant in only one L2 situation and one L4 situation (Table 35). Differences between trilinguals and quadrilinguals in values for the frequency of choice of the L3 to express anger are modest, but the values are markedly higher for the pentalinguals using the L2 (Figure 25).

Another participant in the interviews, Klaus (German L1, English L2, French L3, Russian L4, Spanish L5), has lived in the UK for nearly 20 years and is highly fluent in English. He is married to a native speaker of Catalan and Spanish, with whom he communicates in English. He feels that he can swear in any language he shares with an interlocutor:

K: Because the context is usually English, I swear in English as well (...) if I speak to a German friend of mine and I feel anger, then I would swear in German. (...)

B: So when you argue with your partner you argue in English?
K: English yeah.
B: With any German swearwords?
K: No no, no.

Table 35 The effect of total language knowledge on frequency of choice of the LX to express anger (χ^2)

Anger	L2	L3	L4
Alone	1	19***	1
Letters	4	14**	2
Friends	5*	15**	2
Parents	2	9*	0
Strangers	2	21***	4*
Swearing	2	13**	1

*** p < .0001, ** p < .001, * p < .05

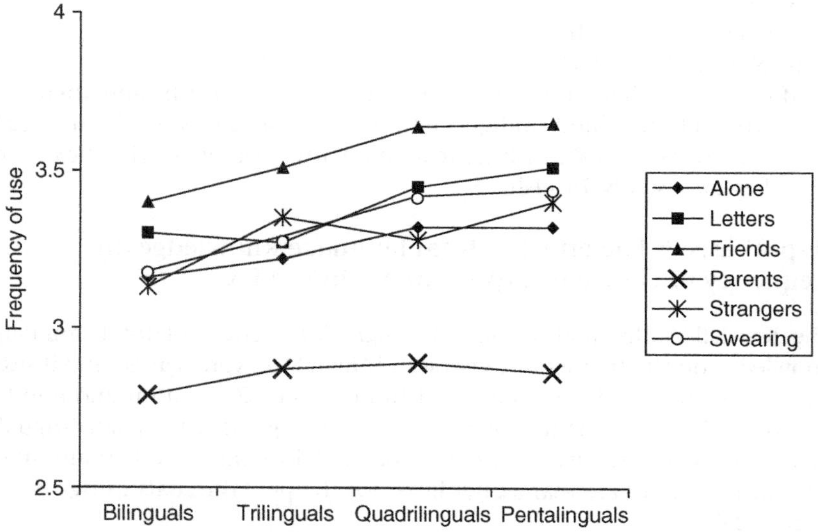

Figure 25 Mean values for frequency of use of the L2 to express anger according to total language knowledge

Hypothesis 8: The effect of Trait Emotional Intelligence on frequency of choice to express anger in the LX

A series of Kruskal-Wallis analyses show no significant effect of TEI on frequency of language choice to express anger, with the exception of expressing anger to strangers in the L2, where the High-TEI group scores significantly higher than the Low-TEI and Medium-TEI groups (Table 36). A similar pattern emerges for swearing in the L3.

Hypothesis 9: The effect of gender, age and level of education on frequency of choice to express anger and to swear in the LX

Gender

A series of Mann-Whitney tests reveal significant differences in frequency of language choice to express anger and swear in the L2 but no effect emerged for the other languages (Table 37). Female participants were more likely to choose the L2 to express anger than males (Figure 26).

Table 36 The effect of TEI on frequency of choice of the LX to express anger (χ^2)

Anger	L2	L3	L4	L5
Alone	0	4	1	1
Letters	5	1	1	1
Friends	2	1	0	1
Parents	0	3	2	1
Strangers	13**	5	5	1
Swearing	1	6*	2	1

** p < .001, * p < .05

Table 37 Differences in frequency of use of language choice to express anger and to swear between female and male participants in the L2, L3, L4 and L5 (Z)

		L2	L3	L4	L5
Alone	Mann-Whitney	177101	122365	55610.5	17366.5
	Z	2.7*	–0.1	–1.7	–1.8
Letters	Mann-Whitney	171308	114227	50456	16565
	Z	2.5*	–0.0	–1.6	–1.0
Friends	Mann-Whitney	174375	113047	51330	17121
	Z	3.4**	–0.7	2.0*	–0.8
Parents	Mann-Whitney	160635	103175	48138	17265.5
	Z	2.6*	–0.6	–1.79	–0.0
Strangers	Mann-Whitney	175581	108938	49654	15861
	Z	0.7	–1.0	2.3*	–1.8
Swearing	Mann-Whitney	176684	104579	46611	15145
	Z	0.7	–0.6	2.5*	–1.0

* p < .05, ** p < .001

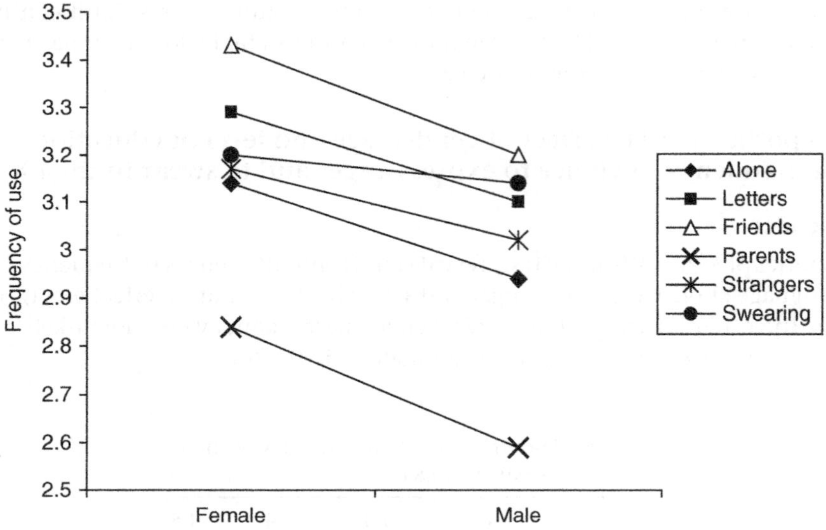

Figure 26 Mean values for frequency of use of the L2 to express anger according to gender

Table 38 The effect of age on frequency of use of the LX to express anger (χ^2)

Anger	L2	L3	L4	L5
Alone	3	7	3	6
Letters	8	3	3	5
Friends	10	6	5	6
Parents	7	10	5	11
Strangers	4	18*	10	18*
Swearing	16*	5	7	2

* $p < .05$

Age

A series of Kruskal-Wallis tests reveal only scattered effects of age on the frequency of use of the L2, L3 and L5 to express anger and to swear (Table 38).

Education

A series of Kruskal-Wallis analyses show an effect of education level on the frequency of language choice to express anger and swear in the L2, but not in any language acquired later (Table 39). Participants with a BA or an MA tended to score higher in the frequency of use of the L2 to express anger compared to participants with an A-level or a PhD (Figure 27).

Table 39 The effect of education level on frequency of use of the LX to express anger (χ^2)

Anger	L2	L3	L4	L5
Alone	3	1	4	3
Letters	8*	5	3	1
Friends	10*	3	2	5
Parents	13*	7	5	1
Strangers	8*	1	2	3
Swearing	5	1	3	4

* p < .05

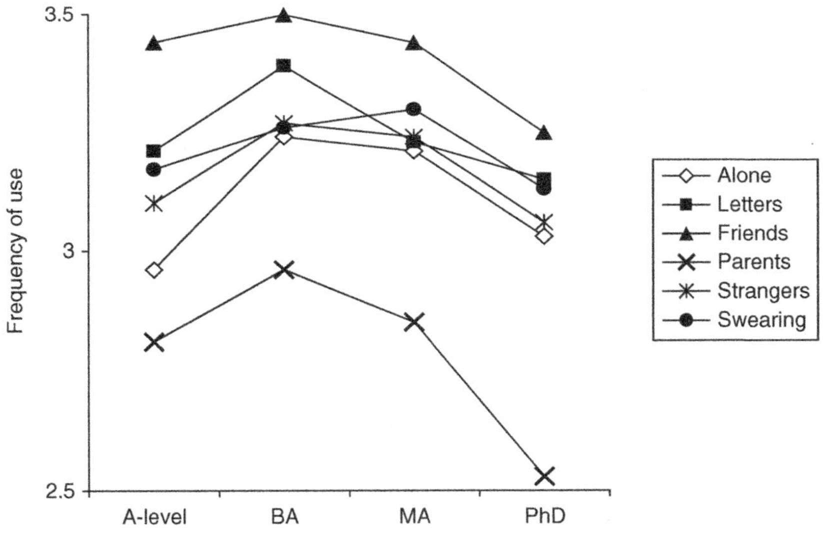

Figure 27 Mean values for frequency of use of the L2 to express anger according to education level

Summing up

Most hypotheses were confirmed, although for some dependent variables the effect was not significant in all situations and in all languages.

Statistical analysis showed that pentalinguals are significantly more likely to vent their anger in their L1 and gradually less so in languages acquired later.

The comments showed that the majority of the respondents prefer the L1 for expression of anger because of its superior emotional force. Anger in the LX felt "fake" to some participants. However, because of the superior impact of swearing in the L1, some participants considered it taboo and avoided swearing in it, which could be linked to both cultural and religious beliefs. The fact that the LX tended to "lack oomph" for some interlocutors increased the likelihood of it being used for swearing. Ilana had even integrated some popular English swearwords into her Russian L1, Andrew used a single Spanish swearword in his English or French to express his anger. For Barbara, the language chosen to express anger depended on the strength of her anger: she felt able to express mild to strong anger in her L2, but switched to her L1 when her anger reached boiling point. Other participants reported being perfectly capable of switching languages to express anger and to swear in the language of their interlocutor. Piero and Klaus reported code-switching between their L1 and L2 to express anger and to swear (see also the final chapter of the present book).

The "history of learning" variables had significant effects on the frequency of use of the LX to express anger. Younger starters were more likely to use their L2, L3 or L4 to express their anger and swear (in the L5 AoA affected only frequency of swearing). Participants who had only learnt an LX through formal instruction were less likely to use that language to express anger compared to mixed or naturalistic learners. Bart commented that learners absorb grammar rules in the LX rather than emotion scripts, which have to be learned outside the classroom during social interactions. This also suggests that instructed learners who might have become fluent LX users never quite close the gap in the frequency of use of an LX to express anger.

Just as for the expression of feelings, the independent variables reflecting current use of the LX had a highly significant effect on the frequency of its use to express anger across situations. Participants who used an LX frequently, were strongly socialised in the language and used it with a wide network of interlocutors were more likely to use it to express anger with various interlocutors.

Several participants, typically of Asian or Arabic origin (Ryoko, Kumiko, Miho, Layla, Mustafa and Michelle) reported that swearing in English allows them to escape the social constraint that weighs on them in Japanese, Arabic, Kurdish and Chinese, where swearing carries strong social stigma. Contact with English had made them more inclined to express anger in the English way, even to use mild swearwords with interlocutors from their home county. Only one participant, Tomomi, claimed that she stuck to her Japanese rule of avoiding swearing in any language.

All the participants, with the exception of Jean, had spent a considerable amount of time in the UK and were highly fluent in English, and could probably be described as multicompetent biculturals, aware of the differences between the L1 norms and the British English norms. Sandra, for example, remarked on the fact that anger scripts cannot be translated literally from one language to another, as they involved different metaphors and imagery.

For participants who use their L2 with their partner, the L2 is also the preferred language for swearing. This could be an illustration of a high level of socialisation in the L2. For participants who do not use English systematically within the family, language preference and swearing practices are somewhere in the middle between L1 norms and English L2 norms. Layla, Michelle and her Chinese friends report using euphemisms rather than the actual English swearwords, but in doing so clearly behave differently than their L1 monolingual peers.

Participants' linguistic profiles, i.e. the number of languages mastered, had a significant effect only on the frequency of use of the L3 to express anger. Participants knowing four or five languages used the L3 more frequently to express anger. Trait Emotional Intelligence had an effect on frequency of use of the L2 to express anger to strangers and the L3 for swearing.

The effects of gender, age and education level on the likelihood to use an LX to express anger are not clear cut. Female participants used the L2 more frequently than males to express their anger (but no other language). The participants' age had limited effects in the L2, L3 and L5. Finally, education level had an effect only in the L2. More highly educated participants were more likely to use the L2 to express anger in certain situations.

8
Results: Attitudes towards Languages and Perception of Emotionality of Swearwords

The present chapter focuses on the complex interaction of independent variables that affect attitudes and perceptions towards multilinguals' languages. It also looks more specifically at the perception of a particular category of words in the different languages, namely swearwords and taboo words.

Multilinguals entertain clear opinions about their languages. I referred in the introduction to Raimund Gregorius, the character in Pascale Mercier's novel *Night Train to Lisbon* who is more passionate about dead languages rather than currently spoken ones. The reader remains in the dark about Raimund's attitudes toward his native German and his French L2, but his dislike of Spanish (at which his ex-wife excelled) is clearly described, as is his sudden infatuation with Portuguese. He just loves the sound of the language and delves into language courses, grammars and dictionaries in order to master it (Mercier, 2007). Research shows that not only in novels do attitudes towards various languages vary dramatically.

Language attitudes

My interest in attitudes toward languages and dialects stems from personal experience. I grew up in a French-speaking family in the Flemish city of Bruges (a monolingual Dutch-speaking environment) in the late 1960s. My grandparents were all fluent Dutch-French bilinguals. My maternal grandfather, Adriaan Vandewalle, whose self-portrait adorns the cover of this book, was a perfect example of the complex attitudes Flemings had toward Dutch and French. In 1914, aged seven, he fled to Rouen in France with his family and came back to Flanders after the war. The family continued to speak Dutch to each other in Rouen, but French was the only language used outside the house. He became a fluent bilingual. Yet, as he continued his studies in Flanders and entered university in Ghent in the 1930s, he developed a strong sympathy for the Flemish call for more respect and autonomy within Belgium. French had been the prestige language in Flanders for much of the nineteenth century and the first half of the twentieth (Vandenbussche,

2004). Flemings had to master French if they wanted to have a career and the Flemish bourgeoisie often raised their children in French, using Dutch (or the local Flemish dialect) with the servants and switching back and forth between both languages when talking to each other. Instruction in primary and secondary schools was in French and only in the late 1930s did Dutch become more common. My maternal grandfather was always keen to tell his grandchildren how his knowledge of French saved him from being beaten up during demonstrations and counter-demonstrations about the introduction of Dutch as a language of instruction. The pro-French lobby argued that it was impossible to use Dutch to discuss highly abstract, philosophical topics, and that the introduction of Dutch would therefore lead to a devaluation of the quality of teaching at university. Pro-Dutch students wore black hats, while pro-French students wore white hats. At some point my grandfather and his friend, Walter Vanbeselaere, were separated from their group and had to flee through the many side streets of Ghent, pursued by a pack of "white hats". At that point my grandfather decided that they could not outrun them, and that they would have to outsmart them. His friend and him thus tucked their black hats deep inside their pockets, turned a corner and started walking calmly towards the advancing group of pursuers. Panting, these asked whether they had seen the "deux flamingants" (a derogatory term for Flemings), running in their direction. My grandfather answered in fluent French that indeed two exhausted Flemings had run past them in the next sidestreet. The pack took up the pursuit and they thanked their good fortune, and the fact that my grandfather's French was so good.

By the time I entered primary education in Bruges in the late 1960s, Dutch was the established language of education and French had lost its prestige. Indeed, French was perceived as an ostentatious language. I learnt Dutch through interactions with friends and teachers. It later turned out that I had absorbed the local variant of "standard" Flemish/Dutch (called "Algemeen Beschaafd Nederlands" – literally "General Civilised Dutch") rather than the dialect used in Bruges, which again made me quite unpopular with dialect speakers in the playground. They would approach me and enquire whether I was a "keeskop" (cheesehead, an insulting reference to the Dutch) or a "franskilion" (an equally derogatory term referring to francophone Flemings). When I moved to Brussels to study French at the Vrije Universiteit (a Flemish university), I discovered that my Dutch had a coastal accent that turned out to be associated with mental retardation by my flatmates from Brussels and Antwerp. Not wanting to sound stupid, I tried to adapt to the new standard norm. After finishing my PhD in Brussels in 1993, I moved to London. For once, I did not encounter any hostility toward my accent and language use: Londoners are used to variety of English L2s, and my British interlocutors rather liked my French accent in English, which they thought was "cute". Yet, when attending the AAAL conference in Washington in 2003, which coincided with the start of the US intervention in Iraq, I discovered that my French accent had become a liability when interacting with Bush supporters.

What I wanted to illustrate with this personal story is that multilingual, or multidialectal, children grow up with an acute sense of the complex attitudes toward the various languages in their environment (cf. Lasagabaster and Huguet, 2006).

Gardner (1985) defined attitude as "an evaluative reaction to some referent or attitude object, inferred on the basis of the individual beliefs or opinions about the referent" (p. 9). The data Gardner obtained from participants through the Attitude Motivation Test Battery (AMTB) is quantitative, namely a value on a five-point Likert scale accompanying a list of statements relating to possible reasons why the participant wants to learn a second language ("Studying the L2 can be important for me because it will allow me to travel to L2 areas; (...) it will allow me to learn about myself; (...) it will help me find a better job; (...) it will allow me to appreciate L2 minority problems"). These items are linked to 11 scales (integrative orientation, attitudes toward the target group, interest in foreign languages, teacher evaluation, course evaluation, motivational intensity, desire to learn the language, attitudes toward learning the language, language class anxiety, language use anxiety and instrumental orientation. These scales form the basis of five constructs, namely integrativeness, attitudes toward the learning situation, motivation, language anxiety and instrumentality (Gardner, 2006: 246). Statistical analysis allows the researchers to calculate the score of each participant on the different scales, and thence provide a unique quantitative profile of that person.

According to Gardner (1985) levels of motivation are influenced and maintained by attitudes toward the learning situation and integrativeness, defined as "an openness to the TL group and other groups in general linked to one's sense of ethnic identity" (Gardner, 2006: 236). Research has shown that second language learners with higher levels of integrativeness tend to obtain better results in the L2 than learners with lower levels of integrativeness. A higher level of instrumentality also tends to correlate positively (albeit not always significantly) with L2 proficiency measures (Dörnyei, 2001; Gardner, 2006). Gardner (2006) rejected the criticism that the AMTB is only appropriate in the Canadian context by demonstrating the similarity in internal consistency reliability coefficients, factor structures and achievements in English L2 with the data collected through the AMTB in four European countries.

Attitudes toward foreign languages in general are not as stable as some early studies have seemed to suggest. This error originated from the fact that most early SLA research into attitudes considered a single foreign language (typically French L2 in the Canadian context). However, recent studies have shown that learners may have widely different attitudes toward the different foreign languages they are studying (Gardner and Tremblay, 1998). Lasagabaster (2005b) considered the attitudes of university students towards three languages (i.e. Basque, Spanish and English). He found that participants showed a very positive attitude towards English and toward their own

L1 (Basque or Spanish). The Spanish L1 participants had more favourable attitudes toward English than those with Basque as their L1. Dewaele (2005a) analysed attitudes toward French L2 and English L3 among Flemish high-school students. Attitudes toward English were found to be much more positive than those toward French, despite the fact that the participants had enjoyed a longer and more intense formal instruction in French. Participants who felt more Flemish (i.e. their regional identity) than Belgian displayed more negative attitudes toward French. These attitudes towards French are the result of the tense sociopolitical relations between Dutch and French speakers in Belgium. Higher levels of self-perceived competence, a higher frequency of use of the TL and lower levels of CA in French and English were found to correlate positively with attitudes toward these two languages.

Kormos and Csizér (2007) investigated attitudes toward English and German among young Hungarian teenagers. The results showed that participants had very little direct contact with English and German and that information about target language speakers and their culture was gained indirectly through various cultural products. The participants displayed a wide variety of attitudes toward a considerable number of aspects of the TL cultures. They also reported that cross-cultural contact helped them become more proficient, increased their motivation and reduced their FLA. Csizér and Kormos (2008) found that contact with English through media had a more important effect on young Hungarian teenagers than direct contact with NSs of English.

Attitudes and perceptions are determined by a complex set of affective, historical, social, political and geographical factors. While these attitudes are relatively stable within speech communities, they can suddenly shift as a consequence of political circumstances (war) or migration patterns, when a new language suddenly emerges in the local soundscape and becomes associated with a particular style of music or activity.

An interesting question is whether attitudes toward foreign languages are always shaped by the people who speak these languages, or whether some inherent characteristic of the language may affect the attitude of a group of people or individuals toward that language. This dissociation between the language and the cultural values that the language represents has been amply documented in the literature. The teacher wants learners to acquire competence in the TL and TL culture without actually feeling any sympathy toward the speakers of that language. In other words, an instrumental motivation is encouraged but an integrative one is strongly discouraged. An illustration of this peculiar situation is provided by Pavlenko (2003). She recounts her first English language class in the former Soviet Union in the mid-1970s. Her teacher framed the objective of the class as the necessity to master English, the language of the enemy, in order better to defeat him:

> My inculcation process started in 1975 when as a fifth grader I chose my foreign language, English, and attended the first class. The teacher welcomed us with a passionate speech: "My dear fifth graders, today is a

> very important day in your life – you are starting to study English. Your knowledge of this language will prove crucial when we are at War with the imperialist Britain and United States and you will have to decode and translate intercepted messages". This was a new idea for me, since my mother, herself an English teacher, conveniently forgot to inform me that one day we would have to confront the capitalist powers and interview their spies. The mission did not particularly appeal to me, neither did the delivery. Thus, I patiently waited until the end of the class and then asked to be transferred to the French programme. French, at the time, was the language of popular singers, Joe Dassin and Mireille Mathieux, of popular movies with Pierre Richard and Jean-Paul Belmondo, and, of course, of popular writers, Balzac, Dumas-père, and Maupassant. It was glamorous and non-threatening and I was delighted to delve into it both in middle and high school and later in college as a French major. (p. 313)

A similar attitude existed toward Russian during the Cold War in the West, and toward German during the two World Wars (Pavlenko, 2003).

Attitudes toward foreign languages, and the cultures they represent, are very often ambivalent. They are also often dependent on the political climate and can shift quite rapidly. Any linguistic group forced to learn the language of another group with whom it co-exists within a nation may learn that language without any desire to adopt the cultural values and attitudes of that group. This so-called language teaching "with a clothespin on the nose" is dictated by political or economic necessity at the level of the group. For example, many Francophones grudgingly accept that English, rather than French, has become the new lingua franca. How enthusiastic, or reticent, will these Francophones be in promoting the learning and teaching of what they consider to be a "rival" language? Dutch probably suffers from an even more negative perception among many young Francophone Belgians who feel they need to learn Dutch because knowledge of both French and Dutch is often required for jobs in Belgium (Mettewie, Van Mensel and Belang, 2006). These Francophone Belgians thus rate Dutch as useful in the Belgian context but they often find it a difficult and ugly language, with very little international stature. Not surprisingly, the motivation to learn a language perceived as ugly and not very prestigious will be low. Emotional attitudes toward languages may thus be quite independent from purely instrumental evaluations.

Attitudes toward foreign languages are often shaped by the global geopolitical and sociopolitical context, but they need not be adopted completely by the individual (Van Essen, 2004). Indeed, "FL learners are not passive 'consumers' of institutionalised ideologies and may engage in resistance and opposition" (Pavlenko, 2003). Her own act of resistance as a pupil was walking away from the English language class and opting for French instead. This obviously had nothing to do with her attitude toward English (which must have been positive considering her mother was a teacher of English) but rather with the attitude toward the teacher. Mettewie (2004) similarly reported that the attitude toward the foreign language teacher to a large extent determines the attitude toward the foreign language, especially for languages that are rare in the usual linguistic landscape of the learners. The decision to learn a particular foreign language and to soak up the cultural and political values attached to that language can be an act of resistance in itself. Pavlenko (2003) refers to the case of Natasha Lvovich, a translator and professional teacher of French in the former Soviet Union, who bitterly regretted being unable to travel to France and for whom French became an intellectual escape from the oppressive communist regime:

> Associating French with intellectualism, sophistication, and nobility, she created an imaginary French identity for herself, learning to speak with a Parisian accent, memorising popular French songs, reading French classics and detective stories in argot, mastering numerous written genres, cooking French food (from locally available ingredients). (p. 326)

An individual's attitude toward a language can also be determined by purely subjective factors: one language may sound repulsive, while another one may sound sexy. Piller (2002) coined the term "language desire" to describe the attraction of language learners. In her study of linguistic practices of bilingual couples, Piller (p. 269) notes that some participants were in love with English or German as an L2 long before they actually met their partners. However, languages may have completely different effects on different people. The American philosopher Richard Watson, a specialist in Descartes, could read French but not speak it. After an invitation to give a paper at a conference in Paris marking the anniversary of Descartes' *Discours de la Méthode* he decided it was time to learn oral French. Six months of conversation classes with a tutor had very little effect and the conference presentation turned out disastrously. Among the affective obstacles to learning oral French he mentioned the fact that French sounded "syrupy" and "effeminate" and a language that "Real Men" would not speak (Pavlenko, 2005: 67).

The opposite happened to Edna, an American student described in Kaplan (1993):

> Edna is just back from a year of study abroad where she took the majority of her classes at "Sciences Po" – the French institute for the study of political science. She is imbued with the style and the tone of a French Sciences Po student. She went even farther than I did to make herself over; her French is indistinguishable from that of a student at Sciences Po. She is every French professor's dream! She acquired all the

> micro-traits of intellectual francophilia: in her notebook, she underlines her main points, marked with Roman numerals "I.", "II.", "III.", in contrasting colored-pencil colors, and for every big point, she's got a little point "a.", a little point "b.", sub-points "i.", "ii.", "iii." This, I imagine, she got from sitting in French university amphitheaters where the professors actually say "aspect number three, second part, small a" as they're talking, to assist the students taking notes. (p. 175)

Edna seems to have been driven, in Gardner's terms, by extreme integrative motivation. Not only does she manage to sound exactly like her French peers at Sciences Po, she seems also to have adopted some specific French academic traits. It is perfectly possible, of course, that she possessed these traits before her stay in France, but Kaplan attributes them to her contact with French academic culture.

Kaplan describes her own infatuation with French and France as a form of addiction: (...) "sometimes I don't want to need French so much. I want to be free of it" (p. 207).

Some American students can also react in a completely opposite way. Kinginger (2008) reports on the case of Deirdre, who had not enjoyed her French classes in the US very much but who wanted to go to France: "basically, the reason that I kept on pursuing French was because I wanted to go abroad. I wanted to go abroad ever since seventh grade. (Pre-departure Interview)" (p. 237). However, once in France, she wrote at length in her journal of her homesickness and self-imposed social isolation. She was also counting the number of days remaining in her programme and moved her return flight three weeks forward in order to leave at the earliest possible moment (p. 240). During her final month in Montpellier she claimed that she "wasn't talking French hardly at all" and was, in fact, no longer interested in it. Deirdre's goal seems to have been to survive the ordeal. In an interview after her return to the US, she declared that she was not really concerned with keeping it up. She was no longer interested in taking any more classes and expected to start losing the little French she had learned: "She had survived her ordeal and was "done" with French" (p. 247).

Kinginger (2004b) analysed the literary and autobiographical work of Nancy Huston. Kinginger observes that for Huston, the French language offers the typical American an alternative frame associated with "adult affect, self-control, and subtle artistry, but also with history, refinement, and civilization" (p. 173).

This attitude toward French is also present among British schoolchildren with clear gender differences in the preferred languages (Williams, Burden and Lanvers, 2002). Participants explained the boys' preference for German in terms of French being a more feminine language and German more masculine: "As a high proficiency year 9 boy put it, 'French is the language of love and stuff' while German is 'the war, Hitler and all that' " (p. 520). A girl from the same year group confirms this: "I reckon girls are really into French: they like the way that French sounds more than boys do" (p. 521).

Kramsch (2003) reports similarly ambiguous attitudes toward French in her study on metaphors and the subjective construction of beliefs of foreign language learners. A second semester student of French at UC Berkeley wrote that learning French is "like eating regurgitated paté". Kramsch notes that this metaphor might evoke and be linked to a cluster of other beliefs such as "France is the country of good food" as well as "learning French is like having phlegm stuck in the back of my throat". The positive side of the metaphor is the choice of word "paté", which indexes deliciously sophisticated French food. This positive connotation is undercut by the adjective "regurgitated" which transforms "paté" into something revolting. Kramsch sees potential irony in the metaphor. She points to the prosodic structure of the metaphor itself, which underscores the ruptured harmony of the experience. "Learning a language / is like eating paté" would be rhythmically pleasing, but the insertion of "regurgitated" breaks the rhythm with too many syllables. She sees a possible reference to the too many words the learner has to ingurgitate, enacting the confusing nature of the experience, which is at once savoury and unsavoury (Kramsch, 2003).

Dewaele (2010a) focused on attitudes toward Francophones, the perception of French and the perception of areas of difficulty in the French language (pronunciation, grammar, syntax, lexicon, politeness, address pronouns and spelling) among 684 native and non-native learners of French in universities in Europe, North America and Australia. The findings suggest that NSs and NNSs of French have different perceptions of the language and of Francophones, and that they also judge the areas of difficulty in French differently. A positive perception of the characteristics of the language was found to be positively correlated with a similar one of the characteristics of Francophones among NNSs but not among NSs. One possible explanation is that for the NNSs French might still be a largely imagined rather than a "lived" language. On the other hand, the NSs, being socialised in French, have fewer illusions about the politeness, the niceness, the openness and the culture of their fellow NSs. However, a highly significant positive correlation emerged between the perceived romantic character of French and the characteristics of Francophones in both groups. French as the language of love thus seems to be an enduring myth among NSs and NNSs alike. Participants (both NSs and NNSs) knowing more languages perceived French to be richer, more poetic, more useful and more difficult than participants knowing fewer languages did. Interestingly, the different perceptions of NSs and NNSs of French did not all go in the same direction. In other words, the NSs were not more globally "positive" about their language. They also considered themselves to be significantly less polite and cultivated than NNSs perceived them to be. Also, the NSs judged French to be generally more difficult than NNSs did.

When focusing on specific areas of difficulty, it turned out that NSs perceived spelling to be more difficult than NNSs did. All other areas of difficulty were judged to be harder by the NNSs. It is possible that for NSs all areas of French that fall under the label of implicit competence are perceived to be easier. The one exception is spelling, which is arbitrary and needs to be learnt consciously. The French "dictée" is a standard exercise in French classes for NSs in primary and secondary school. On the other hand, NNSs need to master all areas of French through conscious learning and intense effort. Because spelling is one of many difficult things that need to be mastered, it does not stand out. Indeed, the average difficulty score that NNSs assigned to spelling was very similar to that for other areas.

Surprisingly, NNSs gave French higher scores on a number of "emotional" dimensions. The explanation probably resides in the specific research design and in the selection of the sample. Participants were not asked to compare the characteristics between their different languages but simply to judge the characteristics of French on a Likert scale. The fact that the NNSs judged French to be more poetic, useful and romantic than NSs did could be explained by the fact that they were actively learning the language and that they had freely chosen to study it. In other words, they had invested time and effort in mastering French. They must have convinced themselves that French possessed all the positive qualities in order to justify their continued effort in studying it. They were therefore likely to have more positive attitudes toward French and more accepting views of speakers of French than peers who were not studying this language (Rubenfeld et al., 2006). They might have not have progressed far enough in their study to judge the richness of the language, the only characteristic where NSs' scores surpassed those of the NNSs. These NNSs were therefore quite different from the high school students reported in Williams, Burden and Lanvers (2002), who were more or less forced to take French and did not seem to enjoy it much. Finally, NNSs judged Francophones to be significantly more cultivated and polite, but not more open or nicer. It was argued that the NNSs' more positive attitudes could be linked to their on-going investment in the foreign language learning process (cf. Peirce, 1995) and the fact that they may have idealised certain aspects of the TL and the TL community.

Attitudes toward languages may also vary widely within a particular country. Dörnyei and Clément (2001) looked specifically at the attitudes of thousands of 13- and 14-year-old Hungarian schoolchildren toward five different languages – English, German, French, Italian and Russian. Except for marked gender differences (with girls scoring higher on most attitudinal/motivational measures), the researchers found strong regional variations: schoolchildren in the capital scored highest on most variables, those living near the Austrian border scored higher for German, those in the east scored higher for French and Russian and Italian was most popular in Budapest. The authors concluded that "macrocontextual, geopolitical factors significantly affect people's language attitudes" (p. 423). In a further study Dörnyei, Cziser and Németh (2006) analysed the effect of sociopolitical changes at the end of the 1980s in Eastern Europe on attitudes toward foreign languages. The researchers investigated whether the strong increase in intercultural contact in Hungary had affected the attitudes of Hungarian schoolchildren toward the same five languages. They found that the rank order between the different languages had remained unchanged after the fall of the Iron Curtain: English was the most popular language, followed by German, then French and Italian at similar levels, with Russian at the bottom of the table (p. 143). Gender differences, which had been strong in earlier studies (English, German and Russian being preferred by males, French and Italian being preferred by females) were weaker and had disappeared for English in 2004. French and Italian were found to have overtaken German in the capital (p. 144).

Håkan Ringbom, a Swedish-Finnish bilingual, and emeritus professor from the university of the southern Finnish town of Turku, observes that despite the fact that his Finnish is good enough to cope "with any everyday situation almost as well as a native" (2001: 61), it has taken him some time before appreciating the aesthetic qualities of Finnish: "Finnish has to me been primarily a means of communication in ordinary situations (the flexibility and beauty of the language dawned on me at a very late stage" (p. 61). He studied Latin and English at school and remembers that his English teacher managed to maintain his interest in the language until he reached university, where an exceptional professor of English got him hooked (p. 63).

Ringbom's experience shows that attitudes, perceptions and the investment in the learning of a foreign language are never static but that "the interplay between sociohistoric, sociopolitical, and linguistic circumstances that shape individuals' investments in particular languages and shows that the languages speakers choose to learn, speak, or abandon are intrinsically linked to their social, political, gender, and national identities and imagined futures" (Pavlenko, 2005: 234).

Considering himself an advanced NNS of English, Håkan Ringbom is aware that English swearwords do not affect him as strongly as Swedish or Finnish swearwords:

> I remember how shocked our (male) native speakers at the English Department were when one of our brightest girl students returned from a year in Britain, speaking very genuine English of a genuinely unacademic type with frequent expletives like "fucking". At our department

> we certainly encourage our travelling students to integrate with the natives, but there may be limits to that! As a non-native speaker I wasn't as shocked as my colleagues were, primarily since English swearwords do not convey the same emotional force to me as they do to native speakers of my generation. In both Finnish and Swedish, though, I am well aware of the emotional force of swearwords, having grown up hearing them all around me at school or on the streets. (Ringbom, 2001: 66)

Emotional resonance of multilinguals' languages

Languages acquire particular emotional connotations among multilinguals. The LX is often perceived as being less emotional than the L1 (Harris et al., 2006; Pavlenko, 2005, 2012a). Huston writes that her French L2 feels less emotional to her than her native English:

> Oui, je crois que c'était là l'essentiel: la langue française (et pas seulement ses mots tabous) était, par rapport à ma langue maternelle, moins chargée d'affect et donc moins dangereuse. Elle était froide, et je l'abordais froidement. Elle m'était égale. C'était une substance lisse et homogène, autant dire neutre. (Huston, 1999: 63, quoted in Kinginger, 2004b: 171)
>
> (Yes, I think that was the essential thing: compared to my mother tongue, the French language was less burdened with emotion and therefore less dangerous. She was cold and I approached her coldly. She was uniform. It was a smooth and homogeneous substance, one might say neutral).

The case of Samuel Beckett is particularly interesting. Many critics see his decision, after World War II, to write exclusively in French, the language he learned as a schoolboy and studied at university, as a way of avoiding the pathos and emotionality he associated with his L1 English and of gaining a greater simplicity and objectivity. Writing in French, he was able to "restrain his native verbal profligacy" (Kellman, 2000: 28). Knowlson (1996) adds that for Beckett: "Writing poetry in French allowed him to get away (...) from the dense allusiveness, wide erudition and 'intimate at arms length' quality of his English poems" (pp. 293–294). Using French enabled him "to cut away the excess, to strip away the color" (p. 357).

The Croatian author Josip Novakovich advances a similar argument to explain his decision to write in English:

> In my own case, English words didn't carry the political and emotional baggage of repressive upbringing, so I could say whatever I wanted without provoking childhood demons, to which Croatian words were still chained, to tug at me and to make me cringe. (Novakovich and Shapard, 2000: 16)

The decision not to write in one's L1 might seem surprising given the typically greater emotionality of that language. However, pragmatic concerns, namely the intended readership, can overcome the "natural inclination" to use the L1. Ilan Stavans (2001) relates how his grandmother, Bobbe Bela, a Polish Jew who emigrated to Mexico to escape persecution, sent him her diary "Mi Diario (...) in broken Spanish" (p. 50). She dedicated it to him in Spanish:

> "Dedico mi (diario) (o un chico relato) de mi juventud a mis queridos nietos, Ilan, Alison y Josh, como recuerdo de Bobe [sic] Bela." (...) And not only is the dedication in Spanish but also the entire narrative. This, in fact, is the most urgent question I have, the one I would love to discuss with Bela. Why not in Yiddish, her mother tongue, the tongue in which she sobs and screams? I know the answer of course: she wants to be read, understood and appreciated; she is eager to reach not only me but my wife and, at some point in the future, my children as well. (p. 51)

The lack of emotionality of insults in the LX can also lead to unexpected illocutionary effects in interactions with NSs. In Dewaele (2005a), I recounted an episode that happened during a schooltrip to Paris when a classmate uttered the words "Avec ta sale gueule" (literally "with your dirty mug", meaning "shut your gob") to a French museum guard. He had clearly underestimated the emotional power of the expression. The guard turned red and threatened to call the police. My classmate was dumbstruck, he could not quite understand how this expression, which meant nothing to him, could have such a powerful impact on this French native speaker (2005b: 532).

The literature on language choices and the perception of emotionality of bi- and multilinguals in emotional interactions is spread across various disciplines with researchers using a wide range of methods to gather data. I will focus on the emergence of this paradigm and then more specifically on both the psycholinguistic, cognitive psychological, approach, and the sociolinguistic-applied linguistic one.

Anooshian and Hertel (1994) measured the ability of Spanish-English bilinguals who were late learners of their L2 to recall neutral and emotional words in both their L1 and L2. The participants were highly fluent in both languages, but half of them had Spanish as an L1 and the other half, English. The participants viewed neutral and emotional words in Spanish and English and were given an unexpected free recall test. They were instructed to write down as many of the words as they could remember. A memory advantage for emotion words was found in all participants' L1 but not their L2. Altarriba (2003) has suggested that emotion words in the L1 of bilinguals benefit from multiple traces in memory, leading to a stronger semantic representation. Emotion words in a less frequently used language may have fewer of these connotations and are less deeply encoded. This could explain why the L2 has often been described as being more detached, more distant than the L1 (Dewaele and Pavlenko, 2002; Marcos, 1976).

Research into bilingual autobiographical memory showed that no single language in more emotional per se, but that emotional intensity depends on whether the memories are told in the language in which they were encoded. Javier, Barroso and Muñoz (1993) asked native Spanish-speaking and Spanish-English bilinguals to speak about a life experience using the language in which the event took place. They then described the event again in their L2. The authors found that the first version was more detailed, more elaborated and more vivid than the second version, regardless of the language involved. Schrauf and Hoffman (2007) looked at emotional intensity and valence in the autobiographical memories of immigrants. The researchers found that memories from youth were recalled with less emotional intensity than memories from old age, and negatively valenced memories were rated as less intense than positively valenced memories. It thus seemed that the immigration event created separate contexts of usage for immigrants' L1 and L2, and that this led "to the formation of different associations between bilinguals' languages and their autobiographical memories" (Knickerbocker and Altarriba, 2011).

Marian and Kaushanskaya (2004) analysed autobiographical memories in Russian and English of bicultural adult Russian-English bilinguals who had immigrated to the US as teenagers. Language choice was found to affect self-construal. The recall of memories in English, a language associated with a more individualistic culture, resulted in more individualistic narratives, whereas memories in Russian, a language associated with a more collectivist culture, produced more collectivist narratives, regardless of the language of encoding or the main agent in the narrative. Participants expressed more intense emotion when retrieving a memory in the language that corresponded to the language used at the time when the event took place. Age also affected the valency of the memories, with memories encoded later in life being rated as more positive than memories encoded earlier in life.

Working in a similar vein, Panayiotou (2004a, 2004b) has investigated differences in the reactions of Greek-English and English-Greek bilinguals listening to the same story read to them in both languages. Participants were found to interpret and relate the "same" events differently, depending on the language context. The Greek version of the story elicited sympathy and concern for the protagonist, whereas in English it elicited indifference and disapproval. Different imagery and cultural scripts were used in the retelling, which suggests that participants were drawing on distinct linguistic repertoires and cultural frames. There was also some code-switching, which was interpreted as evidence that bicultural bilinguals interacting with other bicultural bilinguals can use the full range of their cultural and linguistic repertoires.

Altarriba and Canary (2004) used the word-priming paradigm to investigate the effect of word arousal, an emotional component of words, on the priming effect in bilinguals. The authors developed word pairs, which were presented to the participants individually in sequential order. The latter had to indicate whether the second word was a word or a non-word. Previous research has shown that when the first word, or prime, is related to the target, participants generally exhibit a priming effect evidenced by faster reaction times (RT). This effect also occurs when the prime and target are similarly emotionally charged (negative or positive). Altarriba and Canary (2004) found evidence of affective priming in both English monolinguals and Spanish-English bilinguals. However, the bilinguals had longer RTs and a reduced priming effect in some conditions when compared to monolinguals. The authors suggest that this difference might be linked to the fact that the bilinguals had learned and used English in educational and work-oriented environments and that their English emotion words had fewer emotional connotations and reduced affective priming (Altarriba and Canary, 2004).

The Emotional Stroop Task has also been used to investigate bilinguals for differences in how they process emotion words. The Emotional Stroop Task is similar to the traditional Stroop Task but the printed words are emotionally charged and do not label specific colours. Participants are asked to report the colour of each word instead of the actual words. Emotions typically have an interference effect resulting in an increase in RT on the colour-naming task. Sutton et al., (2007) used this method with highly proficient Spanish-English bilinguals. The researchers found evidence of interference in emotion words on the Emotional Stroop Task in bilinguals. The participants had shorter RTs with neutral words compared to emotion words in Spanish and English. In other words, emotion words captured their attention regardless of the language in which they appeared. The participants responded significantly faster when the words were presented in English but the size of the interference effect was similar in both languages. Eilola, Havelka and Sharma (2007) followed a similar procedure with participants who were proficient in Finnish and English, and were late learners of English. Participants were found to have longer RTs on the Emotional Stroop Task when presented with taboo and negative words. These findings suggest that "language proficiency, rather than age of acquisition, had a larger influence on bilingual performance on the Emotional Stroop Task" and "emotional content in different languages does not result in processing differences in bilinguals when bilinguals have equal levels of proficiency in both languages" (Knickerbocker and Altarriba, 2011).

Caldwell-Harris and her team have carried out some pioneering work on physiological responses to swearwords and taboo words in the L1 and L2 of bilinguals. The researchers were intrigued by the finding that taboo words seem to be more anxiety-provoking and embarrassing when presented in the L1 instead of the L2 of bilinguals (Bond and Lai, 1986; Gonzalez-Reigosa, 1976). Using lie-detector technology, Harris, Ayçiçeği and Gleason (2003) investigated skin conductance responses in the Turkish L1 compared to the English L2 of 32 Turkish-English bilinguals who were students at Boston University. Physiological reactions to taboo words presented auditorily in the L1 Turkish were found to be much stronger than their translation equivalents in the L2 English. Harris (2004) investigated whether emotionality effects would be stronger in an L1 even if it was the weaker language. A comparison of the adult offspring of Latin American immigrants in the US, for whom English was considered L2 but was the dominant language, and more recently arrived immigrants from Latin America to the US showed that only the latter group reacted more strongly to reprimands in Spanish. The early learners of English had similar patterns of electrodermal responses in their two languages. The author thus concluded that languages learnt in childhood elicit similar physiological reactions. To explain why an L1 was not more emotional than an L2, which was acquired in childhood, the author proposed "a mechanism independent of age, namely the emotional contexts of learning hypothesis; where language is experienced as emotional when it is acquired and used in an emotional context" (pp. 276–277). A follow-up study with Turkish-English bilinguals residing in Istanbul confirmed that emotional phrases presented in an L1 elicited higher skin conductance responses than emotional phrases in an L2 (Caldwell-Harris and Ayçiçeği-Dinn, 2009). The researchers also looked more specifically at emotion memory effects (i.e. the fact that emotion words are more frequently recalled than neutral words) among 59 Turkish-English students from Istanbul university (Ayçiçeği-Dinn and Caldwell-Harris, 2009). They found that overall emotion-memory effects were similar in the two languages, with reprimands having the highest recall, followed by taboo words, positive words, negative words and finally neutral words.

Emotionality is not just an inherent property of a word. An applied linguistic study on emotionality ratings of sentences judged by NSs and NNSs (Dewaele and Edwards, 2004) showed that context and grammar determine the emotional intensity of an utterance. Sentences with a verb in the progressive form and in the present tense obtained higher emotionality ratings than non-progressive, past tense forms, i.e. "people are screaming" versus "people scream/ed". NNSs tended to have lower scores than NSs and there was more variation in their scores. We argued that the computation of emotional intensity involves either very fast computing of the relevant semantic, grammatical and contextual cues, or retrieval of the value from long-term implicit memory. NSs may be able to retrieve fixed values, while NNSs may be forced to compute on the spot, which leads to slightly different outcomes.

In sum, the L1 seems to occupy a special position in multilinguals' hearts and minds. Altarriba (2003), Harris et al., (2006) and Pavlenko (2005) suggest that this effect stems from the way the L1 was learnt: emotion words and scripts learnt in childhood acquire rich emotional connotations, may be encoded more deeply, with strong links to the limbic system, and stored in implicit memory. In contrast, similar words and expressions learnt later in life have typically been acquired through classroom learning, with a stronger reliance on declarative memory, with fewer emotional connotations, which would explain why they produce weak physiological responses and a general feeling of detachment. Pavlenko (2012a) suggests that among late bilinguals and foreign language users, the L1 and LX may be "differentially embodied, with the later learned language processed semantically but not affectively" (p. 405).

Operationalising the variable

Data on attitudes and perceptions were collected through closed questions, based on a five-point Likert scale. The first item was formulated as follows:

> "Here are some subjective statements about the languages you know. Please mark to what extent they correspond to your own perceptions. There are no right/wrong answers. (My L1/L2/L3/L4/L5 is…useful, colourful, rich, poetic, emotional)."

Possible answers included: 1 = not at all, 2 = somewhat, 3 = more or less, 4 = to a large extent and 5 = absolutely.

The second question was formulated as follows:

> "Do swear and taboo words in your different languages have the same emotional weight for you? Please circle the appropriate answer."

Possible answers on a 5-point Likert scales included: (1 = does not feel strong, 2 = little, 3 = fairly, 4 = strong and 5 = very strong).

Information was collected for the L1, L2, L3, L4 and L5. The dependent variables are thus the numerical values reflecting agreement with a descriptor for the language or the perceived emotional force of swearwords in that language. As the variables are formulated in a positive way, they will be referred to as "positive language characteristics".

Cronbach alpha analyses revealed high internal consistency reliability for the descriptors of the different languages: L1 (alpha = .83), L2 (alpha = .84), L3 (alpha = .87), L4 (alpha = .89), and L5 (alpha = .90).

A series of one-sample Kolmogorov-Smirnov tests revealed that the values for perception of language characteristics and the emotional strength of swearwords are not normally distributed (Kolmogorov-Smirnov Z values vary between 4.2 and 16.7, all $p < .0001$). As a consequence, Kruskal-Wallis tests were used as non-parametric equivalents to one-way ANOVAs, and Wilcoxon Signed Ranks Tests and Mann-Whitney tests were used instead of t-tests.

Hypothesis 1a: Monotonic decline in perception of language characteristics and emotional strength of swearwords from L1 to L5

Friedman's ANOVA tests for related samples revealed that perception of positive language characteristics and the emotional strength of swearwords decreases highly significantly from the L1 to the L5 (Table 40).

The effect is strongest for the perception of the emotional strength of swearwords, followed by perceived usefulness of the language and the finally the "affective" characteristics. An analysis of the means shows a levelling off between L4 and L5 (Figure 28).

Most participants' comments confirm the general trend of higher values on the characteristics of languages acquired first. Peter (English L1, French L2) teaches English literature at a French university and feels that his L1 is richer than his L2:

> Peter: I feel English is OBJECTIVELY rich compared with French: just compare the headwords in the Shorter Oxford with even the largest Robert: roughly 5 times more.

Kevin (Finnish L1, English L2, Swedish L3, German L4) also confirms that swearwords in his L1 have a greater emotional impact than swearwords in his L2:

> I very rarely swear in Finnish but "oh shit" or "fuck" can easily escape my mouth even in quite trivial occasions – they just don't feel that serious to my (or my hearers') ears, even though I know they would sound quite

Table 40 The effect of chronology of acquisition on perception of language characteristics and emotional strength of swearwords from L1 to L5 (χ^2)

Variable	N	df	χ^2	p
Useful	412	4	308.3	***
Colourful	380	4	101.6	***
Rich	378	4	121.1	***
Emotional	375	4	57.0	***
Swearwords	368	4	709.8	***

*** $p < .0001$

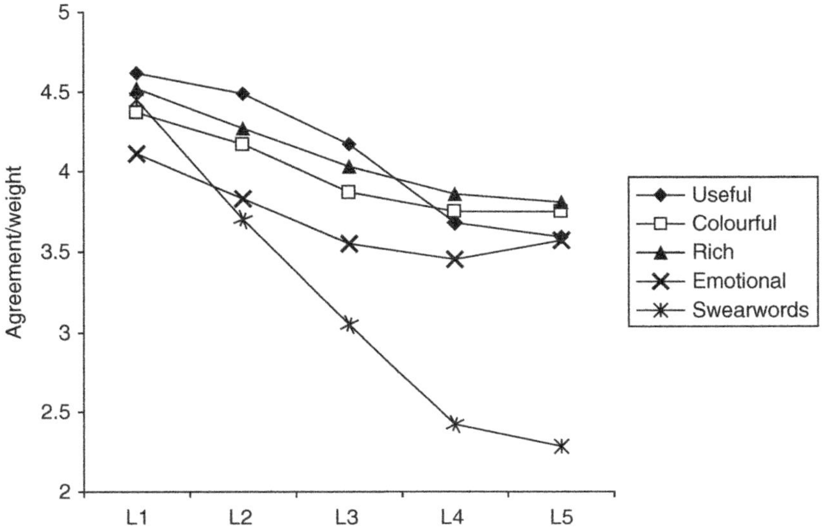

Figure 28 Mean values for language characteristics and emotional strength of swearwords from the L1 to the L5

horrible to a native speaker (milder English swearwords like "damn" for example don't even sound like swearwords to me). If I would happen to hit myself with a hammer the words coming out of my mouth would definitely be in Finnish.

Piero (Italian L1, English L2 and a UK resident for the last ten years), who reported a preference for code-switching when expressing anger alone or to other bilinguals, tells the interviewer that he still feels that his L1 is the more emotional language:

B: Do you think one of your languages is more poetic, more emotional?
P: I think Italian is a bit more poetic, I've got this impression but if it's true or no I don't know [laughs] I don't specialize in languages so...

Yet, to the (Italian) interviewer's surprise, Piero declares that English swearwords are "more aggressive" and "more direct" than Italian swearwords:

P: English has got some very good ways of swearing, sometimes I prefer the English way (...) they're being I think more more aggressive (...)
B: The English ones?
P: Yeah, the English ones, I don't know, I got the idea that they got some very good words to swear

B: Really?

P: Yeah, sometimes I think it's more, you express, you express more your anger sometimes, I got this idea, maybe it's not true but I think it's this more direct.

B: English is more direct?

P: Yeah, Italian is a bit more ehm, I mean, yeah, there is some very good swearing words in Italian as well but sometimes I feel it's more I don't know [laughs] more direct, English is more direct.

A number of participants report that because of their personal history, their L1 is not the language with the most positive characteristics. This is the case of SS (English L1, Spanish L2, Italian L3), who feels dominant in her L1 and L2 but feels that the L2 is endowed with more positive characteristics:

SS: I prefer to use my L2 Spanish, as the part of the family that tended to be more loving and emotional whilst I grew up was the Spanish-speaking side. I find it richer, warmer and more passionate.

Dagmar (Dutch L1, German L2, Serbian L3, Russian L4, Swedish L5, English L6) even feels that her L1 is too cold to be used for writing about emotions in a diary. She feels that she would prefer her L3 or L4:

Dagmar: I do not write in a personal diary but if I would, I would not use my mother tongue, it is too cold. I would choose Swedish, a language I associate with joy and happiness (partner) or Russian because it is so rich (and I adore Russian poetry).

IB (Neapolitan L1, Italian L2, French L3, English L4, German L5) is very proud of her native dialect, Neapolitan, with which she still identifies. The languages she acquired later have their own unique connotations. Interestingly, all her languages combine positive and negative connotations:

IB: Neapolitan (...) is a reflection of my roots, my sunny holidays of who I am. It is my love for fun, good food and family dramas! Italian: austerity, rigidity, coldness, boredom! Just an official language useful for correspondence! However I love reading it for pleasure, watching films and listening to songs! (...) French: it is my education in France, my trying to live in harmony in a society that wasn't mine, my growing-up, lots of regrets. English: Freedom, feeling what is being a "real" foreigner! Wow! The anxiety of not speaking/writing English properly and with an accent! Have met wonderful people/great work experience. Great happiness to be in England. German: (...) Used to be fluent. Forgot it. I would only use it to communicate with my friends.

LH (English L1, German L2, Swedish L3, Spanish L4, French L5, Italian L6) does not seem to conform to the "hierarchy" linked to chronology of acquisition of languages. Indeed she reports that her Italian L6 strikes her as intensely emotional despite her only basic competence in that language. However, when discussing her perception of herself in using her L2, L3, L4 and L5 she clearly does not feel as lively and humorous as in her L1:

> LH: I noticed the most marked change in using a language I don't know very well (L6 Italian). Suddenly a whole range of expression opened up to me having to do with intense emotion. It was really rather startling. When speaking Swedish I become a very cautious person to my own mind rather reserved (though my Swedish friends find me outgoing and gregarious). In German I am serious and rather annoyingly sincere I think. I lose much of my sense of humour. In French I try for formality; I think this has to do with my lack of mastery of the language. Spanish reduces me to childhood since I really know so little of the language and have to trust my interlocutor to forgive errors and understand me.

Zelideth (Spanish L1, English L2; French L3, Japanese L4, Portuguese L5, dominant in L1 and L2) refused to order his languages in a linear way, insisting that each language had unique features and characteristics:

> Zelideth: English is just like an apple tart and crunchy and only good for certain things. Spanish is like a Passion Fruit sweet tart, runny but with seeds so that it's good to express everything.

Hypothesis 2: The effect of Age of onset of Acquisition in the LX on perception of characteristics and emotional strength of swearwords in the LX

The Kruskal-Wallis tests show some significant but largely scattered effects of AoA on language characteristics and emotionality of swearwords in different languages (Table 41). Although the general pattern is that early starters tend to have more positive scores on the different dimensions, the effects are rarely highly significant, and there are no effects for the L5. The pattern of declining values across AoA groups for the L2 is comparable to previous dependent variables: it drops linearly in the first three AoA groups for the L2 – with the exception of usefulness and poetic character of the L2 – (Figure 29), after which it stabilises and even rises slightly for the perception of emotional strength of swearwords in the oldest AoA group.

Table 41 The effect of AoA in the LX on perception scores of language characteristics and emotional strength of swearwords in the LX (χ^2)

Perceptions	L2	L3	L4	L5
Useful	3	20***	4	2
Colourful	11*	6	15**	3
Rich	12*	2	5	2
Poetic	8	10*	9*	3
Emotional	11*	9*	28***	7
Swearwords	35***	17***	1	6

*** p < .0001, ** p < .001, * p < .05

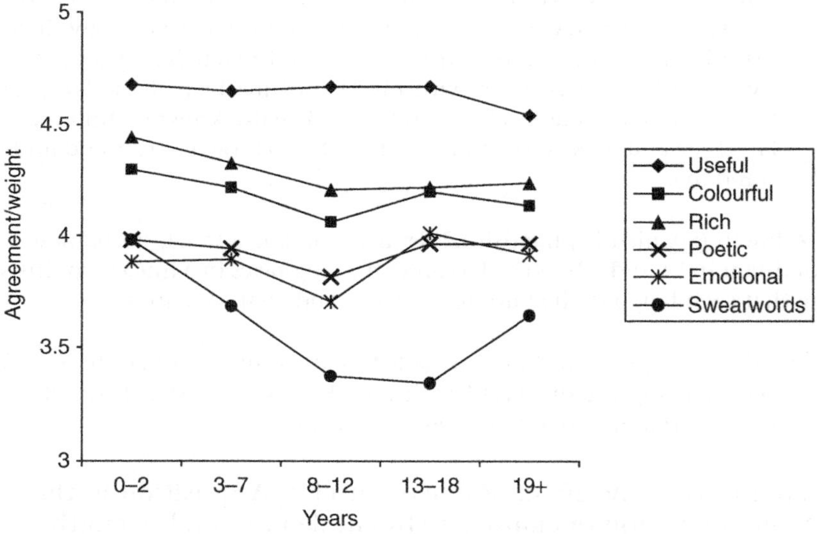

Figure 29 Mean values for language characteristics and emotional strength of swearwords in the L2 according to AoA

Hypothesis 3: The effect of context of acquisition of the LX on perception of characteristics of the LX and emotional strength of swearwords in the LX

The Kruskal-Wallis analyses show a highly significant effect of the context of acquisition on perceptions of the L2. Although the effect was still significant in the L4 – and to a lesser degree in the L3 – it mostly disappeared in the L5, where it only had a significant effect on the perception of the emotional strength of swearwords, Table 42).

Figure 30 shows a linear increase for the perception variables in the L2 from purely instructed context, to mixed context and finally naturalistic

Table 42 The effect of context of acquisition of the LX on perception of language characteristics and emotional strength of swearwords in the LX (χ^2)

Perceptions	**L2**	**L3**	**L4**	**L5**
Useful	26***	19***	25***	6
Colourful	19***	5	12**	2
Rich	9**	6*	6*	1
Poetic	14***	2	6*	1
Emotional	26***	10**	13**	4
Swearwords	55***	42***	39***	29***

*** p < .0001, ** p < .001, * p < .05

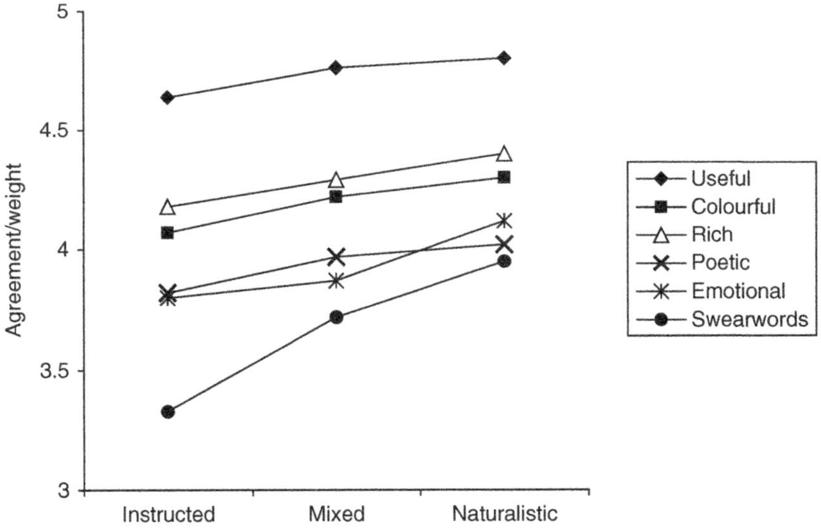

Figure 30 Mean values for language characteristics and emotional strength of swearwords in the L2 according to context of acquisition

acquisition context. The more participants used their L2 outside the classroom while learning it, the higher they situated it on the various dimensions.

SK (Hindi L1, English L2, French L3), a student at an Indian university, learnt English at school from the age of six and feels dominant in Hindi and English. However, Hindi is his preferred language for expressing feelings:

> SK: Many of the Hindi terms of endearment have a greater resonance to them and convey more shades of meaning (...) Many of the English ones seem to be artificial and stilted because I have not often heard them used in real life. They sound like they are words from films or books, not something that is meant by the speaker.

Hypothesis 4: The effect of frequency of use on perception scores of characteristics of the LX and emotional strength of swearwords in the LX

The Kruskal-Wallis tests show significant effects of frequency of use on characteristics of the different languages and the emotional strength of swearwords, with a higher general frequency of use corresponding to higher scores on the various dimensions. The relationship is highly significant for perceived usefulness, but the pattern is slightly more uneven for the other variables (Table 43). While the emotional weight of swearwords is significantly linked to the frequency of use across languages, only the perception of colourfulness is significantly linked to frequency of use across all four languages. Richness is significant for the L2, L3 and L4, emotional character is significant for L3 and L4, while poetic character is significant only for the L2.

An analysis of the means for the L2 (Figure 31) shows a sharp difference between participants who use their L2 only yearly or less and those who use it monthly, after which the scores stabilise.

One participant, KP (Catalan L1, Spanish L2, English L3, Italian L4, German L5), reports that because of his constant use of three languages, these ones have equal emotional status:

> KP: Because of my personal circumstances I constantly use my L1, L2 and L3. I don't really feel there is a significant emotional difference.

Theodora (Greek L1, English L2, German L3) uses Greek with her family and English with her colleagues and students. She feels equally fluent in both languages and uses them constantly, yet, swearwords in English do not feel as strong as the Greek ones:

> T: When I say a swearword in English it won't feel as strong as I say it in Greek, so I could say the worst swearing swearwords in English

Table 43 The effect of general frequency of use of the LX on perception of language characteristics and emotional strength of swearwords in the LX (χ^2)

Perceptions	L2	L3	L4	L5
Useful	177***	241***	119***	45***
Colourful	17**	25***	10*	10*
Rich	22***	26***	10*	7
Poetic	13*	7	7	3
Emotional	6	22***	10*	7
Swearwords	66***	115***	76***	52***

*** p < .0001, ** p < .001, * p < .05

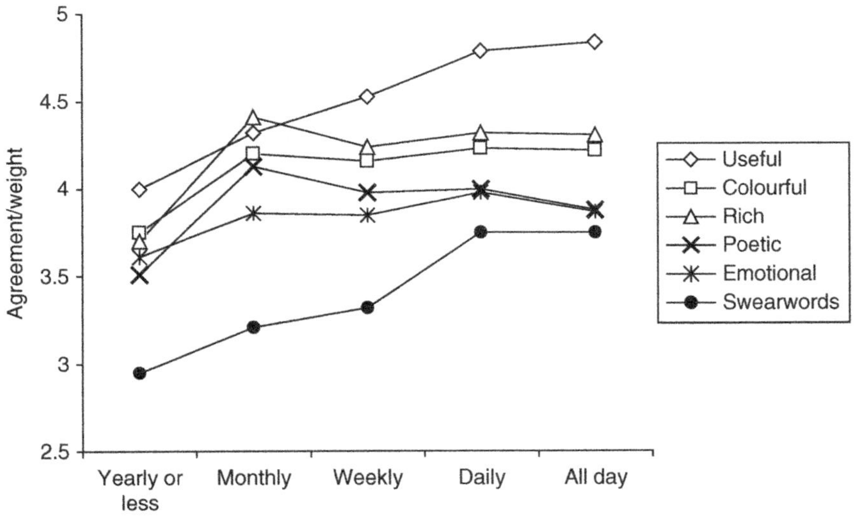

Figure 31 Mean values for language characteristics and emotional strength of swearwords in the L2 according to general frequency of use of the L2

> and it just wouldn't feel, you know it wouldn't feel that strong in me as it would feel to an English person, 'cos it has happened to me for example, someone taught me a very bad English word, and you know I just kept saying it as a joke, because it just doesn't mean anything to me you know, it's it's it's a swearword you know, it's just another foreign word. Of course after some time I lived in England I realized you know that you don't use these words very often, you use it in very specific objects, but still you know if someone provokes me, I have no problems saying this word. Now in Greek there are some words which are very very bad swearwords, but even though I know them I would never ever use them, because I know that they are very very offensive.

The fact that Mustafa (Kurdish and Turkish L1, German L2, French L3, Arabic L4 and English L5) lives in the UK and is surrounded by English colloquial language has not altered his feeling that swearwords in Kurdish are harsher than any other language he knows:

B: Right, so when you hear a swearword in Kurdish, in Turkish or in English, which one sounds stronger, heavier?
Mu: For swearing?
B: Yes, when you hear it?
Mu: Um ... heavier?

B: Yes.
Mu: What do you mean heavier?
B: More you know, more rude.
Mu: Um...well, as I said I mean you know between those 3 languages, Kurdish especially. It is because of kind of cultural context, is a bit heavy, quite heavy, and then comes Turkish and English.

Also, Christina (Spanish and German L1, English L2, Italian L3, French L4), comparing the emotional weight of her five languages, noted that one of her L1s, German, has lost its emotional resonance. She also raises another important point, namely that limited exposure to an L1 and partial attrition may inhibit the use of that language to express emotion:

Christina: Spanish is what I grew up with most and really feels very special inside me when I hear it, read it or speak it. English my third language is also a favourite because I married an English man and have spent all my married life in the UK. German is very rusty and I use it so little that I could not describe it as arousing any emotions in me when I either hear it or speak (try) it.

Christina's observation that her German is no longer emotionally arousing is quite intriguing. In another study of the same corpus (Dewaele, 2004d), I found that self-reported L1 attriters may no longer use the language or feel proficient in it, but that the emotional resonance of their L1 remains largely unaffected. For example, L1 swearwords tend to retain their emotional force, despite being rarely – if ever – used. Christina's case is notably different – it is possible that the loss of affective reactions points to complete attrition of the language.

Hypothesis 5: The effect of degree of socialisation in the LX on perception of characteristics of the LX and emotional strength of swearwords in the LX

A series of Kruskal-Wallis tests showed that socialisation in an LX had a highly significant effect ($p < .0001$) on the perceived usefulness of the different languages and on emotional weight of swearwords in them (Table 44). The effect of socialisation was less pronounced on the "affective" characteristics of the languages. Higher levels of socialisation were linked to higher scores on the perceived richness of the L3 and L5, the perceived colourfulness in the L3 and the perceived emotionality in the L3 (Figure 32).

Strong socialisation in the L2 is linked to higher levels of its perceived usefulness and of the increased emotional force of L2 swearwords. There

Table 44 The effect of degree of socialisation in the LX on perception of language characteristics and emotional strength of swearwords in the LX (χ^2)

Perceptions	**L2**	**L3**	**L4**	**L5**
Useful	83***	106***	33***	22***
Colourful	3	15**	1	5
Rich	7	15**	3	10*
Poetic	5	1	1	3
Emotional	5	8*	4	6
Swearwords	31***	64***	21***	21***

*** $p < .0001$, ** $p < .001$, * $p < .05$

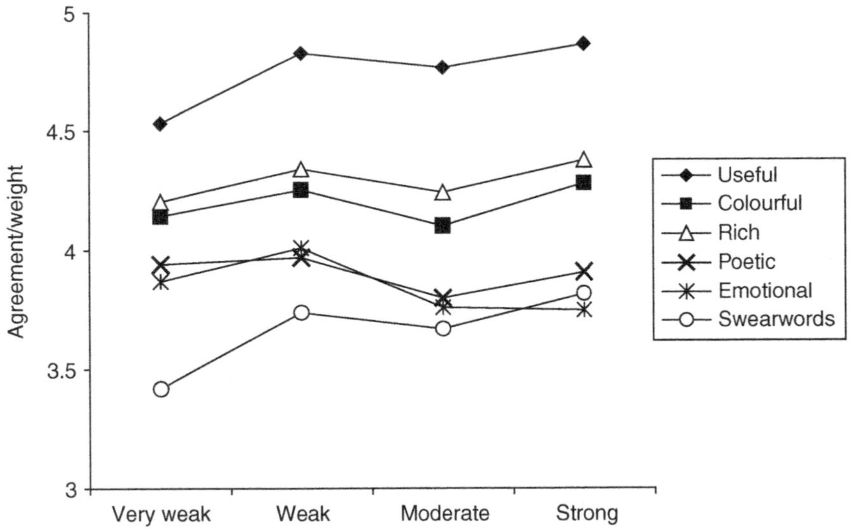

Figure 32 Mean values for language characteristics and emotional strength of swearwords in the L2 according to level of socialisation in the L2

is a strong increase between participants with minimal levels of socialisation in the L2 ("very weak socialisation") and the group with a "weak socialisation" in the L2. However, the trend is reversed when considering the next group ("moderate socialisation"), and tends to pick up slightly for the group with strong socialisation (the exception being perceived emotionality, where mean values tend to decrease in groups with stronger L2 socialisation (Figure 32).

Participants who did not spend their childhood in the L1 environment and are strongly socialised in their L2 may have slightly different perceptions of certain swearwords and taboo words in their different languages. Janne-Elisabeth (English L1, Danish L2, Spanish L3, German L4) reports that some taboo words have a stronger emotional resonance in her L1 despite having spent most of her life in the L2 environment:

> Janne-Elisabeth: I still find words such as "arse" or "prick" less acceptable in English than their Danish counterparts, although a word such as "cunt" doesn't shock me, probably because I never heard it as a child and had no notion when I did hear it for the first time as a young adult that it was an obscene word. (My mother who was a native Danish speaker was shocked by the English words but literally did not know until I told her what the Danish word "pik" ("prick" "dick") meant. When I think about it she probably never realized that "dick" meant anything other than the boy's name in English.

Hypothesis 6: The effect of network of interlocutors on perception of characteristics of the LX and emotional strength of swearwords in the LX

Kruskal-Wallis analyses showed a consistent effect of the network of interlocutors on the perception of usefulness and emotionality of swearwords across all languages. Its effect on "affective" dimensions is more limited and scattered. The network of interlocutors is linked to the perception of richness in the L3 and on perception of emotionality in the L2 and L3 (Table 45). Figure 33 shows that the perceived usefulness, emotionality and emotional weight of swearwords in the L2 increase steadily with networks consisting of more familiar interlocutors.

Some participants report that their love of a language is linked to the love for the people they use the language with:

Table 45 The effect of the network of interlocutors on perception of language characteristics and emotional strength of swearwords (χ^2)

Perceptions	L2	L3	L4	L5
Useful	28***	47***	59***	11*
Colourful	8	7	8	3
Rich	4	11*	6	4
Poetic	2	8	3	2
Emotional	14**	18**	8	2
Swearwords	37***	47***	23***	11*

*** $p < .0001$, ** $p < .001$, * $p < .05$

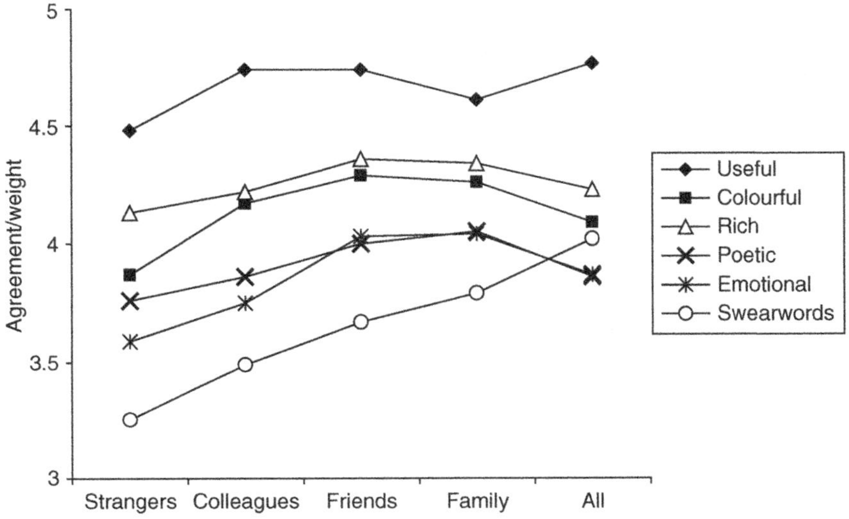

Figure 33 Mean values for language characteristics and emotional strength of swearwords in the L2 according to network of interlocutors

Beatrice: I was born in a bilingual family in a bilingual community (Transylvania) using both Romanian and Hungarian at home and in all matters. Having moved to Hungary at the age of 16, I can only use Romanian when visiting my relatives who remained there. While being in Hungary I miss my Romanian relatives so probably the longing for the ones I love interferes with my attachment to the language they (and myself) speak.

Other participants attach particular values to their different languages, which make them particularly appropriate to express certain emotions, or to interact appropriately with certain interlocutors. FS (Afrikaans L1, English L2, German L3, Xhosa L4) is dominant in Afrikaans but uses her other languages constantly:

FS: Afrikaans is the language to be familiarly friendly in while English is the language to be politely friendly in. Afrikaans and German are good languages to be really angry in (I can only be politely angry in English). I find it easiest to be caring toward adults in English but it is easier to be caring toward children in Afrikaans. Afrikaans is a "feel-good" down-to-earth language English is a polite language. German is a language to be difficult in and Xhosa I only use to show that I am trying to connect with members of other cultural groups in South Africa.

Hypothesis 7: The effect of total language knowledge on perception of characteristics of the LX and emotional strength of swearwords in the LX

The Kruskal-Wallis analyses revealed a significant effect of total language knowledge on the perception of positive language characteristics and emotional strength of swearwords (Table 46). Those knowing more languages perceive the L2 more positively, and, to a lesser degree, the L3 (Figure 34). They also sense the emotionality of the swearwords in the L2 and L3 better than those knowing fewer languages.

Table 46 The effect of total language knowledge on perception of language characteristics and emotional strength of swearwords (χ^2)

Perceptions	L2	L3	L4
Useful	10*	18***	5*
Colourful	14*	3	1
Rich	21***	4	1
Poetic	14*	1	1
Emotional	8*	6*	0
Swearwords	10*	14*	2

*** $p < .0001$, ** $p < .001$, * $p < .05$

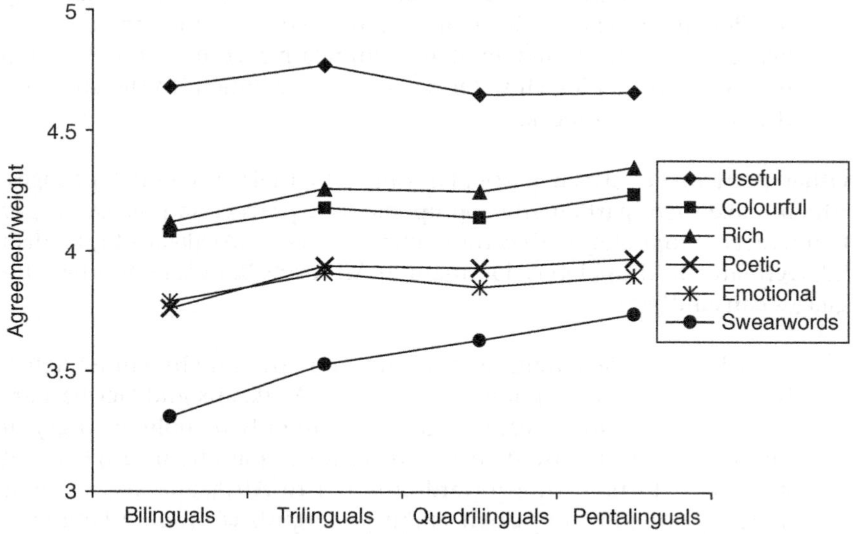

Figure 34 Mean values for language characteristics and emotional strength of swearwords in the L2 according to total language knowledge

Hypothesis 8: The effect of Trait Emotional Intelligence on perception of characteristics of the LX and emotional strength of swearwords in the LX

The Kruskal-Wallis analyses reveal a significant effect of TEI on some perception scores of the positive characteristics of the L2 and emotional strength of swearwords in the L2 (Table 47), where higher levels of TEI corresponded to higher scores on the various dimensions (Figure 35). No such effect was detected in the L3, L4 or L5.

Table 47 The effect of TEI on perception of language characteristics and emotional strength of swearwords in the LX (χ^2)

Perceptions	L2	L3	L4	L5
Useful	7*	1	2	3
Colourful	9*	2	4	1
Rich	13**	2	5	4
Poetic	8*	0	4	5
Emotional	5	1	0	2
Swearwords	3	3	0	0

*** $p < .0001$, ** $p < .001$, * $p < .05$

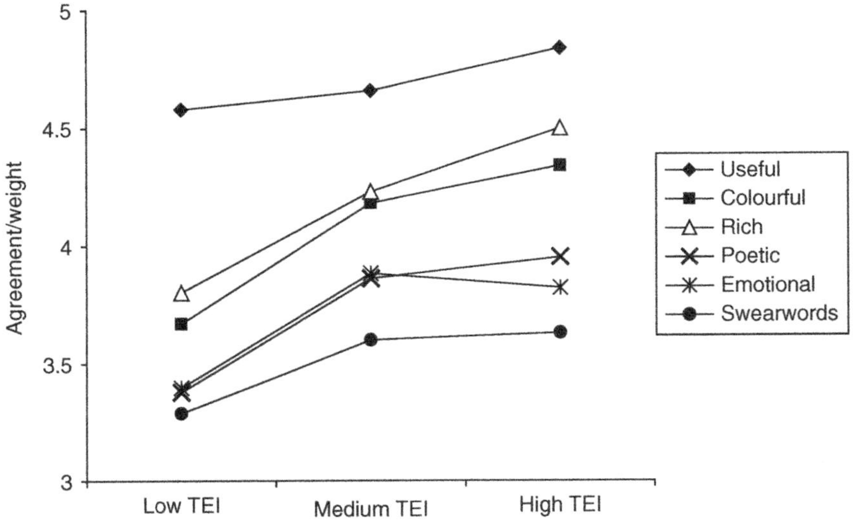

Figure 35 Mean values for language characteristics and emotional strength of swearwords in the L2 according to TEI

Hypothesis 9: The effect of gender, age and level of education on perception of characteristics of the LX and emotional strength of swearwords in the LX

Gender

A series of Mann-Whitney tests highlighted only two significant differences on the perception scores of the positive language characteristics and emotional strength of swearwords in the L2, where female participants scored higher on the perceived usefulness of the L2 and the emotional strength of swearwords in that language (Table 48). No significant difference was uncovered in the other languages.

Age

The Kruskal-Wallis tests reveal that the effects of age on perception of language characteristics and emotional strength of swearwords are limited to the L2 only (Table 49).

A look at the scores of the different age groups shows that increased age is associated with higher scores on the perceived usefulness, and especially with higher scores on colourfulness, richness and poetic character of the L2 (Figure 36).

Education

A series of Kruskal-Wallis analyses showed an effect of education level on the perception scores of several dimensions of positive language characteristics

Table 48 Differences in the perception of language characteristics and emotional strength of swearwords between female and male participants in the LX (Z)

		L2	L3	L4	L5
Useful	Mann-Whitney	237561	142081	62644	19344
	Z	−2.1*	−0.0	−1.8	−0.6
Colourful	Mann-Whitney	240799	127921	59802	17842
	Z	−0.5	−0.9	−0.4	−0.6
Rich	Mann-Whitney	234633	127963	60381	17760
	Z	−1.6	−1.2	−0.3	−0.5
Poetic	Mann-Whitney	239177	125881	60405	18075
	Z	−0.4	−0.9	−0.0	−0.3
Emotional	Mann-Whitney	227217	125785	58456	18259
	Z	−1.7	−0.7	−06	−0.1
Swearwords	Mann-Whitney	170268	95405	42562	11916
	Z	−2.1*	−1.6	−0.5	−0.1

* $p < .05$

Table 49 The effect of age on perception of language characteristics and emotional strength of swearwords in the LX (χ^2)

Perception	L2	L3	L4	L5
Useful	13*	2	6	1
Colourful	24***	4	6	5
Rich	33***	7	3	5
Poetic	19**	4	6	4
Emotional	9	2	3	7
Swearwords	4	8	3	4

*** p < .0001, ** p < .001, * p < .05

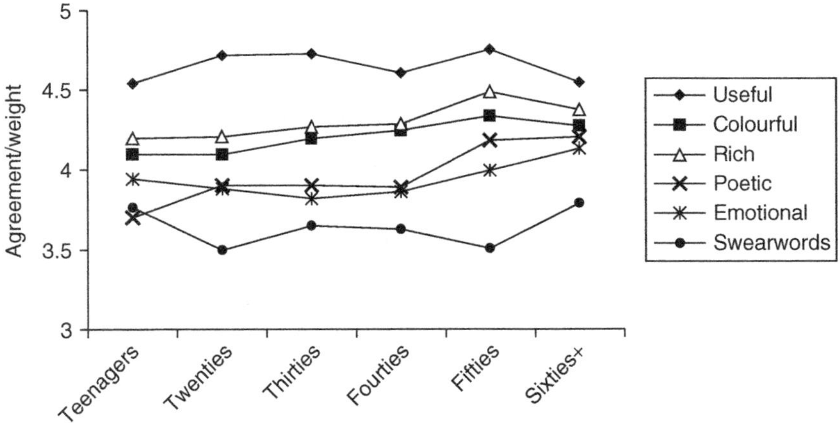

Figure 36 Mean values for language characteristics and emotional strength of swearwords in the L2 according to age

and emotional strength of swearwords in the L2 and L4, but not in the L3 and L5 (Table 50). Mean values for the different education levels shows a steady increase in values for the L2 across education levels, with the exception of swearwords (and emotionality, for which education level fails to show any significance) (Figure 37).

Summing up

The pattern that emerged for the perceived language characteristics and emotional strength of swearwords is quite comparable to previous chapters.

Table 50 The effect of education level on perception of language characteristics and emotional strength of swearwords in the LX (χ^2)

Perception	L2	L3	L4	L5
Useful	15**	4	2	4
Colourful	22***	1	11*	2
Rich	38***	3	9*	1
Poetic	23***	4	16**	2
Emotional	5	1	5	2
Swearwords	2	3	0	2

*** p < .0001, ** p < .001, * p < .05

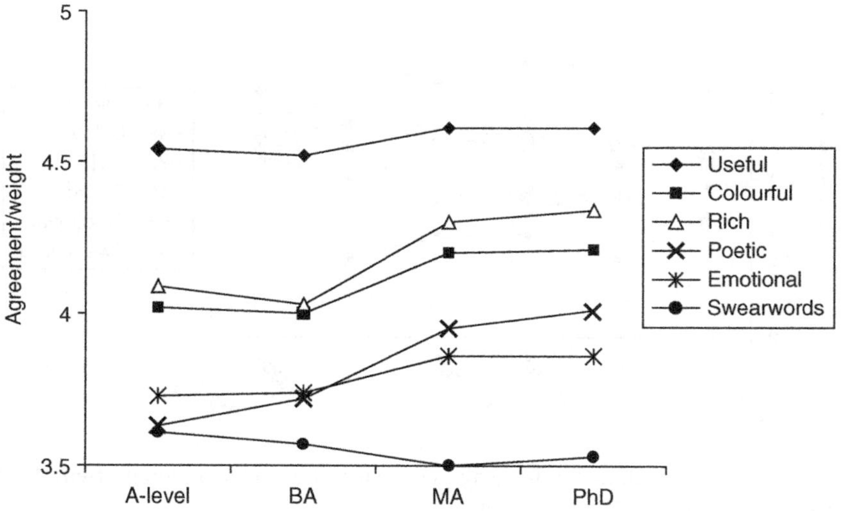

Figure 37 The effect of education level on perception scores of positive characteristics and emotional strength of swearwords in the L2

The hypotheses were generally confirmed, although the effects were systematically different for some dependent variables and often limited to certain languages.

The Friedman ANOVA showed that pentalinguals rate their L1 significantly more positively, and L1 swearwords are felt to be more powerful, with values declining for languages acquired later. This finding was backed up by participants' comments, such as those from Theodora and Mustafa.

The participants' narratives reflected those mentioned in the two previous chapters. Indeed those talking about swearing typically also mentioned the emotional force of swearwords. The superior emotional force of swearing in the L1 corresponded to more emotional weight for L1 swearwords. The same dilemma was mentioned for the expression of anger: the superior strength of swearwords in the L1 meant that for some participants (typically Arabic or Kurdish) these words were taboo, while other participants felt they provided necessary relief to express strong anger. The weaker impact of swearwords in an LX facilitated the use of these words for some interlocutors. Interestingly, the values for the emotional weight of swearwords tended to yield stronger effects from the independent variables than the more abstract dimensions. It is possible that a judgement about a salient group of words, such as swearwords, is relatively speaking easier to formulate than a global judgement about the characteristics of a whole language. One participant, Piero, even felt that his L1 was more poetic but that swearwords in the L2 were "more direct".

The "history of learning" variables had some significant effects on the positive language characteristics and emotional strength of swearwords. Younger starters judged their L2, and to a lesser extent their L3 and L4, as being more positive and stronger than older starters did. The effect for context of acquisition was stronger, with participants who had learnt an L2, L3 and L4 through formal instruction giving lower ratings compared to mixed or naturalistic learners.

The independent variables reflecting current use of the LX had a significant effect on some language characteristics and the emotional strength of swearwords. Participants who used an LX frequently, were strongly socialised in the language and used it with a wide network of interlocutors felt that the LX was more useful and that swearwords were stronger compared to participants who did not use the LX frequently, were weakly socialised and had smaller networks. The subtle gradings of swearwords were typically picked up more easily by immigrant children than their immigrant parents, as Janne-Elisabeth reported. A look at the participants' linguistic history again showed socialisation in the L2 culture is linked to a change in the perception of swearwords. Many participants commented on how LX swearwords had crept into their swearing repertoire without them realising it. The three independent variables reflecting current use of the LX had more scattered effects on perceived richness, emotionality and poetic character of the LX.

For many participants the characteristics of the LX were determined by the groups of people they knew who spoke these languages. Particular languages could thus be invested with strong nostalgic values: these languages were often spoken by family members or friends in a country that had been left behind. Some participants, like FS, attached different values and characteristics to their different languages. Choosing a particular language allowed her to momentarily reconnect with those particular values.

The participants' linguistic profiles, i.e. the number of languages known, had a significant positive and systematic effect on the perception of the usefulness of all languages. The effect on the other dependent variables was more scattered, though more pronounced in the L2, and slightly less so in the L3 and L4. Trait Emotional Intelligence was found to have a significant positive effect in the L2 on the perception of usefulness, colourfulness, richness and poetic character. It had no significant effect on the L3, L4 and L5.

The effects of gender, age and education level on language characteristics and emotional strength of swearwords are relatively limited. No significant gender effect was uncovered. Participants' age had a limited effect in the L2, with older participants scoring higher on the different scales. The finding that age correlates positively with the perception of the positive characteristics of the L2 could be linked with the observation that beliefs become more stable and strongly held with age (Robins and Pals, 2002; Schommer, 1998). The absence of any relationship in the L3, L4 and L5 might suggest that the language must be really familiar in order for this effect to appear.

Finally, education level had an effect in the L2 and L4. More highly educated participants judged the L2 and L4 to be more useful, more colourful, richer and more poetic than participants with lower education levels did.

9
Results: Foreign Language Anxiety

Foreign language anxiety (FLA) has been defined as: "the feeling of tension and apprehension specifically associated with second language contexts, including speaking, listening, and learning" (MacIntyre and Gardner, 1994: 284).

This FLA typically develops in the LX classroom. Horwitz, Horwitz and Cope (1986) report the words of one student: "When I'm in my Spanish class I just freeze! I can't think of a thing when my teacher calls on me. My mind goes blank" (p. 125).

Williams (1991) suggested that FLA in the classroom is "a response to a condition in which the external element is, or is perceived, as presenting a demand that threatens to exceed the student's capabilities and resources for meeting it" (p. 25). As a result of this FLA, the student might lose focus, and be unable to maintain full attentional control of the task in hand.

Research on FLA started in the 1970s (Curran, 1976; Gardner et al., 1976). MacIntyre (2007) observes that there seems to be agreement in the SLA community that FLA is an emotional experience uniquely provoked by L2 situations. MacIntyre and Gardner (1989) attributed inconsistencies in the early research in this area to "an inappropriate level of instrument specificity" (p. 272). This view seems to have evolved, as MacIntyre (2007) now argues that the initial contradictory findings on the link between success in SLA and FLA (as reported in MacIntyre, 1999) would be due to a confusion in levels of abstraction, more specifically the distinction between trait anxiety, situation-specific anxiety and state anxiety, "each of which provides a valuable, but somewhat different perspective on the processes under study" (p. 565).

Traits refer to stable, general patterns of behaviour. In other words, an individual with a high level of trait anxiety is likely to feel anxious in a variety of situations. Eysenck et al., (2007) point out that anxiety occurs if an existing goal is being threatened. This causes a diversion of attentional resources of the central executive to the source of anxiety and the decision on how to react. The anxious person might thus be distracted from his/her goals by internal (troubling thoughts) or external (threatening task-irrelevant distractors) stimuli.

Spielberger (1983) defined state anxiety (A-state) as "a transitory emotional state or condition of the human organism that varies in intensity and fluctuates over time" (p. 39). He distinguished it from trait anxiety (A-trait), which referred to "relatively stable individual differences in anxiety proneness, (...) differences in the disposition to perceive in a wide range of stimulus situations as dangerous or threatening, and in the tendency to respond to such threats with A-state reactions" (p. 39). Spielberger developed a Trait Anxiety Scale, which was not specifically designed for language production and showed no consistent link with L2 variables (MacIntyre and Gardner, 1989, 1994).

At the situation-specific level of conceptualisation, "the concern is for concepts that are defined over time within a situation" (MacIntyre, 2007: 565). The Foreign Language Classroom Anxiety Scale (FLCAS) developed by Horwitz et al., (1986) measures this situation-specific anxiety. For Horwitz and colleagues FLA is "a distinct complex of self perceptions, beliefs, feelings and behaviors related to classroom learning arising from the uniqueness of the language learning process" (p. 128). Negative correlations emerged between scores on the FLCAS and measures of L2 performance (Aida, 1994; Horwitz, 1986, 2001; Rodriguez and Abreu, 2003).

Finally, at the state level, "the concern is for experiences rooted in a specific moment in time without much concern for how frequently those experiences occurred in the past or whether they might occur again in the future" (MacIntyre, 2007: 565). L2 performance seems negatively correlated with higher levels of state anxiety (Gregersen, 2003; MacIntyre and Gardner, 1994). MacIntyre (2007) speculates that there are fewer studies on state anxiety in SLA because of the complicating factor that learners attempt "to cope with and compensate for the effects of anxiety" (p. 565).

Dewaele (2002) noted that the apparent stability of CA/FLA could be related to the fact that the studies in question considered only individuals with a single LX (Horwitz, 1986; MacIntyre and Charos, 1996; Onwuegbuzie, Bailey and Daley, 1999). Only recently has the construct of FLA been tested on samples of participants learning two LXs simultaneously (Rodriguez and Abreu, 2003). The second part of MacIntyre and Gardner's definition seems to suggest that CA/FLA is specific to experienced learners only. However, this seems to imply that beginners do not experience CA/FLA or that they experience a state-like CA/FLA, which gradually becomes a trait. As Dörnyei (2005) points out, when talking about anxiety "it is surprising how ambiguous the conceptualisation of the concept becomes when we go beyond the surface" (p. 198). Therefore, it seems necessary to go back briefly to the sources of the concept.

In their exploratory study of the relations between language anxiety and other anxieties in English as an L1 and French as an L2, MacIntyre and Gardner (1989) subjected their different anxiety scales to a Principal Components analysis, which yielded two orthogonal factors accounting for 48 per cent of the total variance (p. 261). These factors were labelled

"General Anxiety" and "Communicative Anxiety", respectively. The former factor was defined by scales of trait, state, and test anxiety, whereas the latter was defined by French class anxiety, French use anxiety, English class anxiety, and audience sensitivity. General anxiety was found to have little effect on the dependent variables in the L2 (multiple-choice test, free vocabulary recall test in both high- and low-pressure situations). However, CA/FLA did have a significant negative effect on the recall of French L2 words. Negative correlations were observed between written proficiency scores and French class anxiety and French use anxiety. Similar results emerged for the oral proficiency measures, which were negatively correlated with both French class anxiety and French use anxiety (1989: 267). The authors concluded that CA/FLA is the direct cause of "performance deficits" (p. 270).

The foregoing results confirmed earlier findings by Horwitz (1986) on the orthogonal nature of language anxiety and trait anxiety. Similar results emerged from MacIntyre and Gardner's (1991b) study into the factor structure underlying 23 scales, assessing both language anxiety and other forms of anxiety. French L2 tasks were judged to be more anxiety provoking than their English L1 equivalents by students who had had an average of eight years of being taught French as an L2. Subjects with higher levels of language anxiety in the L2 (but not the L1) obtained significantly lower scores on a Digit Span test (a measure of short-term memory) and on a Thing Category test (vocabulary production). The authors suggested that impaired performance among more anxious students could be related to short-term memory loss and problems in long-term memory retrieval, both of which are attributable to anxiety (p. 530).

MacIntyre (1999) reviewed the literature on FLA and concluded that a moderate negative relationship exists between language anxiety and various measures of language achievement. Krashen (1981) had already identified anxiety as an "affective filter" that blocked easy acquisition of the TL during classroom instruction. Further studies have confirmed this trend (Abu-Rabia, 2004; Dewaele, 2007f; Frantzen and Magnan, 2005; Matsuda and Gobel, 2004; Onwuegbuzie, Bailey and Daley, 2002). Interestingly, FLA does not disappear among more advanced learners (Dewaele, 2007; Ewald, 2007; Onwuegbuzie et al., 1999; Saito and Samimy, 1996). Bernaus, Moore and Cordeiro Azevedo (2007) have looked at FLA and the motivation levels of multilingual students learning Catalan in a bilingual Catalan-Spanish environment, and reported that while motivation decreased across year groups, levels of FLA increased.

However, an extended overseas experience in the TL country seems to increase self-confidence in it and, as a result, decrease LX classroom anxiety (Matsuda and Gobel, 2004).

FLA has been found to be related to a number of sociobiographical and affective factors and even to broader cultural factors. Onwuegbuzie et al., (1999) identified eight variables that collectively accounted for 40 per cent of FLA variance (i.e. age, academic achievement, prior history of visiting foreign countries, prior high school, experience with LXs, expected overall average for current language course, perceived scholastic competence and perceived self-worth).

Gardner and MacIntyre (1993) have suggested that reciprocal paths exist between language anxiety and motivation. High levels of motivation inhibit anxiety and high levels of anxiety depress motivation. Dewaele (2005a) found that Flemish students' attitudes toward certain LXs were linked to FLA in these languages. Participants who reported low levels of FLA when speaking French L2 were found to have significantly more positive attitudes toward French than those who reported moderate or high levels of FLA. However, no such pattern emerged for English L3 (Dewaele, 2005a). Given the correlational nature of the design, it was impossible to determine whether attitudes or FLA were the cause or effect.

FLA has also been linked to personality characteristics such as perfectionism. Gregersen and Horwitz (2002) made audio recordings of comments by anxious and non-anxious language learners as they watched themselves interact in a videotaped oral interview. The anxious learners were found to set higher personal performance standards, tended to procrastinate and were more fearful of evaluation and more concerned about errors. In other words, the more anxious participants tended to be the more perfectionist.

Dewaele (2002) looked at the effect of personality traits on FLA in the French L2 and English L3 speech production of Flemish students and found that FLA was affected by both individual and contextual effects. The perception of French as the former prestige language in Flanders and its function as a social marker were found to be linked to participants' social class, which, in turn, was negatively linked to levels of FLA in French, but not in English. This social effect appeared to be a stronger predictor of FLA in French than the three Eysenckian personality dimensions (extraversion, neuroticism and psychoticism). However, these four independent variables together explained only 9 per cent of the total variation in FLA. In the same study, psychoticism, extraversion and, to a lesser extent, neuroticism, significantly predicted levels of FLA in English L3 production, explaining 20 per cent of variance. Students who scored high on the extraversion and psychoticism scales reported significantly lower levels of FLA in English. Those who scored low on neuroticism had overall lower levels of FLA in English. It was argued that the higher FLA of introverts follows logically from the observation that they tend to be reserved, quiet and unassertive, in contrast to the more outgoing and talkative extraverts (Furnham and Heaven, 1999). The extraverts' more optimistic side might limit their fear of speaking an LX. Extraverts were also found to possess higher levels of self-perceived competence in English L3. The study further showed that generalised trait anxiety (as measured by the neuroticism scale) and FLA are moderately positively correlated, despite having been considered as orthogonal dimensions by MacIntyre and Gardner (1989). Speakers who scored higher on the neuroticism scale also reported higher levels of FLA in English. This result was in contrast to the findings of

MacIntyre and Charos (1996), who reported no link between neuroticism/ emotional stability and FLA. ADD: Dewaele (2013) reported that Neuroticism correlated significantly with FLCA sharing between 9% and 25% of variance. Moderately significant relationships were also found between Psychoticism, Extraversion and FLCA. Dewaele and Shan Ip (2013) found that FLCA, Second Language Tolerance of Ambiguity and Self-rated English proficiency of Chinese learners predicted half of the variance in each other. Students who were more tolerant of second language ambiguity were less anxious in their English classes and they also felt more proficient.

FLA may be linked to sociobiographical and affective factors, but situational factors can also affect levels of FLA. Dewaele (2007f) found that the situation in which the interaction was taking place affected FLA levels of adult multilinguals in all languages. Private speech with friends was felt to be significantly less anxiety-provoking than interaction with strangers. Public speech appeared to be the most anxiety-provoking activity, especially in an LX. FLA levels were highly correlated across the various languages. While values varied in intensity, the rank order remained very similar across languages, supporting the position that FLA is a stable personality trait. FLA also seems to be highly infectious; in other words, a speaker may react to and reflect the interlocutor's FLA (Dörnyei and Kormos, 2000). If both interlocutors are anxious this will significantly affect the L2 output; if one interlocutor is sufficiently confident however: "he/she might 'pull along' the more anxious speaker and therefore the impact of anxiety may not reach statistical significance" (p. 296).

A large-scale study by Liu (2006, 2009) revealed relatively high levels of reticence to use English and FLA among Chinese undergraduate students in ESL classes at a top university in Beijing. The author suggests that the reticence and the high FLA may be caused by cultural factors as well as the educational system, which focuses strongly on written English in the middle school and does not allow much oral interaction (2009: 233). The emphasis on keeping face in Chinese culture, combined with the importance of test scores, may have increased students' anxiety about making mistakes and being laughed at (p. 220).

While levels of FLA may fluctuate in the space of a few minutes (MacIntyre, 2012), they can also fluctuate over longer periods if the individual is involved in intensive language learning and gains self-confidence and self-perceived competence. One study to have considered variation in FLA over a nearly two-year period is van Daele's (2007) analysis on the effects of FLA on the French L2 and English L3 of Flemish students (Dutch L1). FLA was found to correlate negatively with lexical richness in English and French, and positively with grammatical accuracy in English at the start of the study. FLA was not significantly linked to lexical and grammatical accuracy in French. Interestingly, the effects were strongest for English L3, the language for which participants reported lower levels of FLA than French L2. The effects of FLA faded and disappeared completely at the last data collection point (van Daele, 2007).

Several researchers suggest that skill in one's native language (e.g., reading, vocabulary and group achievement) may affect anxiety levels in the LX (Sparks et al., 1998). Students with overt or subtle native-language difficulties in reading, writing, listening and speaking are likely to experience similar difficulties in learning an LX (Sparks et al., 1998: 209; Horwitz, 2000). Contrary to MacIntyre and Gardner (1991b), these researchers argue that FLA does not play a causal role in individual differences in foreign-language learning, but is merely the consequence of differences in native-language skill.

The cultural background of learners has also been found to determine levels of FLA. English language learners from Confucian Heritage Cultures (China, Korea and Japan) typically suffer more from FLA than other ethnic groups (Woodrow, 2006).

In sum, it appears that CA/FLA is a highly complex constellation of interacting variables, and this supports MacIntyre's (1995) assertion that CA/FLA is simultaneously influencing and being influenced by other variables: "aptitude can influence anxiety, anxiety can influence performance, and performance can influence anxiety" (p. 95). Levels of CA/FLA fluctuate both in the very short term (minutes) and in the long term (years) and seem to be associated with various situational, social, biographical, cultural and psychological variables.

FLA is an enigma that merits being cracked because "the potential of anxiety to interfere with learning and performance is one of the most accepted phenomena in psychology and education" (Horwitz, 2000: 256). Indeed, FLA has been shown to be a significant predictor of oral achievement (Woodrow, 2006). It is therefore necessary to understand why a language learner feels anxious, in order to control such anxiety and alleviate its effects (MacIntyre and Gardner, 1991a, 1991b). High levels of FLA in the classroom cause negative affective reactions and can induce negative attitudes and discourage students from continuing their language study (Philipps, 1991, 1992). Research on FLA has potentially strong pedagogical implications and many researchers have argued that LX teachers should learn to recognise explicit anxiety-indicating cues, so as to identify learners who struggle with high levels of FLA (Gregersen, 2007; Gregersen and MacIntyre, 2013; Horwitz, 1996; Young, 1990, 1991). The consequences of FLA extend beyond the classroom. A person who has studied an L2 until graduation but suffers from high levels of FLA may actually never speak it after leaving school. This is a shame for the individual and for the whole school system that has invested money, time and energy in the teaching of a skill that will ultimately not be used. It would also have economic consequences for the individual in many countries where active multilingualism is a prerequisite for well-paid jobs, and it could ultimately affect the economy as a whole (Mettewie, Van Mensel and Belang, 2006). Finally, the non-use of the L2 may also have political consequences in bilingual countries where the ability to use the L2 is perceived by members of the L2 community as a sign of goodwill toward them.

Operationalising the variable

The data were obtained through the following closed question:

> "How anxious are you when speaking your different languages with different people in different situations?" (Circle appropriate number, 1 = not at all, 2 = a little, 3 = quite anxious, 4 = very anxious and 5 = extremely anxious).

Information was requested for every language known to the participant in the following situations: speaking with friends, with colleagues, with strangers, on the phone and in public.

Information was collected for the L1, L2, L3, L4 and L5. The dependent variables are thus the numerical values reflecting self-perceived competence in four language skills.

Cronbach alpha analyses revealed that internal consistency reliability was extremely high for the five items linked to FLA in the different languages: L1 (alpha = .91), L2 (alpha = .91), L3 (alpha = .90), L4 (alpha = .94) and L5 (alpha = .94).

A series of one-sample Kolmogorov-Smirnov tests revealed that the values for FLA in the five situations in up to five languages are not normally distributed (Kolmogorov-Smirnov Z values vary between 2.4 and 15.1, all $p < .0001$). As a consequence, Kruskal-Wallis tests were used as non-parametric equivalents to one-way ANOVAs, and a Mann-Whitney test was used instead of a t-test.

Hypothesis 1b: Monotonic increase in CA and FLA from L1 to L5

The Friedman ANOVA showed that pentalinguals experience significantly more FLA in languages acquired later in life. The effect is highly significant for the five different situations (Table 51). Figure 38 shows a near linear increase in FLA across situations in the different languages.

Table 51 The effect of chronology of acquisition on CA and FLA from L1 to L5 (χ^2)

Variable	N	df	χ^2	p
Friends	248	4	305.9	***
Colleagues	210	4	298.7	***
Strangers	270	4	371.4	***
Phone	238	4	388.4	***
Public	196	4	309.2	***

*** $p < .0001$

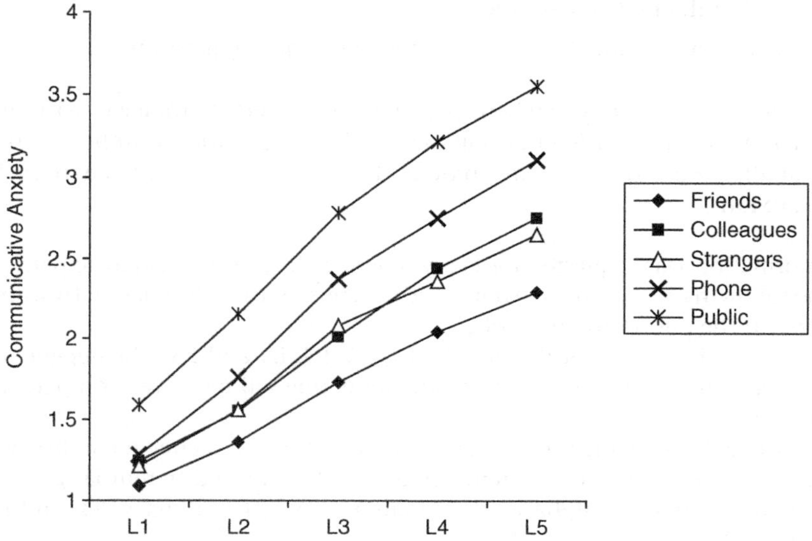

Figure 38 Mean values for CA and FLA values from L1 to L5

Yaprak, a young female PhD student (Turkish L1, English L2), confirmed the general trends, reporting increased communicative anxiety in her L2 compared to her L1:

> Yaprak: While speaking Turkish I feel more relaxed and it is easier for me to express myself. But in English I feel anxious and get tired because I need to think all the time the right words to say.

Jesus (Spanish L1, Catalan L2, English L3, German L4) feels more at ease in his L1:

> Jesus: I feel more comfortable in L1, but L2 is my language too.

A majority of participants report feeling more anxious when using languages learned later in life:

> Sonia (English L1, French L2, German L3, Russian L4): I feel much more shy and quiet when speaking languages (L2, L3, L4) I'm not as comfortable in.

Several participants explained that speaking on the phone in an LX made them particularly anxious. IE (Japanese L1, English L2) explains that several factors contribute to his anxiety in using his L2 on the phone:

IE: I thought that anxiety might involve not only the use of the language and content of the message/emotion but also the context of the language situation (perceived status of interlocutors) and consequences (motives). I get nervous speaking on the telephone because I am afraid I might not understand the import of a message given.

However, for participants like Eric (German L1, English L2), who has stopped using his L1, which has partly attrited as a result, communicative anxiety in the L1 is actually higher than in his L2:

Eric: When speaking German I feel either immature or unprofessional to a certain extent. I feel like my German has been frozen at the age of 18. When speaking German I feel as if I should be expressing myself more maturely though I'm not sure exactly in what way. I feel less confident when using German than English now never having had to function professionally completely in German.

Hypothesis 2: The effect of Age of onset of Acquisition of the LX on FLA in the LX

The Kruskal-Wallis tests show highly significant effects of the AoA on FLA in the L2 and L3 but not in the L4 and L5 (Table 52). Figure 39 shows that early starters suffer less from FLA in their L2 and L3 compared to older starters. FLA values for the L2 increase across AoA groups and stabilise at different points (with the exception of speaking in public where it increases across all groups). FLA levels in conversations with friends and colleagues remain stable from the AoA 8–12yrs group on, while the levelling off happens a little bit later in conversations with strangers and on the phone (i.e. the AoA 13–18yrs group).

Some participants, like Paola (Italian L1, English L2, French L3), did link their early AoA of an LX with lower levels of FLA and more self-confidence:

Paola: The acquisition of L2 at an early age meant for me to be able to speak calmly with less emotional anxiety.

Table 52 The effect of AoA in the LX on FLA in the LX (χ^2)

FLA	L2	L3	L4	L5
Friends	28***	12**	7	6
Colleagues	46***	14**	8*	2
Strangers	56***	17***	6	3
Phone	84***	31***	6	7
Public	57***	15**	4	2

*** $p < .0001$, ** $p < .001$, * $p < .05$

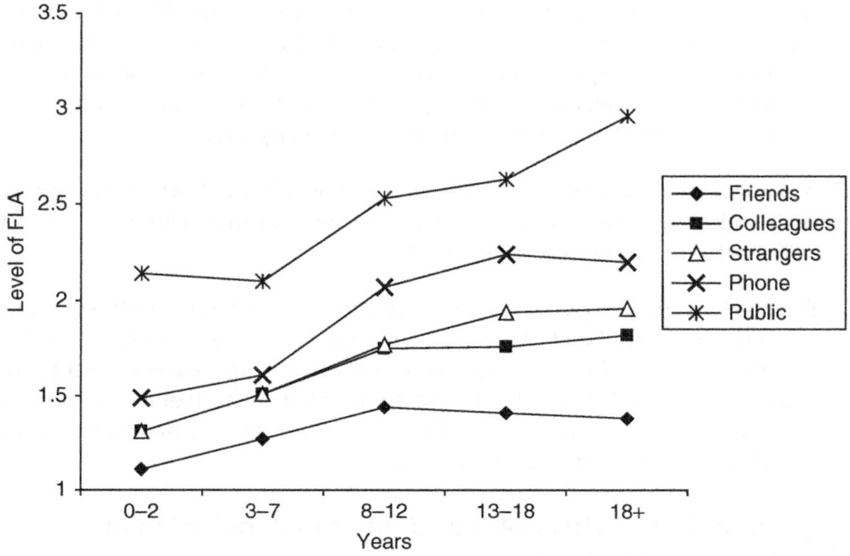

Figure 39 Mean FLA values in the L2 according to AoA

Hypothesis 3: The effect of context of acquisition of the LX on FLA in the LX

The Kruskal-Wallis analyses revealed a highly significant effect of the context of acquisition across the languages on levels of FLA experienced in various situations (Table 53). Interestingly the difference is most striking between purely instructed learners on the one hand, and mixed and naturalistic learners on the other (Figure 40). While the former report much higher levels of FLA across all situations, the latter report lower levels of FLA, and this, on average, two decades after finishing learning the language. Interestingly, the difference in the means of the mixed and naturalistic learners is very small.

Participants confirmed that they suffered more from FLA when speaking languages that they had only used within the LX classroom:

> Jenny (English L1, German L2, French L3, Australian Sign Language L4, Italian L5): I live in a monolingual English environment. With the exception of some of my friends in language classes at university and the lecturers, I have no choice but to communicate in English; when I get the opportunity to converse in other languages I take it, but because of this lack of contact with my second, third, fourth and fifth languages, I have no contact with any speakers of my L3 or L4 and this is why I am so anxious to use them.

Table 53 The effect of context of acquisition of the LX on FLA in the LX (χ^2)

FLA	L2	L3	L4	L5
Friends	66***	52***	54***	14***
Colleagues	89***	49***	50***	22***
Strangers	90***	62***	58***	27***
Phone	101***	56***	45***	21***
Public	62***	41***	32***	15***

*** p < .0001

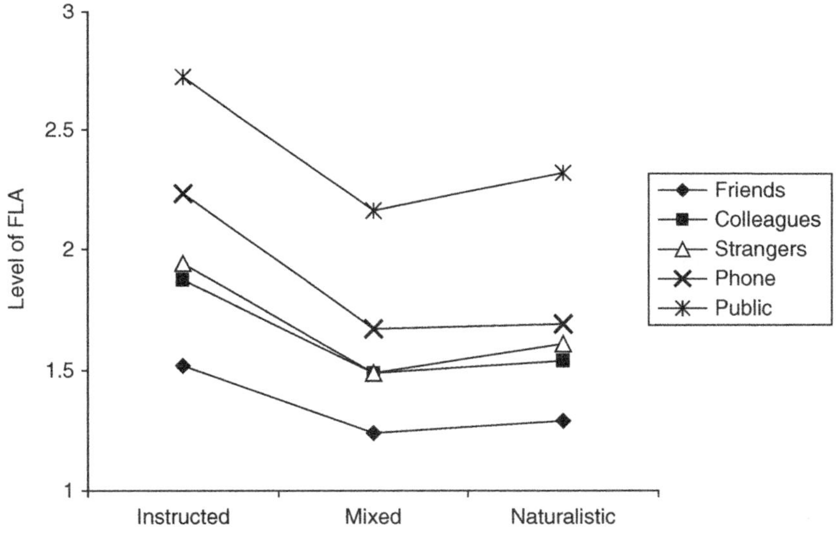

Figure 40 Mean FLA values in the L2 according to context of acquisition

Hypothesis 4: The effect of general frequency of use of the LX on FLA in the LX

The Kruskal-Wallis tests show highly significant effects of the general frequency of use on FLA in the different languages, with a higher general frequency of use corresponding to lower levels of FLA with various interlocutors and in different situations. The χ^2 values are highest for the L2, and slightly lower for the L3, L4 and L5. Yet, even for the L5 they remain highly significant (Table 54).

An analysis of the means for the L2 shows a graded difference between groups of participants: those who use their L2 yearly or less score higher than those who use it monthly (Figure 41). However, the FLA values are

Table 54 The effect of general frequency of use of the LX on FLA in the LX (χ^2)

FLA	L2	L3	L4	L5
Friends	184***	183***	86***	59***
Colleagues	213***	198***	100***	56***
Strangers	204***	172***	77***	54***
Phone	235***	193***	104***	62***
Public	181***	135***	69***	51***

*** p < .0001

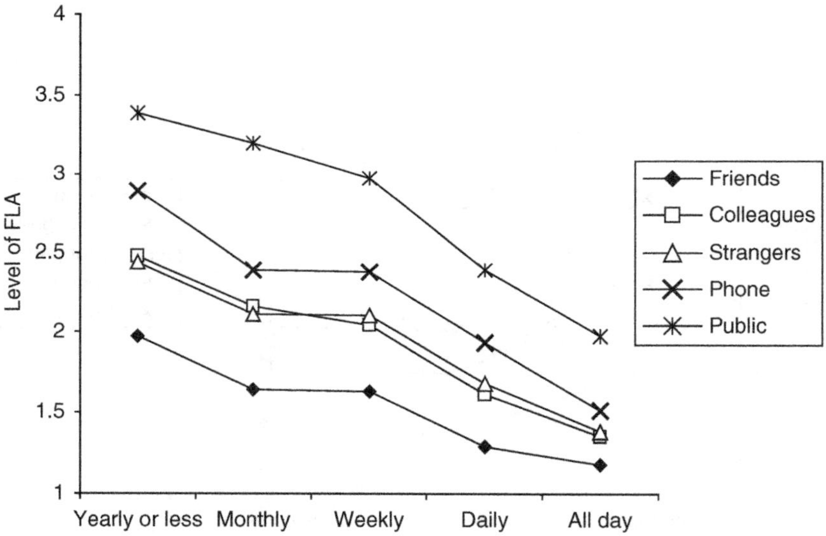

Figure 41 Mean FLA values in the L2 according to general frequency of use of the L2

quite similar between those who use the L2 monthly and those who use it weekly. This is followed by a steady decline in FLA levels across all situations for those who use the L2 daily or all day.

Participants spontaneously observed that levels of FLA dropped for LXs that they used frequently. Theodora reported feeling much less anxious using her English L2, which she learned in Greece, after a period of intense use:

> Theodora (Greek L1, English L2, German L3 – dominant in Greek): I've been living in UK for the last 4 years. I certainly feel much more comfortable and relaxed and familiar speaking in English now rather than when I spoke English when I was back at home.

Kristina, reported that her FLA in L2 English had almost completely disappeared after several years in the UK, despite the fact that her English remains non-native-like:

> Kristina (German L1, English L2): Apparently I make German sounds when arguing and getting angry such as "ach". I don't feel inferior or disadvantaged though nowadays. I did when I first came to live in Britain and had arguments in L2. I also had native English speakers picking on my accent or grammatical mistakes when arguing. That has stopped bothering me so much now.

Hypothesis 5: The effect of socialisation in the LX on FLA in the LX

A series of Kruskal-Wallis tests shows that socialisation in an LX has a highly significant effect ($p < .0001$) on FLA in the different languages (Table 55). Higher levels of socialisation are linked to lower FLA values in the different languages (Figure 42).

Strong socialisation in the L2 is linked to lower levels of FLA in various types of L2 interactions. The strongest decrease occurs between participants with minimal levels of socialisation in the L2 ("very weak socialisation") and the group with a "weak socialisation" in the L2. However, the effect is less pronounced and even absent at higher levels of socialisation.

Deborah (English L1, French L2, German L3, Finnish L4, Italian L5) feels dominant in both her English L1 and her Finnish L4. She has been living in Finland for a long time and feels totally socialised in her L4. However, she remembers how anxious she was about talking about emotions in Finnish to a Finnish therapist, not because of linguistic difficulties, but rather because of the fear of being misperceived by the therapist:

> When I was undergoing therapy and also marriage counseling, I found it quite difficult to speak about things in Finnish and went out of my way to try and find a therapist whose English was excellent enough that I felt

Table 55 The effect of socialisation in the LX on FLA in the LX (χ^2)

FLA	L2	L3	L4	L5
Friends	109***	101***	52***	31***
Colleagues	139***	107***	62***	32***
Strangers	146***	92***	43***	29***
Phone	198***	124***	61***	33***
Public	143***	103***	35***	32***

*** $p < .0001$

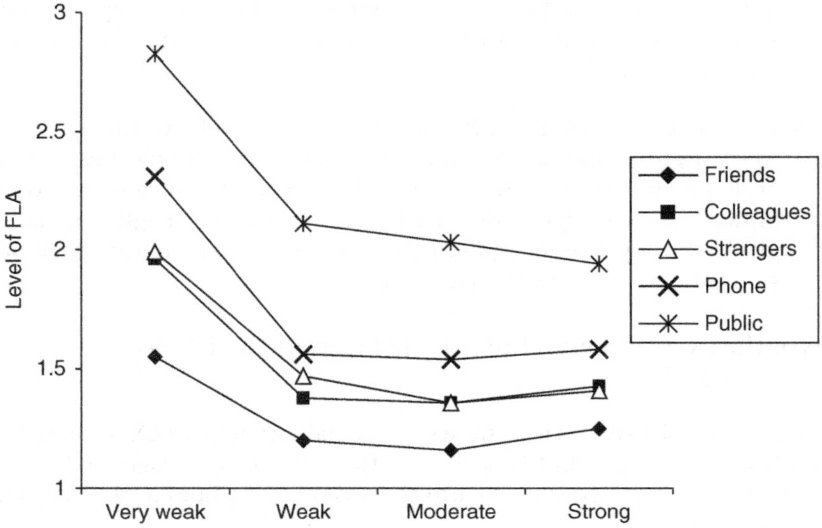

Figure 42 Mean FLA values in the L2 according to level of socialisation in the L2

> I was understood. The problem was not really with the language per se I think as it was with being afraid of not being understood; I'm putting this badly what I think I mean is that *I* knew I could express myself perfectly well in Finnish but I was afraid the therapist might have difficulties with the *way* in which I was expressing myself and also with the fact that I was speaking Finnish.

FLA can arise from a perceived decrease of L2 language socialisation, with infrequent use of the L2 leading to a loss in proficiency:

> Nancy (English L1, American Sign Language L2): I recall a dream in which a dear friend (L2 speaker) was speaking to me under poor lighting conditions which made it difficult to see him. I had to ask him to repeat himself several times (in the dream) and he reprimanded me that I "never understand him". I take this to be anxiety about my current level of contact in the L2 community and fear of loss of fluency with diminished contact.

Hypothesis 6: The effect of network of interlocutors in the LX on FLA in the LX

The Kruskal-Wallis analyses reveal a highly significant effect of the network of interlocutors on levels of FLA experienced in various situations in all languages except in the L5 (Table 56). A language that is only used with

Table 56 The effect of network of interlocutors in the LX on FLA in the LX (χ^2)

FLA	L2	L3	L4	L5
Friends	40***	64***	40***	5
Colleagues	69***	59***	33***	5
Strangers	47***	53***	27***	4
Phone	59***	45***	31***	5
Public	44***	29***	27***	7

*** p < .0001

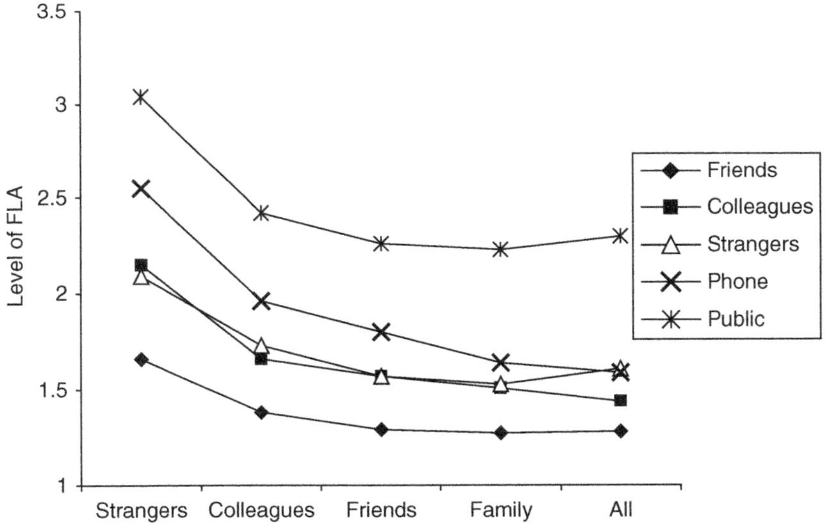

Figure 43 Mean FLA values in the L2 according to network of interlocutors in the L2

strangers, i.e. interlocutors who do not constitute a regular network, is associated with higher levels of FLA. Levels of FLA decrease gradually from use with colleagues, friends, family and "all" (Figure 43).

Linda explains why she experiences higher levels of FLA when speaking with colleagues rather than friends:

> Linda (English L1, German L2, French L3, American Sign Language L4, Lakota L5): I use the research languages frequently: one primarily for reading (although I do coincidentally have occasion to speak it), the other for documentation (...) speaking with colleagues in a research language evokes more anxiety than speaking that language with friends but the reverse is true for a non-research language. It has to do I think

with how the listener evaluates my efforts. The colleague is gauging my proficiency (high anxiety), the friend (or language research consultant) is pleased that I am making the effort, especially when the language is an endangered language (low anxiety).

Hypothesis 7: The effect of total language knowledge on FLA in the LX

The Kruskal-Wallis analyses show highly significant effects of total language knowledge on FLA in the different languages except the L5 (Table 57). Bilinguals report consistently higher levels of FLA in their L2 in various situations while pentalinguals report the lowest levels of FLA in their L2 (Figure 44).

Table 57 The effect of total language knowledge on FLA in the LX (χ^2)

FLA	L2	L3	L4	L5
Friends	40***	64***	40***	5
Colleagues	69***	59***	33***	5
Strangers	47***	53***	27***	4
Phone	59***	45***	31***	5
Public	44***	29***	27***	7

*** $p < .0001$

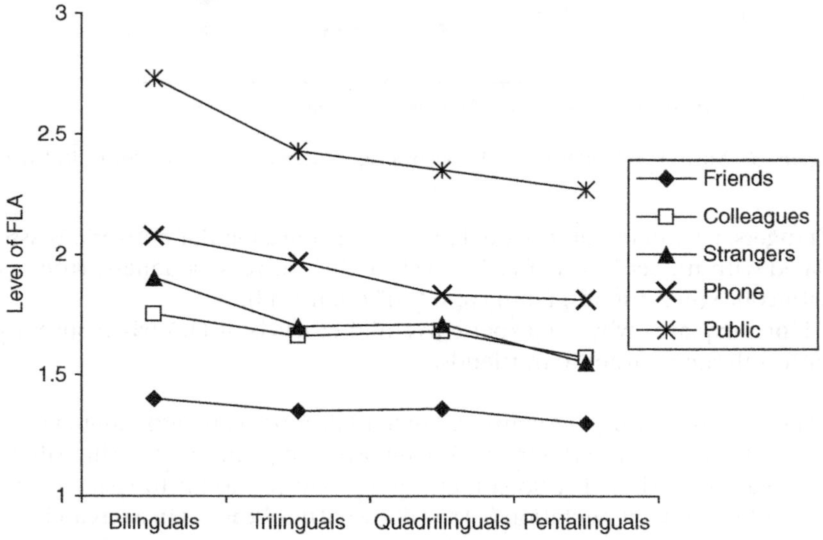

Figure 44 Mean FLA values in the L2 according to total language knowledge in the L2

Hypothesis 8: The effect of Trait Emotional Intelligence on FLA in the LX

The Kruskal-Wallis analyses reveal significant effects of TEI on FLA values in the various languages (Table 58). The effect is systematic in the L2 and L3, and more scattered in the L4 and L5. Participants with higher levels of TEI experience lower levels of FLA across situations (Figure 45).

Some participants displayed characteristics of high TEI in their narratives, namely adaptability, assertiveness, self-esteem, self-motivation, social competence, emotion management, relationship skills, happiness and optimism (Petrides and Furnham, 2003). Ellen (English L1, Russian L2, German L3) belongs to the "High TEI" group. She explains how much she enjoys being

Table 58 The effect of TEI on FLA values in the LX (χ^2)

FLA	L2	L3	L4	L5
Friends	8*	13**	11*	9*
Colleagues	6*	10*	4	6*
Strangers	11**	13**	11*	2
Phone	10*	11*	8*	3
Public	10*	16***	11*	3

*** $p < .0001$, ** $p < .001$, * $p < .05$

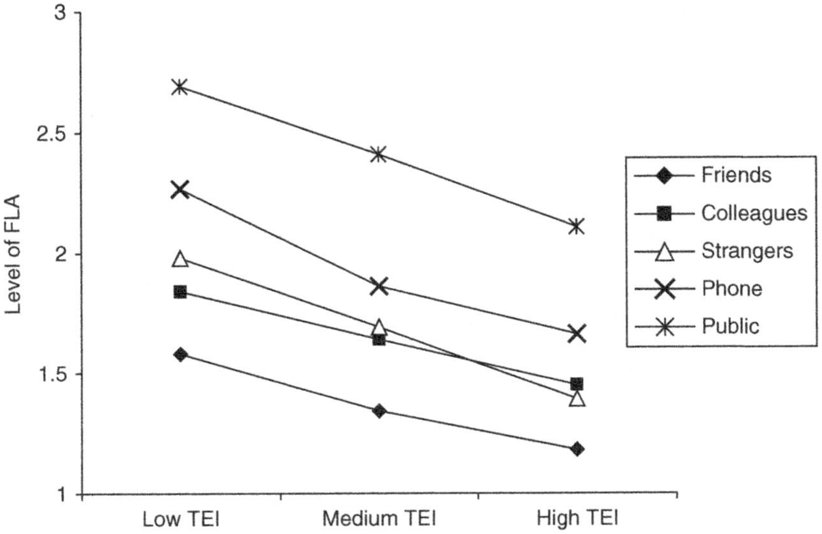

Figure 45 Mean FLA values in the L2 according to TEI

successful in using her L2 and L3, yet very occasionally she experiences a peak of FLA when confronted with unfamiliar technical vocabulary in her German L3. She experiences this as a brutal reminder that she is an NNS of German, pretending to be an NS:

> Ellen: Speaking my L1 is like being in my own skin – a completely natural and comfortable feeling. Using my L2 is perhaps like wearing gorgeous clothes and evening make-up – a not completely natural state of affairs but one which allows me to shine and appear "beautiful." When speaking German I am aware that I do so well and that my listeners are usually quite impressed (they often tell me so). This gives me a feeling of accomplishment and pride as well as being admired for a unique skill. I know many other native English speakers living and working in Germany but few of them have mastered the language as I have according to reliable witnesses – the Germans. So yes I often feel rather clever when speaking German except in situations where I am suddenly confronted with unfamiliar technical vocabulary. That's when the bubble bursts and I feel like the pretender that I am – a bumbling clod!

Hypothesis 9: The effect of gender, age and level of education on FLA in the LX

Gender

A series of Mann-Whitney tests showed only two significant differences between male and female participants in the L4 (on the phone and in public), but none in the other languages (Table 59).

Table 59 Differences in FLA between female and male participants in the LX (Z)

FLA		L2	L3	L4	L5
Friends	Mann-Whitney	226484	105544	39879	11033
	Z	−0.5	−0.3	−0.7	−1.1
Colleagues	Mann-Whitney	210260	95305.5	31806	8870
	Z	−0.2	−0.4	−1.6	−0.6
Strangers	Mann-Whitney	229136	115730	44832	12552
	Z	−0.7	−0.1	−1.0	−0.5
Phone	Mann-Whitney	221064	104585	34837	10254
	Z	−1.0	−0.8	−2.8*	−0.4
Public	Mann-Whitney	211229	84541	26409	7486
	Z	−0.9	−1.0	−2.5*	−0.6

* $p < .05$

Age

A series of Kruskal-Wallis tests showed highly significant and systematic effects of age on FLA in the L2 and L4, with more scattered effects in the L3 and no significant effects in the L5 (Table 60). A look at the mean values reveals that participants in their twenties suffer most from FLA, after which levels of FLA decrease linearly with age (Figure 46).

Education

A series of Kruskal-Wallis analyses showed a significant effect of the education level on FLA in four out of five situations in the L2, in two situations in the L3, three in the L4 and none in the L5 (Table 61). Participants with higher education levels are generally reporting lower levels of FLA (Figure 47).

Table 60 The effect of age on FLA in the LX (χ^2)

FLA	L2	L3	L4	L5
Friends	25***	10	12*	6
Colleagues	33***	15*	12*	5
Strangers	40***	28***	30***	1
Phone	28***	17*	23***	5
Public	29***	22**	23***	4

*** p < .0001, ** p < .001, * p < .05

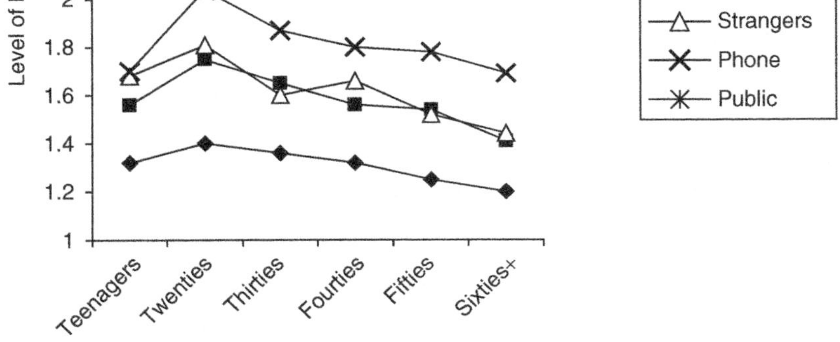

Figure 46 Mean FLA values in the L2 according to age

Table 61 The effect of education level on FLA in the LX (χ^2)

FLA	L2	L3	L4	L5
Friends	17**	3	9*	4
Colleagues	16**	2	2	0
Strangers	27***	8*	9*	2
Phone	4	1	4	2
Public	16**	9*	11*	3

*** p < .0001, ** p < .001, * p < .05

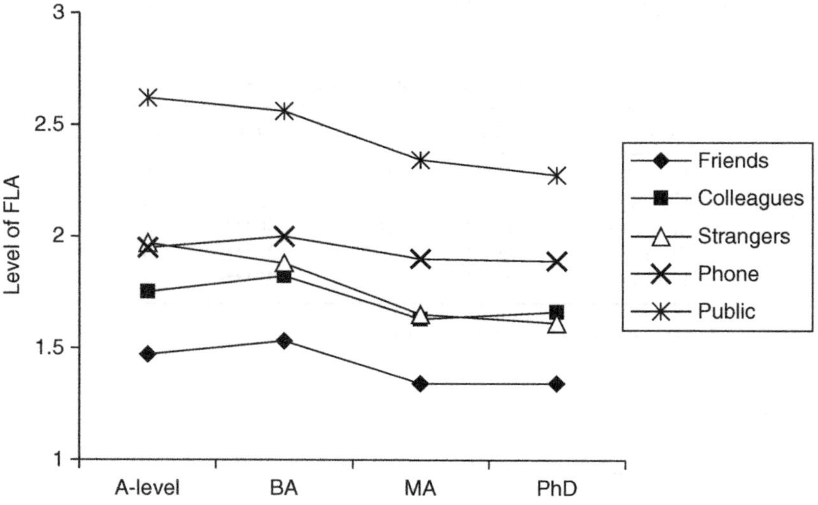

Figure 47 Mean values of FLA in the L2 according to education level

Summing up

Most hypotheses were confirmed for FLA, with most independent variables having significant and systematic effects on FLA in the different languages.

The Friedman ANOVA showed that pentalinguals experience significantly less communicative anxiety in their L1 than in languages acquired later. Participants' comments confirmed this.

The "history of learning" variables had significant effects on FLA. Younger starters experienced significantly less FLA in the different situations in their L2 and L3 and to a lesser extent in their L4 compared to older starters. The effect for context of acquisition was stronger and extended to all situations in all languages. Formal instruction always resulted in higher levels of FLA compared to mixed or naturalistic learning.

The independent variables reflecting the current use of the LX had highly significant effects on FLA. Participants who used an LX frequently, were strongly socialised in the language and used it with a wide network of interlocutors (with the exception of the L5) suffered significantly less from FLA than those who did not use the LX frequently, were weakly socialised and had smaller networks. Participants such as Kristina observed that FLA in English L2 had decreased after spending several years in the UK. She was no longer worried about what interlocutors might say or think about her grammatical mistakes and her German accent. Interestingly, the biggest difference in FLA was found between those with a very weak level of socialisation and those with a merely "weak" level of socialisation. Higher levels of socialisation did not cause a further drop in FLA.

The participants' linguistic profiles, i.e. the number of languages known, had a significant positive and systematic effect on FLA in all languages. The more languages a person knew, the less FLA he/she experienced across situations in the different languages. Trait Emotional Intelligence was found to have a highly significant positive effect in the L2 and the L3, and more scattered significant effect in the L4 and L5. In other words, participants who scored higher on TEI suffered less from FLA, a finding that was reported in Dewaele, Petrides and Furnham (2008).

Interestingly, this effect was significant even in relatively stress-free conditions (such as communication with friends), where the high TEI group showed the lowest FLA levels. It thus seems that "the constellation of emotion-related self-perceptions that trait EI encompasses is inversely related to CA/FLA levels" (p. 947).

We argued that this is evidence that "trait EI might be one of a number of basic ("upstream") personality variables, partially determining CA/FLA levels" (p. 951).

Participants with higher levels of TEI, like Ellen, possess strong belief in their ability to communicate in different languages while regulating their stress levels. Although individuals with high levels of TEI may experience FLA in very specific situations, these participants typically remain optimistic and confident in their ability to overcome the communication difficulty.

No significant gender effect on FLA was uncovered. However, age and education level did have effects on FLA. The non-linear relationship with age was significant in the L2, L3 and L4. Participants in their twenties scored highest on FLA, with both younger (teenagers) and older participants scoring lower. It is possible that prolonged experience in using LXs lowers levels of FLA from the age of 30 on. The lower FLA values of the teenage group could be linked to the fact that most of these participants were probably still involved in LX learning, and were probably often using the LX within the safe environment of the classroom. Participants in their twenties had to deploy their skills in the LX in order to survive socially and professionally, which may have triggered higher anxiety.

Finally, education level had an effect in the L2, L3 and L4. More highly educated participants reported significantly lower levels of FLA than participants with lower education levels in four situations in the L2, two situations in the L3 and three situations in the L4. It is possible that a longer education involved longer instruction in an LX, that participants with higher degrees had been forced to use an LX more intensively to carry out their studies or research and that participants with a lower education level had a more limited formal instruction in LXs, making them, on average, slightly more anxious when using these LXs.

10
Results: Code-Switching and Emotion

Introduction

When Nancy Huston, the Canadian writer who has been living in France since her student days at the Sorbonne, was asked by an interviewer on the radio (France Inter) on 30/09/2006 what language she would prefer to express a strong emotion in, she answered that she would prefer English, her L1, and when prompted to imagine what she would say in a situation of sudden terror, she uttered three swearwords in English, followed by a common swearword in French: "merde" ("shit"). She seemed surprised herself by the presence of the French swearword:

> Nancy: Quand j'ai véritablement besoin d'exprimer une émotion forte, comme comme la peur, s'il y a un chauffard qui qui manque m'écraser dans la rue ou si je laisse tomber un marteau sur mon pied, je vais jurer en anglais.
> "If I really need to express a strong emotion, like anxiety, if a bad driver almost runs me over in the street or if I drop a hammer on my foot, I swear in English."
>
> Journalist: Vous dites quoi?
> "What do you say?"
>
> N: Je dis *Christ fucking shit merde*!
> "I say Christ fucking shit *merde*!"
>
> N: Ah je peux ajouter *merde*!
> "Ah, I can add merde!"
>
> J: Hahaha, vous êtes bilingue mais vous xxx?!
> "Haha, you're bilingual but you xxx?!"
>
> N: Le *merde* a dû faire le voyage!
> "The *merde* must have travelled over"

This sudden code-switch seems to have taken Nancy Huston by surprise. She engages in a metalinguistic reflection and seems to realise that the sudden occurrence of that French swearword might in fact be an illustration of her secondary socialisation in French. She realises that her belief that English is her preferred language for expressing strong emotions needs to be qualified. This code-switch is thus an illustration of shifting language preferences, something that often escapes the bilingual speaker's conscious attention, especially when they get emotional.

In this next-to-last chapter, I aim to investigate the matter raised by the anecdote on Nancy Huston's sudden and apparently subconscious code-switch in a more systematic way. Is it true that code-switching (CS) is more likely to occur in emotional interactions? Does it depend on the type of interlocutor the multilingual is talking to? Could the fact that Nancy Huston is a highly educated female bilingual be linked to the probability of CS occurring in the interview situation? In other words, do gender, education level and knowledge of other languages have an effect on the frequency of CS? Finally, adopting an emic perspective, I want to investigate whether multilinguals are aware of the reasons behind their CS practices.

The chapter is organised as follows: after a short literature review on the reasons for CS and for particular language choices, I will focus on studies that considered CS in emotional interactions. I will present Grosjean's concept of language mode and the Complementarity Principle as a broad theoretical background to understanding the phenomenon of CS in emotional communication. The results of the quantitative analyses will be presented and linked to the participants' metalinguistic comments on their self-reported CS behaviour.

Literature review

CS – changing from one language to another in the course of conversation (Li Wei, 2007: 14) – is a typical feature of the speech of bilinguals; it is "neither unusual nor abnormal; it is an ordinary fact of life in many multilingual societies" (Cook, 2008: 175). Being a member of a multilingual family and a node in an international network of friends and colleagues, I can testify that CS is widespread and considered to be totally acceptable. Researchers at applied linguistic conferences do present their papers in the same language, but CS is not uncommon in the following discussion.

CS is more likely to happen when the speaker is in a bilingual language mode (Grosjean, 2001), i.e. when both languages are maximally activated, and can happen abruptly. CS happens in articulated speech as well as in inner speech (Dewaele, 2006b). It has become clear from the research that CS is not necessarily the sign of a problem, but rather the illustration of "skilled manipulation of overlapping sections of two (or more) grammars, and that there is virtually no instance of ungrammatical combination of two languages in code-switching, regardless of the bilingual ability of the speaker" (Li Wei, 2007: 15).

There is a large body of research on the reasons underlying CS (Auer, 1998; Basnight-Brown and Altarriba, 2007; Gardner-Chloros, 2009; Milroy and Muyskens, 1995). CS can occasionally be linked to a momentary loss for words in one language, but there are many pragmatic reasons for CS (see Cook, 2008). CS can signal that the speaker is reporting someone else's speech. It can also serve to highlight particular information, indicate a change in the speaker's role, qualify a topic or single out one person at whom to direct speech.

The reasons for CS may also be linked to specific contexts. For example, classroom CS is closely linked with teaching and learning activities (e.g., Martin-Jones, 1995) where CS to the learner's L1 may signal a metalinguistic explanation or the translation of a word in the TL. Family interactions are also conducive to CS (Edwards and Dewaele, 2007; Lanza, 1997). Heredia and Altarriba (2001) have pointed out that CS might also be linked to the specialised knowledge individuals have of specific topics. This idea is also at the core of Grosjean's (2008) Complementarity Principle. He describes it as follows: "Bilinguals usually acquire and use their languages for different purposes, in different domains of life, with different people. Different aspects of life often require different languages" (p. 23). Grosjean points out that as a consequence of this principle, bilinguals may vary in their level of proficiency in a language according to the need and the type of domain for which the language is needed (p. 23). A language that is spoken with a limited number of interlocutors in a reduced number of domains "may be less fluent and more restricted than a language used extensively" (p. 24).

Gardner-Chloros (2009) states that CS does not seem to be linked to gender, although "it intersects with a large number of intervening variables which are themselves connected with gender issues" (p. 82). A study by Cheshire and Gardner-Chloros (1998) failed to uncover a link between gender and frequency of CS among Greek Cypriots and Punjabis living in London. Dewaele's (2004b, 2006a) studies on multilinguals' language choices to express anger and to swear reported no clear effects for gender and education level. In a study on the same database, Dewaele (2004a) found that female participants gave higher scores on the perceived strength of swearwords in the L1, L2 and L3. Education levels had no effect on perceived strength. Finally, gender and education levels were found to have no significant effect on the perception of the phrase "I love you" in multilinguals' different languages (Dewaele, 2008a). In a study on attitudes toward CS among London Greek Cypriots, Gardner-Chloros, McEntee-Atalianis and Finnis (2005) found that attitudes were linked to level of education, occupational group and age. Participants with lower levels of education, from lower occupational groups and at younger ages had more favourable attitudes toward CS compared to those who were more highly educated, from higher occupational groups and older. Dewaele and Li Wei (2013b) investigated intra-individual variation (linked to type of interlocutor) and inter-individual variation in the self-reported CS of 2116 multilinguals. Participants who scored high on Extraversion and Cognitive Empathy reported significantly more frequent CS. Those who grew up and worked in a multilingual environment, knew a lot of languages, which they learnt from a young age, had advanced proficiency in various languages which they used frequently also reported more frequent CS. Female participants used significantly more CS with friends, family and colleagues compared to their male peers.

As Pavlenko (2005) points out, the affective functions of CS have long been examined only as a peripheral issue in CS studies (cf. Breitborde, 1998; Grosjean, 1982; Scheu, 2000). Moreover, the existing research tends to present "a somewhat oversimplified portrayal of affective functions of code-switching" (Pavlenko, 2005: 131). CS to the L1 is posited to signal intimacy and group membership, or to express emotions, while CS to the L2 has been found to mark distance or an out-group attitude, or to describe emotions in a detached way (2005: 131). Pavlenko (2005) argues that different languages can have different affective meanings depending on the interlocutors and the situation). In other words, the L1 is not always the language of intimacy and the L2 the language of detachment: "Speakers may use these languages to index a variety of affective stances, and they may also mix two or more languages to convey emotional meanings" (p. 131). Pavlenko (2005) suggests that the relative scarcity of studies on CS in emotion talk could be linked to the fact that these are "among some of the most private speech acts and are as such close to impossible to capture for research purposes" (p. 131). Language choice can thus be highly significant in interactions between clients and their psychotherapist (Costa, 2010; Costa and Dewaele, 2012).

The seminal work in the area of the affective functions of CS is the study by Bond and Lai (1986) on using CS to hide embarrassment over the use of taboo words in the L1. The authors examined language choices of 48 female Chinese students in a Hong Kong university who had been asked to interview each other in L1 Cantonese or L2 English on two neutral and two potentially embarrassing topics. The first topic was economic, the second was political, the third was sociological (differences in sexual attitudes between Chinese and Westerners) and the fourth was a personal story about a recent embarrassing episode. The study showed that participants used more English for the latter two topics, which the authors interpreted as an indication that the use of the L2 allowed participants to distance themselves more from the embarrassing topic. Pavlenko (2005) wonders whether the Bond and Lai (1986) study provides such clear-cut evidence about the L2 detachment effect. She points to the fact that while six participants reported anxiety while discussing the embarrassing topics in Cantonese, three participants reported anxiety while discussing the topics in English. In a similar vein, Javier and Marcos (1989) found that CS to an L2 allowed participants to distance themselves from what they were saying, hence reducing their anxiety.

Pavlenko (2004) used a subsample of the BEQ database to look at language choice in emotional parent-child communication. She used the feedback of

389 parents on closed questions about the frequency (through a five-point Likert scale) with which they used their different languages with their children in general, and also in typically emotional interactions, namely disciplining and praising them. She also considered the spontaneous comments of 141 participants on parent-child communication. Statistical analysis of the quantitative data revealed that language dominance is the key factor affecting language choices, overall and in emotional expression. Parents who were dominant in the L1 reported a preference for L1 in communication with their children, but those dominant in an LX were less likely to use the L1 (p. 186). A significant effect also emerged between the perceived emotionality of the L2 and the choice of that language for disciplining and praising the children. No such relationship existed between the perceived emotionality of the L2 and general use of the L2 (p. 188). Pavlenko found a strong emotional tie of many parents to their L1 and hence their preference to use that language with their children. However, some parents reported feeling perfectly comfortable communicating in their L2 with their children, though they might occasionally switch to their L1 when feeling very emotional (p. 193). Other parents reported the opposite pattern, using their L1 with their children, but switching to their L3 (the partner's L1) to scold the children because they would react faster (p. 196). Interestingly, parents who used their L2 very frequently overall also used the language most frequently to discipline their children. The L2 was used less frequently to praise the children (p. 188).

I have already discussed the issues of language choice in emotional interactions in previous chapters, without focusing exclusively on CS. Many participants reported CS to their L1 – and sometimes to another language – when expressing particularly strong emotions to their multilingual partner.

Grosjean's model of language modes is a very useful theoretical model for discussing CS. It is based on the fact that the bilingual's languages are active to varying degrees when an interaction takes place. There is usually a base, fully active, language and there are the other language(s), which can be active to varying degrees. Grosjean defines language mode as "the state of activation of the bilingual's languages and language processing mechanisms at a certain point in time" (2001: 3). The bilingual has to decide at any given point in time, usually quite unconsciously, which language to use and how much of the other language is needed (p. 2). A speaker thus chooses a base language, which is the most highly activated language, while the other languages can range from being activated to being practically deactivated depending on their position on the language mode continuum. Grosjean notes that these two factors are usually independent of one another and that a change in the activation level of one language does not imply a change in the activation level of the other language (p. 4). A bilingual speaking language X to a monolingual in X is in "X monolingual mode", whereas the same person speaking X to another X-Y bilingual, and code-switching to Y regularly, will be in "X bilingual mode". They could even choose Y as base language and continue their conversation in "Y bilingual mode". Grosjean lists a number of factors that influence language mode. These include:

> the participant(s), that is the person(s) being spoken or listened to (this includes such factors as language proficiency, language mixing habits and attitudes, usual mode of interaction, kinship relation, socio-economic status, etc.), the situation (physical location, presence of monolinguals, degree of formality and of intimacy), the form and content of the message being uttered or listened to (language used, type of vocabulary needed, amount of mixed language), the function of the language act (...) and specific research factors (the aims of the study taking place) (...), the type and organisation of the stimuli, the task used etc.). (p. 5)

Speakers might often occupy intermediate positions on the language mode continuum due to different combinations of the determining factors: the interlocutor might not be very proficient, the topic might be covered in the base language but occasional switches are necessary or a situation could be more formal (p. 6). Grosjean points out that movement along the continuum is usually an unconscious behaviour that takes place smoothly and effortlessly. He compares it to changing speech style or register based on the context and the interlocutor (p. 6).

Grosjean concludes that intra-individual variation in activation levels also needs to be investigated, especially the occasional inability of bilinguals who are highly dominant in one language to their control language mode the way less dominant or balanced bilinguals can (p. 17). He presents the example of a dominant bilingual speaker having to use a weaker language (A) in a monolingual mode. Having realised that his/her competence in language A is too low, s/he shifts to bilingual language mode, where the stronger language (B) is more active and can be used to step in (through short code-switches) if difficulties arise in the production of language A. This CS will not hinder communication if the interlocutor understands language B. Grosjean (2008) points out that "future research will have to investigate the underlying mechanism (...) that makes the stronger language 'seep through' despite the fact that it has been deactivated, at first at least" (p. 77). This is exactly what we propose to investigate in the present study. To sum up, the existing research on CS suggests that a multitude of situational and pragmatic variables can be linked to CS. These variables also affect CS in emotional interactions, but an extra set of factors may become relevant such as the perceived emotional strength of words and expressions in the different languages, the degree of emotionality of the topic under discussion, as well as the amount of control that the speaker retains over language choice.

Research questions

In this final chapter, I propose to investigate the following research questions:

1) "What is the effect of the interlocutor on the frequency of self-reported CS?"
2) "What is the effect of the emotionality of the topic of conversation on the frequency of self-reported CS?"
3) "Is there an effect of gender, age, education level, profession, number of languages known or self-perceived oral proficiency on the frequency of self-reported CS?"
4) "Are multilinguals who are dominant in two or more languages more likely to engage in CS?"

Hypotheses

1) A stronger familiarity with the interlocutor will be linked to increased CS.
2) CS is more frequent when talking about emotional topics compared to neutral topics
3) Sociobiographical factors could be linked to self-reported frequency of CS with different types of interlocutor and different topics, but given the lack of systematic findings in the literature, no directional hypothesis can be formulated.
4) Multilinguals who are dominant in two or more languages are more likely to engage in CS than multilinguals who are dominant in one language only.

The dependent variables

The two dependent variables selected in the present chapter are values on a 5-point Likert scale answering the two following questions:

1) "Do you switch between languages within a conversation with certain people? When speaking with: 1) friends and family, 2) strangers, 3) colleagues or 4) in public?"
2) "Do you switch between languages when talking about certain matters? When speaking about: 1) neutral matters, 2) personal matters or 3) emotional matters?"

Possible answers for both questions were: Never, Rarely, Sometimes, Frequently and All the time.

A series of one-sample Kolmogorov-Smirnov tests showed that the values for self-reported CS frequencies are not normally distributed (Kolmogorov-Smirnov Z-values vary between 6.0 and 9.5, all significant at $p < .001$). The non-parametric option was used as a result of the severe violations of the normality assumption. As a consequence, Friedman's ANOVAs were used as non-parametric equivalents of the repeated-measures ANOVA. Kruskal-Wallis analyses were used instead of ANOVAs.

Results

Comparison of self-reported frequency of self-reported CS across types of interlocutors

A Friedman's ANOVA reveals an extremely significant effect of the type of interlocutors on self-reported CS ($N = 1279$, $df = 3$, $\chi^2 = 126.2$, $p < .001$). Figure 48 presents the mean values for self-reported CS across types of interlocutors and illustrates a significant increase in the frequency of self-reported CS with interlocutors who are more familiar to the speaker.

There might be a relatively simple explanation for this finding. CS typically implies that the speaker is aware of the linguistic repertoire of the interlocutor. It is therefore unlikely to happen before the speakers have established which languages they share. Similarly, when speaking to a larger audience, it is generally impossible to know which languages are known by the members of the audience (except maybe in certain community groups or language schools), hence the logical avoidance of producing stretches of speech in a language that only few may understand. CS is thus a sign of relative linguistic and cultural intimacy.

Comparison of self-reported frequency of self-reported CS across topics

The Friedman's ANOVA shows a highly significant effect of the emotionality of the topic of conversation on the frequency of self-reported CS

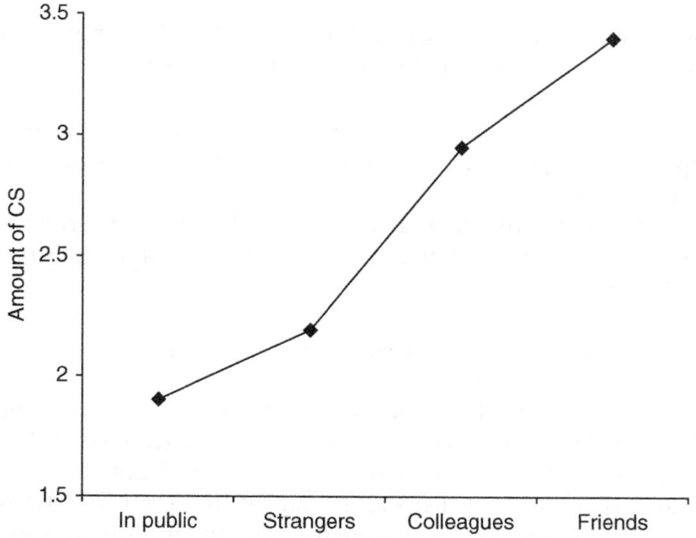

Figure 48 Mean value of frequency of self-reported CS according to interlocutor

(N = 1343, df = 2, $\chi^2 = 65.2$, $p < .001$). The difference is most striking between neutral topics on the one hand, and personal and emotional topics on the other. The latter types of topics display increased levels of self-reported CS (see Figure 49).

The higher frequency of self-reported CS in emotional interactions could have psychological, psycholinguistic or purely linguistic causes. Pavlenko (2005) noticed in the feedback from the participants from the BEQ that instances of self-reported CS could not just be explained by interactional goals and needs, but that they "also serve to satisfy speakers' personal needs, independent of the interlocutors' proficiency or accomplishment of any discursive business other than self-expression and self-satisfaction" (p. 140). It is possible that in a state of higher emotional arousal the speaker becomes more self-centred and hence less inclined to respond to the interlocutor's needs by tending toward the shared language. Of course, CS can be a conscious and strategic decision in emotion talk: a word or expression or utterance in another language may be felt to be more appropriate to convey a specific emotion to the listener. Sometimes CS may not be a strategic decision at all, but rather the result of an emotional outburst.

It is possible that the greater emotional arousal of the multilingual affects the balance of the language mode. A highly activated background language may momentarily become the main language for processing. The sudden

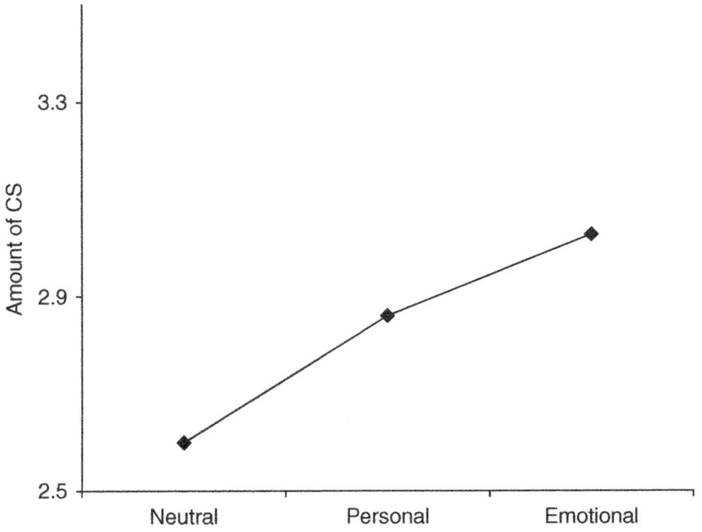

Figure 49 Mean value of frequency of self-reported CS according to topic of conversation

emotional arousal of the speaker may automatically activate expressions with the highest emotional resonance, which may cause CS (cf. Grosjean, 2008). The speaker may thus switch from a monolingual mode to a bilingual mode without realising it. The sudden CS could also be linked to a sudden drop in inhibitory control of the background languages.

The effect of gender on self-reported frequency of self-reported CS

A Mann-Whitney test shows significant differences between males and females in our data for two types of interlocutor, and for two types of topic. Female participants report more CS in conversations with friends, while males reported more CS in conversations with strangers. Female participants report more CS while talking about personal and emotional topics (see Table 62).

The fact that female multilinguals reported more CS when speaking to friends and when speaking about personal and emotional topics will come as no surprise to those researchers who investigate the emotional nature of males and females (cf. Barrett et al., 2000). Indeed, women consistently describe themselves as more emotionally intense than do men when emotionality is defined as a global disposition largely independent of the social context. Barrett et al., (2000) suggest that for some researchers there are gender differences in emotional experience, primarily linked to differential socialisation experiences, while others suggest that differences are inconsistent and exist mainly for emotional expressions (p. 1027).

A less predictable result was the fact that men report more CS when talking to strangers. This could be interpreted as a reduced inclination to accommodate the interlocutor by "imposing" certain language choices.

The effect of age on self-reported frequency of CS

A Spearman correlation analysis revealed positive correlations between the participants' age and the self-reported frequency of CS on all three types

Table 62 The effect of gender on self-reported frequency of CS (Z)

Interlocutor/topic	Female	Male	*Z*
Friends	3.50	3.20	–3.95***
Strangers	2.26	2.41	–2.34*
Colleagues	2.98	2.93	–0.60
Public	1.94	1.96	–0.60
Neutral	2.70	2.69	–0.22
Personal	2.92	2.71	–3.28**
Emotional	2.96	2.74	–3.26**

* $p < .05$, *** $p < .001$, *** $p < .0001$

of topics and two types of interlocutor (Table 63). The fact that no correlation emerged for interactions with friends or strangers, but that very strong correlations emerged for conversations with colleagues and public speech, as well as neutral topics of conversation could indicate that that older participants more often find themselves in professional interactions with members of other speech communities where CS is an accepted practice.

The effect of education level on self-reported frequency of self-reported CS

The Kruskal-Wallis analyses reveal significant differences in self-reported CS between the various education levels for three types of interlocutors and two types of topic. The strongest effect is for participants with higher levels of education reporting more CS with colleagues. The effect is less systematic for the other variables, and hence difficult to interpret (see Table 64).

The fact that participants with higher levels of education reported more CS in interactions with colleagues could reflect their professions, and possibly

Table 63 The relationship between age and self-reported frequency of CS (Spearman Rho)

Interlocutor/topic	Spearman Rho
Friends	–0.010
Strangers	0.016
Colleagues	0.112***
Public	0.101***
Neutral	0.102***
Personal	0.056*
Emotional	0.068*

* $p < .05$, *** $p < .001$, *** $p < .0001$

Table 64 The effect of education level on self-reported frequency of self-reported CS (χ^2)

Interlocutor/topic	A-level	BA	MA	PhD	χ^2
Friends	3.43	3.42	3.51	3.24	8.23*
Strangers	2.42	2.38	2.25	2.21	4.63
Colleagues	2.47	2.88	3.05	3.04	16.18**
Public	1.79	1.94	1.95	1.96	7.93*
Neutral	2.43	2.62	2.81	2.71	13.4*
Personal	2.65	2.92	2.99	2.77	8.56*
Emotional	2.81	2.93	3.02	2.79	7.06

* $p < .05$, *** $p < .001$, *** $p < .0001$

their frequent interactions with people outside their own speech community or with documents in other languages. The same pattern occurred also in their neutral and personal interactions. However, the relationship did not seem to be linear: those with the lowest level of education reported less CS than the three other groups (who did not differ that much among themselves).

Could the level of education be correlated with the level of proficiency in the different languages? In other words, might CS be better explained by the level of proficiency rather than the level of education?

A Spearman correlation analysis suggests that no such relationship exists (Table 65).

The effect of profession on self-reported frequency of self-reported CS

A Mann-Whitney test reveals that the majority of participants who worked in language-related professions reported significantly more CS with strangers and colleagues and in public speech compared to the 299 participants who did not work in language-related professions (Table 66). No significant differences between the two groups emerged for the frequency of CS according to the topic of conversation. This suggests that CS is linked to the nature

Table 65 The relationship between level of education and level of oral competence in the LX (Spearman Rho)

	L2 proficiency	L3 proficiency	L4 proficiency	L5 proficiency
Spearman Rho	0.04	–0.016	0.055	0.005
N	1444	1221	859	469

All p values > 0.05

Table 66 The difference between language-related and non-language related professions on self-reported frequency of CS (Z)

Interlocutor/topic	Language-related	Non language-related	*Z*
Friends	3.38	3.52	–1.49
Strangers	2.34	2.21	–2.00*
Colleagues	3.13	2.30	–5.08***
Public	2.01	1.71	–9.30***
Neutral	2.72	2.60	–1.79
Personal	2.88	2.78	–1.46
Emotional	2.91	2.83	–1.09

* $p < .05$, *** $p < .001$, *** $p < .0001$

of the workplace, and that language professionals are more likely to use CS within that context but less so in the private sphere.

The effect of number of languages known on self-reported frequency of CS

The Kruskal-Wallis analyses show two significant differences in self-reported CS between participants knowing fewer languages and those knowing more languages. Bilinguals clearly report using less CS with strangers than trilinguals, quadrilinguals and pentalinguals do. The same pattern emerges for self-reported CS with colleagues, where participants with more languages report higher levels of CS (see Table 67).

The effect of the number of languages known on self-reported CS in interactions with strangers and colleagues could again be linked to the economic and tourist activities of the participants knowing more languages.

The link between self-perceived oral proficiency and self-reported frequency of CS

In order to find out whether higher levels of oral competence in the different languages are linked to more frequent self-reported CS, a series of Spearman correlation analyses were carried out. The results suggest that levels of self-perceived competence in the L2 and L3 are indeed positively linked to self-reported frequency of CS, especially in interactions with known interlocutors about personal or emotional matters (Table 68). This is a clear indication that CS is not an indication of a deficit in the LX, but, on the contrary, a characteristic of participants who feel proficient in their LXs.

The effect of language dominance on self-reported frequency of CS

A Mann-Whitney test shows significant differences between monodominant multilinguals and multidominant multilinguals for all types of topic

Table 67 The effect of number of languages known on self-reported frequency of CS (χ^2)

Interlocutor/topic	Bilingual	Trilingual	Quadrilingual	Pentalingual	χ^2
Friends	3.36	3.34	3.39	3.46	2.62
Strangers	2.07	2.31	2.31	2.38	24.63***
Colleagues	2.58	2.91	2.97	3.09	25.96***
Public	1.87	1.90	1.92	2.01	3.58
Neutral	2.62	2.7	2.62	2.75	2.76
Personal	2.77	2.94	2.82	2.91	6.28
Emotional	2.79	2.92	2.86	2.97	7.20

* $p < .05$, *** $p < .001$, *** $p < .0001$

Table 68 The relationship between self-reported frequency of CS and level of oral competence in the LX (Spearman Rho)

Interlocutor/topic	L2 Competence	L3 Competence	L4 Competence	L5 Competence
Friends	0.131***	0.069*	0.042	0.041
Strangers	0.033	0.076*	0.026	0.060
Colleagues	0.075*	0.097**	0.072*	0.003
Public	0.065*	0.055	0.069	0.009
Neutral	0.071*	0.040	−0.068	−0.029
Personal	0.072*	0.092**	0.012	0.073
Emotional	0.065*	0.095**	0.052	0.050

* $p < .05$, *** $p < .001$, *** $p < .0001$

Table 69 The effect of language dominance on self-reported frequency of CS (Z)

Interlocutor/topic	One language	Two or more languages	*Z*
Friends	3.27	3.67	−5.86***
Strangers	2.27	2.37	−1.70
Colleagues	2.84	3.19	−4.65***
Public	1.88	2.07	−3.20**
Neutral	2.62	2.84	−3.61***
Personal	2.72	3.11	−5.87***
Emotional	2.76	3.15	−5.84***

* $p < .05$, ** $p < .001$, *** $p < .0001$

and with all interlocutors except strangers. Multidominants report more frequent CS than monodominants (see Table 69).

Given the strong difference between monodominant and multidominant multilinguals, I checked whether the effects of interlocutor and topic are equally significant within each group considered separately. The Friedman's ANOVA shows a significant effect of the conversation topic on the frequency of self-reported CS among the monodominant participants (N = 868, df = 2, $\chi^2 = 16.9$, p < .0001), and an even stronger effect among the multidominant participants (N = 475, df = 2, $\chi^2 = 62.5$, p < .0001).

The effect of the interlocutor is highly significant among the monodominant participants (N = 822, df = 3, $\chi^2 = 729.3$, p < .0001) and the multidominant participants (N = 457, df = 3, $\chi^2 = 550.2$, p < .0001).

Narratives from the participants

The freedom of CS for multicompetent and multicultural participants

CS is a preferred mode of communication for participants like Stefanie, who revel in their ability to switch from language to language with other multilinguals:

Stefanie (German L1, English L2, Spanish L3, French L4, Irish L5; dominant in L1+L2+L3):

> Stefanie: I find it sometimes very strenuous to strictly keep to one language. For instance when speaking with my parents who are monolingual, it takes me some time to feel comfortable speaking only German. Normally I speak to people who are multilingual too and I enjoy switching languages even just for a more colourful word or because one word occurs to me first in another language. I therefore feel more comfortable and at ease speaking with other multilingual friends because I can relax and don't have to think about what exactly I am saying.

Some participants love to have a choice between words and expressions in their different languages. As Zelideth (Spanish L1, English L2; French L3, Japanese L4, Portuguese L5, dominant in L1 and L2) reports, emotion words in different languages have their own unique flavour, deployed according the mood and the situation:

> Zelideth: Honestly, I'd have to say that Spanglish is my language of preference. The person who just cut me off on the highway is a "fucking pendejo". Terms of endearment fluctuate between Spanish and English. My girlfriends are "ma" but my significant other is usually "baby". The Spanish term of endearment "pa" seems like I'm giving him permission to boss me around just like a father and almost places him higher than me and I just refuse to use it. Overall I prefer Spanish for emotional terms but if you want to punctuate it with a harsher tone just add an English word to it.

A number of participants resort to CS for comic effect. Elena (Greek Cypriot L1, Greek L2, English L3, dominant in L1 and L2) explains that the juxtaposition of standard language and dialect offer comic contrasts:

> Elena: I use mostly Standard Greek with my boyfriend (that is the typical situation among a Dialect and a Standard speaker) but I often switch to the Dialect especially when I say a funny story or when I joke.

As Cook (2008) noted, CS can occur when a speaker feels that certain topics are better broached in a specific language. However, once the conversation has started, CS can happen more freely:

> Darrin (English L1, Afrikaans L2; dominant in L1): I have noticed several times when I want to discuss a heavy topic with my wife I will switch to Afrikaans at least to bring up the topic. Then, once the topic is started, we may switch back and forth.

Using an LX allows speakers to produce different voices, assuming a different personality (Pavlenko, 2006; Wilson, 2008). Uttering declarations of love in an LX does not necessarily have the same resonance as in the L1, however they had enough charm for Jane (English L1, French L2, Spanish L3, Portuguese L4; dominant in L1+L3+L4) and her partner to try them out for the very first time. Moreover, the declaration of love in the LX did not have the same resonance as that in the L1, in other words, they did not commit the interlocutors in the same way that a declaration of love in the L1 would have done. It was more an (enjoyable) experiment in words and emotions:

> Jane: When my partner and I first "got serious" we used to switch into Spanish (which we were both studying) to make declarations of love. Like putting on a "funny voice", it seemed to create a certain distance which felt safer. Since then Spanish has become such a part of me that such a declaration in Spanish or English would carry equal weight. In some circumstances I could imagine myself switching into English from any of these languages to give a declaration of love more weight and seriousness – even if the hearer didn't speak much English.

The distancing effect of CS can be used un/consciously to talk about topics that might be too painful in the first language (Altarriba and Santiago-Rivera, 1994; Amati-Mehler, Argentieri and Canestri, 1993; Santiago-Rivera and Altarriba, 2002):

> Vally (Greek L1, English L2, French L3, Turkish L4; dominant in L1+L2): I think when I talk about emotional topics I tend to code-switch to English a lot. I remember when I was seeing a psychologist in Greece for a while I kept code-switching from Greek to English. We never really talked about this (...) To my mind it may have been some distancing strategy because at the time I was trying to figure out what to do with my life (...). I also noticed I code-switched a lot (again from Greek to English) when I was in a crisis situation a couple of years ago and I had just met my current partner and I was trying to explain things to him.

While the statistical trends show that multilinguals talking about emotions are more likely to resort to CS, some multilinguals go somewhat against the general trend, preferring to discuss emotions as much as possible in the shared language which is the L2 for both, while remaining in bilingual mode:

> Silvia (Italian L1, English L2, French L3, German L4, Spanish L5): I live with my Spanish partner. We talk generally in a terrible mixture of Spanish, English and Italian. We realised that we were speaking this

mixture only when a friend heard us talking and told us. Since then it looked perfectly natural to us thus we hadn't noticed. We argue in English though with very few words in Spanish and Italian. Probably because when we argue we need to understand every word we are saying there is no space for further linguistic misunderstandings.

CS to L1 to express strong emotion

Multilinguals often feel that some of their languages are more appropriate to express their anger in. The preferred language is typically the L1, as Evy testifies. The interesting thing is that her partner's CS to the L1 when angry seems to happen unconsciously:

> Evy (Dutch L1, English L2, French L3, dominant in L1): My partner's L1 is Berber but he's also good at Dutch (his L2). So we argue in Dutch. However he sometimes switches to Berber without being aware of it.

One participant, Andrew (English L1, French L2), was interviewed by Benedetta Bassetti on his language preferences when talking about intellectual and emotional matters. It turns out that Andrew who had declared earlier that he is equally at ease in English and French, which he speaks without the trace of a foreign accent, does in fact have a preference for a specific language depending on the topic of the conversation, which is a perfect illustration of Grosjean's Complementarity Principle.

B: So my question then is, you switch from which language to which language?
A: OK, well sometimes if I'm speaking, having an emotional conversation with a French person, for example we are speaking in French, if I, the more emotionally worked up I get the more I want to speak in English.
B: OK.
A: And I think it's quite natural.
B: OK.
A: Yeah.
B: So you would use English words?
A: Yeah.
B: Or just say the whole thing in English?
A: I might have to just spit out a whole sentence in English and then try to retranslate if the person can't understand what I'm saying.
B: Aha, so you do that even with people who don't speak English?
A: Yeah.
B: All right, oh that's interesting, and that's only for emotional and personal matters only?
A: Yeah.

B: And what about the other way round, do you ever feel the need to speak French when you're talking in English about emotional matters? (...)

A: Not really emotional matters no, I sometimes feel the need to speak French rather than English even with an English person who doesn't speak French to try to explain some intellectual ideas, I find French easier.

B: Aha.

A: Ehm, certain abstractions, but not emotions no, I don't see, for me my emotional language is English, and my intellectual language is often, even though it bizarrely it's my second language, it's become French.

In a second interview, Benedetta asked Sophia (Greek L1, English L2) about her language choices to express anger to her partner. She reports that she usually starts in the common language (her L2) before CS to her L1 when she feels incapable of conveying the strength of her emotion in the L2:

S: We start with English, 'cos I want him to understand, obviously every time we have an argument I don't swear at him I'm not a woman that does that, but you know, when he gets me really really angry, then I start, I start in English but I usually get frustrated, because the emotion that I wanna convey doesn't really happen, yeah, so I switch in Greek.

This CS to the L1 in a situation of extreme anger is also reported by Cristina (Catalan L1, Spanish L2, English L3, Italian L4, German L5, she has been living in the UK for nearly 20 years):

B: So when you are angry and speaking in English, do you ever use words or swearwords from Spanish or Catalan?

Cr: Yeah if they are very, if I mean they're very critical situation, if I'm kind of, it's not something, anger that comes from within but something I react to, then I would swear in in Catalan, my mother tongue.

The CS to the L1 is not always linked to the interlocutor, Silvia (Italian L1, English L2, French L3, German L4) reports engaging in CS to the L1 when swearing under her breath:

S: I've said that I tend to talk to myself in English slightly more often than in Italian, so I would probably be swearing at myself in English first and then a colourful translation in Italian if I wasn't satisfied [laughs].

B: [laughs] what do you mean by that?

S: I mean that I could sort of say to me "you fucking idiot" and then go back saying "ma porca madonna avrai un cervellaccio", something like that you know.

Asked by the interviewer whether he can express anger with the same ease in his different languages, Chris (German L1, English L2, French L3, Spanish L4), who has been living for a year in the UK, explains that strong emotion can block his speech production in English L2:

B: Can you express the same?
C: Certainly not
B: So why not?
C: Because the situations you have to react very rapidly and you don't have the vocabulary and it's not ready often.
B: In English.
C: Yeah in English...yeah so...your feelings may prevent you from saying anything because you are too emotional.
B: OK, so when you're emotional you don't control your languages.
C: Yeah yeah yeah you're more...you're blocked.

CS to L2 in emotional exchanges

Finally, some participants declared at first in their interviews that the L1 was the preferred language to express emotions in, however, after a little probing by the interviewer, Tomomi (Japanese L1, English L2, Italian L3, Spanish L4, married to an Italian but still dominant in Japanese) revealed a much more complex reality:

B: When you are angry, which language do you use to express your anger?
T: To who?
B: Ah well, suppose you're alone, like you bump into...
T: I'm by myself?
B: Yeah.
T: Ah, I think, in Japanese.
B: Ah-ah. And if you're writing to friends, like bilingual friends, and you're angry, do you prefer to use English or it, or Japanese, or Italian?
T: I think um...I think Japanese or English, but no Italian.
B: OK. So um, why do you prefer English or Japanese? Do you prefer English or Japanese, and why?
T: Because it's comfortable for me, first, and I can express more what I feel, like you know Italian I can, but it's not like English or Japanese.
B: Ah-ah. But you have no problems expressing your anger in English?
T: English yeah, I think. But maybe if I want to you know, if I wanna express more deep then it's better in Japanese, but I feel like Japanese

> language is not really straight, so if if I wanna show really anger to somebody it's much better in English actually.
>
> B: I see. OK, so if you're really really angry you may prefer English because it's more direct?
>
> T: Yeah.
>
> B: I see. And ... so, so, do you swear?
>
> T: I don't, no, never, in any language

Michelle (Chinese L1, English L2) reflects on her language choices when asked by the interviewer whether she switches to English for swearing. She reports using mild English swearwords in Chinese conversations.

When the interviewer inquires about the reasons for this CS to English, Michelle answers that it is a cultural thing, namely that it is much more acceptable to use "mild" swearwords in English than in Chinese:

> M: I just think English is much more, if you like if you speak something like emotions in Chinese sometimes, you don't feel so comfortable but I think that's a cultural reason, it's not because of the language itself, of course I can say those words but I don't intend to do that so much, although I do, that's because my personality I think, ehm I try to be quite transparent to my friends you know, also my family, but English is something about English I find easier to express, but I think that could be cultural not because of language.

Dorothea (Serbian L1, English L2) explains to the interviewer that she is perfectly at ease in using either her L1 with her mother or her L2 with her partner to talk about emotional topics without CS. However, she admits that occasionally she may switch to her L2 when using her L1:

> D: Most of my time I speak English, because my partner is English, then I do think about emotional issues and expressing emotional issues very often in English, so um sometimes when I want to say something the English way of putting it comes, and because I know they would understand it I just put it that way, but most of the conversation and most emotional discussions would be in Serbian, and you know I don't normally don't have problems expressing myself in Serbian but sometimes an English phrase will just come because, yeah I'm thinking about emotions particularly.

Consistent use of L1 or L2 in emotional exchanges

Miho (Japanese L1, English L2, Thai L3, German L4, dominant in L1 and L2) explains that she prefers English to express strong emotions but that she sticks to either English or Japanese if the interlocutor is not bilingual. She is a bit lost when asked what she would say in Japanese to express anger, and explains that she would communicate her feelings non-verbally, which happens to be the L1 way to express anger:

B: You use English, OK. And you're angry at a bilingual friend, which language do you use?
M: Bilingual, oh, English
B: English. And you're angry at a Japanese friend who doesn't understand English, which language do you use?
M: Um, Japanese.
B: Ah-ah.
M: but I don't know how to say.
B: [laughs]
M: [laughs]
B: So what do you say?
M: I just show angry face?
B: Ah ah.
M: Yeah.
B: OK. You don't use English?
M: No.

Dagmar (German dialect L1, German L2, English L3) explains that she does not engage in CS to either the L1 or the L2 when talking about emotions:

B: When you are saying something in English and you can't find the appropriate word for describing an emotion, would you use a first language word?
D: Like if I would use, if I was speaking English and I couldn't find a word in English then I would use a German word?
B: Yeah or provide a kind of description of this German word
D: No, generally I would try to reword it, like and and because, no I wouldn't, I mean I would generally, and I've never been, in English I've never been um in that kind of situation when I wanna to express I'm like angry or sad or happy or in love or whatever yeah? so so this doesn't really occur to me.

Discussion

The quantitative analysis revealed that self-reported CS is most frequent when talking about personal or emotional topics with known interlocutors (friends or colleagues) and is significantly less frequent when talking about neutral topics to strangers or to larger audiences. I suggested that the reasons for this might be quite simple. Once the speaker knows which languages the interlocutor masters – information that is typically shared by friends and colleagues – the speaker may choose to resort to CS to establish a common multilingual identity or to create specific illocutionary effects.

Pavlenko (2005) suggests that in emotional interactions multilinguals need quick access to the largest and richest linguistic arsenal, typically in their dominant or most proficient language.

I have argued that a highly emotionally aroused speaker might become more self-centred and momentarily diverge from the shared language. Grosjean (personal communication) suggests that the Complementarity Principle could also explain, in part, which language is used when expressing emotions (i.e. does the bilingual have the vocabulary needed to do so in the "wrong" language?). He thinks (p.c.) that a lack of vocabulary may force bilinguals to revert back to the other language when expressing their emotions. It is also possible that the emotion vocabulary is present in both languages, but that the speaker may be aware of the non-equivalence of emotion concepts in both languages. A realisation that the emotion concepts in the weaker language may be incomplete (Pavlenko, 2008a), combined with possible gaps in the prototypical scripts, may push the speaker to switch to the language in which emotion concepts are more complete, where the emotionality and valence of an emotion word – or an emotion-laden word – are known and where they will have the intended illocutionary effects (Dewaele, 2008b, 2008c). This would explain why many participants said that their stronger language felt more appropriate for conveying strong emotion. Emotional outbursts may thus happen in the other language. It is also possible that the emotional arousal might disturb the equilibrium of the language mode, where a highly activated background language may momentarily be selected for processing. Sudden emotional arousal may also activate expressions with the highest emotional resonance, typically in the strongest language. I also wondered whether this type of sudden CS might result from a brief drop in the inhibitory control of the background languages.

The effect of sociobiographical variables on self-reported CS turned out some surprising and some more predictable results. Female participants reported more CS with friends and on more emotional topics, while male participants reported more CS with strangers. This finding is consistent with earlier research showing that women describe themselves as more emotionally intense when emotionality is defined as a global disposition (cf. Barrett et al., 2000). The higher frequency of CS among males when speaking with strangers could be interpreted as an indication of less willingness to accommodate the interlocutor in language choice.

The finding of a positive correlation between the participants' ages and the frequency of self-reported CS when speaking to colleagues, in public and when discussing neutral as well as – to a lesser extent – personal and emotional matters is harder to explain. Age might be linked to a specific type of professional interaction with members of other speech communities for which CS is an accepted practice. However, that does not explain why the link is also significant in personal and emotional interactions. It is also a result opposite to that uncovered in Gardner-Chloros, McEntee-Atalianis and Finnis (2005), in which younger bilinguals reported more positive attitudes toward CS compared to older participants.

More highly educated participants also reported more CS on certain topics with certain interlocutors, which could reflect the more international nature of their profession. A closer look at the effect of profession (categorised as language-related or not) confirmed that CS was more frequent among participants in language-related professions in their interactions with strangers and colleagues and in public speech. No such effect emerged for interactions with friends, or in conversations about neutral, personal or emotional topics. The same pattern emerged for the variable "number of languages known": participants knowing more languages reported more CS in interactions with strangers and colleagues. Knowing more languages increases the probability of finding interlocutors sharing several languages. Language dominance also emerged as an important predictor of CS. Multidominant participants reported higher levels of CS with all interlocutors except strangers and on all conversation topics compared to monodominant multilinguals. A separate analysis was carried out on the groups of monodominant and multidominant participants in order to find out whether the effects of interlocutor and topics of conversation remained significant within these two subgroups. This turned out to be the case.

Two correlation analyses were carried out to check whether the independent variables might have been linked to another variable. A first analysis showed that no relationship exists between education level and oral competence in the various languages. A second analysis showed that higher levels of self-perceived competence in the L2 and L3 were linked to a higher frequency of CS, especially in interactions with known interlocutors about personal or emotional matters, which was interpreted as an indication that CS is favoured by highly proficient multilinguals.

An analysis of the narratives of 20 participants shows that CS can allow multilinguals to feel at ease in both neutral and emotional interactions. The feedback from Stefanie and Zelideth suggests that CS contributes to the establishment of a common ground and a common identity with an interlocutor. CS fulfils many functions in the multilingual repertoire: for Darrin, CS indicates an emotional topic coming up or can be indicative of an emotional state. Participants like Vally also reported that CS can soften the impact of emotion words and expressions allowing her to talk about painful topics, much as Javier and Marcos (1989) reported. For Jane and Elena, CS communicates an air of playfulness and can have a comic effect. For Silvia, CS to the L1 when swearing to herself comes as a complement to the swearwords already uttered in the L2.

For some participants, like Chris, strong emotional arousal can block the output in the L2. The only solution in that situation is CS to the L1, even if the interlocutor does not know that language (Andrew, Sophia and Cristina), as could be expected following Grosjean's Complementarity Principle. This phenomenon of expressing anger in the L1 to a partner who does not know that language also emerged from the data in the BEQ (see the Chapter 7). Grosjean (p.c.) remarked that it is intriguing that CS can happen from a monolingual language mode. Indeed, verbal understanding "breaks down" at the moment of CS (the interlocutor does not understand the words being spoken), but communication does not (the power of the emotion is carried by the other language and by a host of prosodic and non-verbal cues). It does not matter in that case that the interlocutor (typically a partner) does not speak or understand that language.

Some participants, often of Asian origin like Tomomi and Michelle, reported CS in the opposite direction, especially for the expression of anger. CS to English allows them to escape from the social constraint that weighs on them in Japanese and Chinese, where anger cannot be displayed as openly as in English and where swearing carries strong social stigma. Having spent a considerable amount of time in the UK and being highly fluent in English, Tomomi and Michelle are probably multicompetent biculturals, aware of the differences between the L1 norms and the English norms. Their practice for expressing anger is thus somewhere in the middle between L1 norms and English L2 norms. Tomomi likes the directness of English for the expression of anger but would never swear. Michelle and her Chinese friends report CS to English for swearing, but they use euphemisms rather than the actual English swearwords.

Some participants, like Dagmar and Miho, reported suppressing CS in emotional exchanges and sticking to the language of the interlocutor. Miho added an interesting nuance, explaining that she would display anger in the Japanese way (i.e. non-verbally) with a monolingual Japanese speaker and verbally in her English L2 with another English-speaker, but that she would definitely code-switch to English in emotional interactions with other Japanese-English bilinguals.

In sum, these observations seem to fit in nicely with Grosjean's (2001) concept of language modes and his Complementarity Principle. According to the language knowledge of the interlocutor, speakers can function in either monolingual or bilingual language mode. Although Grosjean has considered a range of variables that could affect language mode (2001), especially language dominance (Grosjean, 2008), he has not considered emotional arousal. I thus suggest that emotional arousal affects language mode. When a topic becomes more personal and emotional, participants may prefer to use certain languages that the interlocutor would not understand. As a result they can find themselves torn between languages, and seem to move automatically into bilingual or trilingual language mode.

This does not necessarily mean that they automatically start CS, only that the background languages become more activated, increasing the probability of an occasional CS.

The typical preference for the L1 to communicate emotion in can enter into conflict with the need to stick to the L2 because the interlocutor does not share the speaker's L1. Strong emotional arousal might either activate a background language or wreck the inhibition of it, thus allowing it temporarily to become the output language. This instance of CS would thus be non-strategic and probably uncontrolled. It thus seems that strong emotions can disturb the balance of the language modes, leading to increased CS.

Summing up

The present chapter is the first large-scale investigation on self-reported CS patterns combining data obtained through a questionnaire with those obtained through in-depth interviews. The two-pronged quantitative and qualitative approach allowed me to establish general trends about self-reported CS in a very large sample of adult multilinguals, and also to focus in more detail on the metalinguistic comments of participants. The picture that emerges from the analyses shows that strong emotional arousal can disturb the position on the language mode continuum and can alter habitual language choices.

The quantitative analysis revealed that the topic of conversation is significantly linked to the frequency of self-reported CS. More specifically, the frequency of self-reported CS was found to be much lower when speaking about neutral topics compared to personal or emotional topics. In terms of Grosjean's language mode theory, I have argued that a higher emotional arousal could force a bilingual speaker out of his/her monolingual mode into a bilingual or trilingual language mode. The sudden emotional avalanche needs to be verbalised quickly, and the speaker may realise that his/her emotion concepts are incomplete in the weaker language (Pavlenko, 2008a, 2008b), which might result in unwanted illocutionary effects. Rather than trying to steer the wave of emotion through the bottleneck of the weaker language, the emotions "spill over" and get verbalised in whatever language allows the speaker channel his/her feelings in a satisfactory manner. The strong emotional state of the speaker probably also affects his/her executive control over language choice. As a result, the activation/inhibition of certain languages is no longer under strict control, and unplanned CS happens.

The statistical analysis also revealed a significant effect of the interlocutor on the frequency of self-reported CS. Self-reported CS was found to be much more frequent in interactions with known interlocutors than with unknown or multiple interlocutors. This difference is likely to be the result of conscious, strategic choices of the speaker. If the speaker is not aware of the languages she/he shares with the interlocutor(s), the most logical option is to stick to the language in which the interaction was started. On the other hand, if the speaker is aware of the languages shared with the interlocutor, CS may happen more freely with a multitude of effects.

Individual variation in the frequency of self-reported CS was found often to be linked to gender, age, education level, profession, number of languages known and type of language dominance.

Finally, the analysis of the narratives of the participants confirmed the general trends uncovered in the quantitative analyses, while adding rich information about the reasons for the CS with certain interlocutors and its direction. As reported in previous chapters, CS is strongly linked to the perceived emotionality of the multilinguals' languages and hence allows the speaker to create a range of illocutionary effects. The preferred direction of the CS in situations where strong emotion had to be expressed was from the LX to the L1. Some participants reported CS in the opposite direction, typically to overcome social constraints on the overt expression of emotion in their L1. A few participants also reported that emotional arousal did not cause CS and that they maintained the habitual language of interaction with their interlocutor.

11
Concluding Remarks

I propose briefly to recapitulate and reflect on the main findings now that I have come to the end of a complex set of analyses on the effects of independent variables related to the history of learning an LX and its present use, as well as the effects of sociobiographical and psychological factors on dependent variables reflecting self-perceived competence in the LX, self-reported frequency of its use for communicating emotion, perception of it and communicative anxiety in using it.

A recapitulation

The first part of hypothesis 1 concerned the monotonic decline from L1 to L5 in self-perceived competence, frequency of language use for the communication of emotion, attitude and perception scores. The second part of the hypothesis predicted a monotonic increase in CA and FLA values from L1 to L5. The hypothesis was fully confirmed. Friedman's ANOVA tests showed that values decreased significantly from the L1 to the L5 for the variables covered by the first part of the hypothesis and increased significantly from the L1 to the L5 for the anxiety scores. This finding needs to be interpreted with caution. It suggests that for our sample of multilinguals – two-thirds of whom claimed to be dominant in one language (typically the L1) – the dominant language stands out from the others on a range of dependent variables. The feedback to the open questions and the interview data add a useful nuance to the quantitative finding, namely that for a minority of participants the L1 was no longer the dominant language, nor the preferred language to communicate emotions in. This fact adds an important nuance to "the popular and oversimplified assumption that in late bilingualism, L1 is always the language of emotions and LX the language of distance or detachment" (Pavlenko, 2004: 200). It means that the emotional preponderance of the L1 does not reflect a law of nature, but is rather a reflection of the probability that multilinguals often remain dominant in their L1, as was the case for a large majority in the present sample.

Hypotheses 2 to 9 cover so many different variables in so many languages that it might be good to present the following general overview of the number of significant effects ($p < .05$) that emerged between independent and dependent variables for the L2, L3, L4 and L5 (Table 70). The first value in a case thus shows the total number of significant values for the four languages, followed by the total number of cases. The first case in the table, the effect of AoA on self-perceived competence, shows 14/16, which means that a significant effect of AoA was found for 14 out of 16 cases (i.e. 4 skills × 4 languages), largely confirming the hypothesis.

The statistical analyses revealed that events at the beginning (AoA) and during the language learning process (context of acquisition) reverberate for years in multilinguals' linguistic behaviour, the perception they have of their LX, their self-perceived competence and their FLA.

The effect of AoA was most consistent across all languages for self-perceived competence in oral and written skills, with early starters reporting higher levels of competence in the four skills. The effect of AoA was slightly more scattered for the communication of emotions, perception and FLA, but it was typically significant in more than half of the cases. Early starters tended to use the LX more frequently to communicate emotions; they rated the positive characteristics of the LX higher and felt less anxious when using it. This finding needs to be interpreted with caution, as the lower AoA may be linked to other factors – such as LX socialisation, frequency of use of the LX or length of LX instruction – that are the ultimate cause of the observed variation.

The effect of context of acquisition is consistently significant on our dependent variables. Languages that have been learnt only through formal classroom instruction are less frequently used to communicate emotions than languages that were learnt naturalistically or were also used to communicate outside the classroom. The same pattern emerged for self-perceived

Table 70 The number of significant relationships ($p < .05$) between independent and dependent variables in the LX out of the total number of cases

	Competence	Feelings	Anger	Perception	FLA
AoA	14/16	8/16	14/24	11/24	11/20
Context	16/16	16/16	24/24	17/24	20/20
Frequency	20/20	16/16	24/24	18/24	20/20
Socialisation	16/16	16/16	24/24	12/24	20/20
Networks	13/16	13/16	19/24	11/24	15/20
More Ls	12/12	6/12	8/18	10/18	15/15
TEI	0/16	0/16	2/24	4/24	16/20
Gender	8/16	4/16	7/24	2/24	2/20
Age	8/16	0/16	3/24	4/24	14/20
Education	7/16	3/16	4/24	6/24	9/20

competence in the four skills and FLA in different situations: instructed learners felt less competent and more anxious than mixed and naturalistic learners. The fact that context of acquisition does resonate for years after the end of the active "learning phase" is, however, remarkable. Maybe this is because context of acquisition roughly equates with the type and intensity of exposure to an LX and the opportunity to use it in authentic interactions. If contact with an LX had been limited to the classroom, a user's stylistic range and emotion scripts would inevitably be more limited compared to others who have experienced and used the language in a wider variety of situations. Emotion scripts and emotion vocabulary rarely figure in second language textbooks. When they are, they tend to be polite and emasculated. Loaded expressions, especially if they are vulgar or slang, are banned from the classroom because of their offensive character. Participants reported experiencing difficulties in expressing nuanced emotions in languages they solely or mainly learned at school. The data of the present study offer support for the "emotional contexts of learning" hypothesis put forth by Harris, et al., (2006), which posits that a language learned, or habitually used, in an authentic context may have acquired a stronger emotional resonance than languages learnt in the classroom only.

The next cluster of independent variables covered the present use of the various languages. One of the strongest variables in this cluster was "frequency of use of the LX". Unsurprisingly, it turned out to have a significant effect in every LX for the choice of language to express emotions, for FLA and for most of the "perception" variables. This suggests that the more frequently an LX is used, the higher the probability that it will be used for both non-emotional and emotional speech. Participants also pointed out in the interviews that after years of regular use of the LX they no longer felt worried about possible grammatical or pronunciation mistakes or of the reactions of their interlocutors.

A similar pattern emerged for the effect of LX socialisation. This variable reflects a trajectory rather than an event in the participant's life, namely the increased use of an LX compared to the L1. The analyses and the feedback from participants showed that language preferences for emotional expression, perception of the languages and FLA do evolve as LX users becomes more socialised in an LX. In other words, the LX can become the most emotional language, and this was the case for participants who reported shifts in language preference linked to new partners or simply to the fact of having moved to a different country and, subsequently, having acculturated to the new language and culture. The effect of socialisation was less consistent on perception of the characteristics of the LX. This suggests that usage precedes feelings in the LX. In other words, a highly socialised LX user may be perfectly capable of communicating emotions in an LX, feeling both competent and confident in using it, but it takes years before the positive language characteristics and emotional strength of swearwords in the LX will equal those of the L1. Participants confirmed that it is often only after decades of living in an LX environment that they dared to use some of the swearwords in that language, and even then only the mild ones. Feedback also showed considerable variation between individuals, with cultural background playing an important role in the perception and use of emotional language.

The final variable in the cluster reflecting present use of the various languages is "networks of interlocutors", which was also found in most cases to have a significant effect on language choice. It was also linked to perception and FLA. This suggests that participants who have a large network of interlocutors in an LX will be more likely to use it for the communication of emotions, and that their perceptions and FLA will evolve toward that of the interlocutors. The interviews also revealed that some participants maintain different networks for their different languages. Some expatriates kept in regular contact with other compatriots and reported a lot of CS between the L1 and the LX at their meetings.

The third cluster of variables focused on the sociobiographical and psychological variables. The significant relationships between these independent variables and the dependent variables were more scattered. One of the strongest variables in this cluster turned out to be the number of languages spoken by participants. Those knowing more languages were found to be consistently less anxious in using an LX and felt more competent. This also had an effect in over half of the cases for the communication of emotion and the perception of the characteristics of the LX, with a tendency for the pentalinguals to use the LX more often to express emotion and to judge it more positively, especially the strength of its swearwords.

Trait Emotional Intelligence had only a very limited effect on self-perceived competence, language choice and perception but was more consistently significant in relation to FLA. Participants who scored high on Trait Emotional Intelligence reported lower levels of FLA across situations, which could be ascribed to the fact that these individuals possess a strong belief in their ability to communicate in different languages while regulating their stress levels. These individuals seem to be able to control their FLA by remaining optimistic and confident in their ability to communicate. Moreover, their capacity to judge the emotional state of their interlocutor and to empathise means that they are more aware of how successful they are, and are able to adapt their linguistic behaviour if necessary (Dewaele, Petrides and Furnham, 2008).

The relatively low number of consistent effects for gender, age and education suggest that these factors explain relatively little variance in the data.

The analysis of participants' comments suggests that the communication of emotion covers a wide range of speech acts, which vary according to the home culture; yelling can be acceptable for the expression of anger in southern Europe, but it is taboo in Asia. Multilinguals have a unique capacity to navigate between the taboos and sociopragmatics norms. By using CS with other multilinguals, they can avoid upsetting interlocutors, using words in a language that has less emotionality. They can thus use their multi-competence to develop multilingual speech acts and emotion scripts that are quite unique to them, or are shared by their partner, family or ethnic group. They can also do so with relative confidence thanks to their ability to navigate the treacherous waters of intercultural emotion communication. Participants reported that speech acts and emotion scripts are not static but reflect the changes in their linguistic environment. It is also likely that a growing awareness of sociocultural and sociopragmatic norms in an LX contributes to an evolution in the LX user's repertoire for expressing emotions in it (Pavlenko, 2005).

The chapter on self-reported CS in the BEQ and in the *Multilingual Lives* corpus showed that CS seems to be much more frequent when talking about more emotional topics with familiar interlocutors compared to neutral topics being discussed with unknown interlocutors. An analysis of the feedback to the open questions in the web questionnaire and the interview data confirmed the findings of the quantitative analysis while adding rich detail about the multiple reasons behind CS, as well as its direction. It seems that multilinguals may prefer to talk about certain topics in certain languages (Complementarity Principle) and can use CS strategically. However, in some instances strong emotional arousal can force the speaker from monolingual into bilingual language mode with more CS (Grosjean, 2001, 2008).

Implications for teaching

While no direct implications for teaching can be drawn from the findings, as no experimental design was used to gauge the effect of various teaching methods on the communication of emotion, nor on the emotions underlying teaching and learning, a number of tentative, indirect implications can be formulated.

First, LX users who had learned a language only through formal instruction had a clear disadvantage compared to those who had combined classroom learning and authentic interaction or had learned the language naturalistically.

Could the lower use of the LX to communicate emotions in later life be linked to the absence in LX teaching material of emotional discourse? It thus seems imperative to introduce learners to the communication of various emotions in the LX, including both positive and negative emotions. Moreover, as the vocabulary of emotions and emotion scripts differ from language to language, and culture to culture, it seems doubly important to focus on the differences and similarities between the L1(s) and the LX. Emotion-free LX classes do not prepare LX learners to become proficient LX users.

Language teachers need to be aware that the cultural/typological distance between the learners' L1(s) and the LX is an important obstacle to mastery of emotional speech. The research by Rintell (1984) and Graham, Hamblin and Feldstein (2001) shows that learners from cultures that are relatively further from the target culture experience significantly greater difficulties in identifying emotion in an LX and in judging its intensity compared to fellow learners with similar levels of proficiency. Being able to judge the interlocutor's emotional state is crucial for successful communication (Rintell, 1984). It will also add to sense of competence in the LX and to lower levels of FLA. Foreign language teaching thus needs to broaden the emotional range of the linguistic input. It seems crucial to go beyond a literal decoding of text and speech in an LX to include the reading of the interlocutor's face and an awareness of vocal cues, body language, situation, interlocutors, etc. There seems to be a growing awareness among applied linguists and foreign language teachers that foreign language learning is more than the acquisition of a tool for communication with allophones. Through foreign language classes, learners identify and start to grasp the norms and values for a TL culture. In short, learners develop emotional "intercultural competence" (Byram, 1997). They develop a critical understanding of sociocultural norms, culturally derived attitudes, beliefs, ways of thinking and ways of communicating (Byram, 1997). This learning process alters their view of the world, their sense of self and their personality profile (Dewaele and van Oudenhoven, 2009; Dewaele and Li Wei, 2012, 2013a). Byram (2009) points out that foreign language teachers should be encouraged to stimulate "tertiary socialisation" among the learners, namely to "help learners to understand new concepts (beliefs, values and behaviours) through the acquisition of a new language, new concepts which, being juxtaposed with those of the learners' other language(s), challenge the taken-for-granted nature of their existing concepts" (p. 203). As a result, learners would develop social identities unconstrained by their dominant language(s), which would be more internationally oriented: "a sense of belonging to one or more transnational social groups" (p. 203). The description fits the participants of the BEQ and the *Multilingual Lives* interview corpus quite well. They were almost always proud of their multilingualism and multicompetence, their open-mindedness and their intercultural experience and thus clearly belonged to what Kramsch calls the "Third Culture", namely "a symbolic place that is by no means unitary, stable, permanent and homogeneous. Rather it is, like subject positions in post-structuralist theory, multiple, always subject to change and the tensions and even conflicts that come from being 'in-between'" (Kramsch, 2009: 238).

Another implication of the findings is that practice matters in developing the ability to communicate emotions. Role-plays and experiences of authentic communication might enhance the learners' understanding of the communication of emotion. Evans and Fisher (2005) showed that even short exchange visits (up to 11 days) of British schoolchildren to France lead to significant increases in their use of expressive language. Longer stays abroad have the potential to have even greater effects on an LX user's ability to communicate emotions appropriately. A certain amount of LX socialisation seems to be the prerequisite for the communication of emotion (Dewaele, 2011c; Kinginger, 2008, 2009).

LX learners/users who have managed authentic communication in the LX have sharpened their judgements on sociopragmatic norms and on appropriateness. They may also have become more aware of the multiplicity of norms linked to contextual factors. They may have become better at making subjective appraisals in the course of an interaction, and revising them if necessary. Their understanding of the norms also makes them better able to violate the norms if necessary, doing so in an appropriate way.

Should LX teachers encourage the learning and use of swearwords in the LX? Should course books contain lists of emotion-laden words and expressions with ratings of their intensity? These are difficult pedagogical if not ethical questions: just what and how much of it should be taught to learners? Should these include the many synonyms in the LX referring to genitals and sexual behaviour? Can words with racist connotations be taught?

One could argue that knowledge of these words and expressions constitutes an essential part of sociocultural competence in an LX and that they should be taught with the necessary words of caution. However, teachers, and authors of course books, who included these emotion-laden words and expressions might become the target of angry parents and the press. I pointed out in Dewaele (2005c) that it is hard to imagine course books with a red warning sticker "offensive texts, not appropriate for under-18s" or, as BBC presenters warn viewers, "you may find some of the expressions in this book offensive". Yet, can teachers remain silent about a vibrant and crucial part of and LX and its culture?

Personally, I think it is possible to prepare learners to a certain extent for the communication of emotion. By using authentic material such as film extracts learners can learn how to combine words with body language, vocal cues, gestures, common collocations, and so on (Planchenault, 2005). Another means is through role-plays in the language classroom. I feel that emotion-laden words and expressions need to be explained in the LX classroom with the necessary warnings about their offensive character. Learners need to understand these words and expressions, but not necessarily use them.

This leads to a second ethical question that merits more attention in SLA, namely learner "resistance" towards cultural assimilation and problems of cultural stereotyping on the part of both learner and members of the LX culture (Kinginger, 2008; Ohara, 2002; Siegal, 1996). The LX teacher expects learners to acquire an LX and gradually approximate NS norms. This can be difficult if it involves a conflict with the learner's presentation of self and face. LX users may be aware of the sociopragmatic and sociocultural norms of an LX, but they may decide that they are in conflict with their own beliefs and hence consciously deviate from the NS norm when they become LX users. I am, for example aware of the ambiguous nature of "piropos" in Spain. Some male Spanish friends describe it as friendly banter in which males express their admiration for the looks of a female; other friends, both male and female (depending on age, class, education and political persuasion) find "piropos" unacceptable and offensive. Coming from a culture where this type of speech act is considered inappropriate, I would never utter a single piropo in Spain.

Some LX users may overcome an initial unwillingness to conform to NS norms after realising that an approach modelled on their L1 was unsuccessful. Evans (1988) quotes a British student who had spent a semester in Italy declaring: "The Italians are so different, and if they want something they will go out and get it. I've been taught that you ask for it politely. You realize that unless you do what they do, shout, nothing will come out of it" (Evans, 1988: 45). This is a nice illustration of "tertiary socialisation", namely the coexistence of different sets of pragmatic norms, to be mobilised according to the context in which the interaction takes place.

Strengths and limitations

Research designs are incomplete by nature. In other words, the phenomena under consideration in social sciences are always larger and more complex than can be captured in a single research design. It is thus inevitable that only a glimpse of a multifaceted reality can be provided.

However, I feel that by combining questionnaires with open and closed questions from more than 1500 multilingual participants and in-depth interviews with 20 participants sufficient data could be gathered to answer the initial research questions.

The present design is unique in that it enquired about the various languages of multilinguals. As the BEQ sample consisted of 323 bilinguals, 376 trilinguals, 377 quadrilinguals and 503 pentalinguals, feedback was gathered from 323 × 2, 376 × 3, 377 × 4, 503 × 5 language learning and usage experiences, which totals 646 + 1128 + 1508 + 2515 = 5797 opinions and information about individual languages, including the L1s, which could be linked to a range of independent variables reflecting language learning history, present language use and the participants' socioprofessional and psychological background. The large amount of data allowed me to use statistical techniques to uncover relationships between dependent and independent variables. However, because the dependent variables were generally not normally distributed, I had to resort to less powerful, non-parametric techniques. As a result it became impossible to judge the amount of variance explained by individual independent variables, and it was impossible to use regression analyses, which could have allowed me to check whether all independent variables remained significant when they were entered simultaneously into an analysis.

Another limitation of the present design is that data were collected at a single point in time, thus presenting a snapshot of an on-going evolution. This cross-sectional design does not allow the capture of change in participants' feedback. The open questions and interviews partly remedied this problem, as participants often spontaneously reported how their language practices had evolved over time, and how their self-perceived competence and FLA had evolved over the years.

Questionnaires also have inherent limitations, as a compromise needs to be found between the amount of detail sought and the total length of the questionnaire (Dörnyei, 2003). As a result, only general trends could be identified and the reasons why some participants deviated from these patterns remained open to discussion. The open questions and the in-depth interviews did partially allow me to overcome this problem, and to understand why some participants differed from the average.

A clear strength of the present design is that most participants had finished school some time earlier and were functioning as legitimate LX users. This population is thus quite different from the typical research designs that focus on children or young adults still engaged in learning an LX. The disadvantage, of which we were aware when putting the BEQ online, is that memories about the language learning process may have faded somewhat and it is probably difficult to remember one's attitudes and motivation for studying an LX. The data from the BEQ are therefore less suited to investigating the interplay of factors in the LX learning process, but they are perfect for looking at the post-learning phase, namely how authentic LX users use their languages in daily life and how they feel about them.

Appendix

Dewaele, J.-M. and Pavlenko, A. (2001–2003) Web questionnaire *Bilingualism and Emotions*. University of London.

Bilingualism and Emotions

Preferences

Please choose one of the options listed below to indicate how you would prefer us to proceed with the information you supply

Give you credit if we cite you in our work.

Use your responses but to keep your name and other identifying information confidential.

Use your responses in our analysis but not to quote them in any work that may appear in press.

Background Information

All information will be kept confidential. If you would rather not identify yourself, please use random initials and a number, e.g., AV38.

1. Name
2. Contact address (preferably e-mail)
3. Gender
4. Age
5. Education level (highest diploma or degree)
6. Which ethnic group/community do you belong to or most identify with
7. Occupation/Profession
8. Is your occupation related to your bilingualism or languages in any way

____

Linguistic information

9. Which **languages** do you know and what order did you learn them in? Was acquisition **naturalistic** (outside of school), **instructed** (at school), or both?

Language	Age at which you started learning the language	Context of Acquisition
1st LANGUAGE (L1)		
2nd LANGUAGE (L2)		
3rd LANGUAGE (L3)		
4th LANGUAGE (L4)		
5th LANGUAGE (L5)		

10. Which do you consider to be your dominant language(s)? _____
11. What language(s) does your partner speak?

____

12. On the scale from 1 (least proficient) to 5 (fully fluent) how do you rate yourself in speaking, understanding, reading, writing in all of the languages in question?

	Speaking	**Comprehension**	**Reading**	**Writing**
L1				
L2				
L3				
L4				
L5				

---

13. How frequently do you use each of the languages and with whom? Never=0, every year=1, every month=2, every week=3, every day=4, several hours a day=5)

	With whom	**Frequency**
L1		
L2		
L3		
L4		
L5		

---

14. Which language (s) do you use for mental calculations/arithmetic? (Click where appropriate)

	Never	**Rarely**	**Sometimes**	**Frequently**	**All the time**	**Not applicable**
L1						
L2						
L3						
L4						
L5						

---

15. Do you switch between languages within a conversation with certain people? (Click where appropriate)

	Never	**Rarely**	**Sometimes**	**Frequently**	**All the time**	**Not applicable**
When speaking with friends and family						
When speaking with strangers						
When speaking in public						
At work						

---

16. Do you switch between languages when talking about certain matters? (Click where appropriate)

	Never	**Rarely**	**Sometimes**	**Frequently**	**All the time**	**Not applicable**
When speaking about neutral matters						
When speaking about personal matters						
When speaking about emotional matters						

If you have **no** children click here and go to **question 20**

17. If you have children, what language do you typically use with:
    a) the oldest? (Click where appropriate)

	Never	**Rarely**	**Sometimes**	**Frequently**	**All the time**	**Not applicable**
L1						
L2						
L3						
L4						
L5						

b) the youngest? (Click where appropriate)

	Never	**Rarely**	**Sometimes**	**Frequently**	**All the time**	**Not applicable**
L1						
L2						
L3						
L4						
L5						

---

18. What language do you favor in scolding or disciplining them? (Click where appropriate)

	Never	**Rarely**	**Sometimes**	**Frequently**	**All the time**	**Not applicable**
L1						
L2						
L3						
L4						
L5						

---

19. What language do you select for praise and/or intimate conversations with them? (Click where appropriate)

	Never	**Rarely**	**Sometimes**	**Frequently**	**All the time**	**Not applicable**
L1						
L2						
L3						
L4						
L5						

Languages and Emotions

20. Here are some **subjective statements** about the languages you know. Please mark to what extent they correspond to your own perceptions. There are no right or wrong answers. (Click where appropriate)

Which is your first language? _____

	Not at all	**Somewhat**	**More or less**	**To a large extent**	**Absolutely**
My L1 is useful					
My L1 is colourful					
My L1 is rich					
My L1 is poetic					

My L1 is emotional
My L1 is cold

Which is your 2nd language? _____

	Not at all	Somewhat	More or less	To a large extent	Absolutely
My L2 is useful					
My L2 is colourful					
My L2 is rich					
My L2 is poetic					
My L2 is emotional					
My L2 is cold					

Which is your 3rd language? _____

	Not at all	Somewhat	More or less	To a large extent	Absolutely
My L3 is useful					
My L3 is colourful					
My L3 is rich					
My L3 is poetic					
My L3 is emotional					
My L3 is cold					

Which is your 4th language? _____

	Not at all	Somewhat	More or less	To a large extent	Absolutely
My L4 is useful					
My L4 is colourful					
My L4 is rich					
My L4 is poetic					
My L4 is emotional					
My L4 is cold					

Which is your 5th language? _____

	Not at all	Somewhat	More or less	To a large extent	Absolutely
My L5 is useful					
My L5 is colourful					
My L5 is rich					
My L5 is poetic					
My L5 is emotional					
My L5 is cold					

---

21. If you are **angry**, what language do you typically use to express your anger? (Click where appropriate)

a) When alone

	Never	Rarely	Sometimes	Frequently	All the time	Not applicable
L1						
L2						
L3						
L4						
L5						

b) In letters and e-mail

	Never	Rarely	Sometimes	Frequently	All the time	Not applicable
L1						
L2						
L3						
L4						
L5						

c) When talking to friends

	Never	Rarely	Sometimes	Frequently	All the time	Not applicable
L1						
L2						
L3						
L4						
L5						

d) When talking to parents/partners

	Never	Rarely	Sometimes	Frequently	All the time	Not applicable
L1						
L2						
L3						
L4						
L5						

e) When talking to strangers

	Never	Rarely	Sometimes	Frequently	All the time	Not applicable
L1						
L2						
L3						
L4						
L5						

---

22. If you **swear** in general, what language do you typically swear in? (Click where appropriate)

	Never	Rarely	Sometimes	Frequently	All the time	Not applicable
L1						
L2						
L3						
L4						
L5						

---

23. Do **swear** and **taboo words** in your different languages have the same **emotional weight** for you? (Click where appropriate)

	Not strong	Little	Fairly	Strong	Very strong	Not applicable
L1						
L2						
L3						
L4						
L5						

---

24. What language do you express your **deepest feelings** in? (Click where appropriate)

a) When alone

	Never	Maybe	Probably	Certainly	Without any doubt	Not applicable
L1						
L2						
L3						
L4						
L5						

b) In letters and e-mail

	Never	Maybe	Probably	Certainly	Without any doubt	Not applicable
L1						
L2						
L3						
L4						
L5						

c) When talking to friends

	Never	Maybe	Probably	Certainly	Without any doubt	Not applicable
L1						
L2						
L3						
L4						
L5						

d) When talking to parents/partners

	Never	Maybe	Probably	Certainly	Without any doubt	Not applicable
L1						
L2						
L3						
L4						
L5						

---

25. How **anxious** are you when speaking your different languages with different people in different situations? (Click where appropriate)

	Not at all	A little	Quite anxious	Very anxious	Extremely anxious	Not applicable
When speaking L1 with friends						
When speaking L1 with colleagues						
When speaking L1 with strangers						
When speaking L1 on the telephone						
When speaking L1 in public						

	Not at all	A little	Quite anxious	Very anxious	Extremely anxious	Not applicable
When speaking L2 with friends						
When speaking L2 with colleagues						
When speaking L2 with strangers						
When speaking L2 on the telephone						
When speaking L2 in public						

	Not at all	A little	Quite anxious	Very anxious	Extremely anxious	Not applicable
When speaking L3 with friends						
When speaking L3 with colleagues						
When speaking L3 with strangers						
When speaking L3 on the telephone						
When speaking L3 in public						

	Not at all	A little	Quite anxious	Very anxious	Extremely anxious	Not applicable
When speaking L4 with friends						
When speaking L4 with colleagues						
When speaking L4 with strangers						
When speaking L4 on the telephone						
When speaking L4 in public						

	Not at all	A little	Quite anxious	Very anxious	Extremely anxious	Not applicable
When speaking L5 with friends						
When speaking L5 with colleagues						
When speaking L5 with strangers						
When speaking L5 on the telephone						
When speaking L5 in public						

26. If you form sentences silently **(inner speech)**, what language do you typically use? (Click where appropriate)

	Never	Really	Sometimes	Frequently	All the time	Not applicable
L1						
L2						
L3						
L4						
L5						

27. Does the phrase **"I love you"** have the same emotional weight for you in your different languages? Which language does it feel strongest in?

28. Do you have a **preference** for emotion terms and terms of endearment in one language over all others? Which language is it and why?

29. Do your languages have different **emotional significance** for you? if yes, then how do you see this significance for each language? Is one more appropriate as the language of your emotions than others?

30. If you do write in a **personal diary** – or were to write in one – what language(s) do you or would you use and why?

31. If you were to recall some **bad or difficult memories**, what language would you prefer to discuss them in and why?

32. If you are married to or living with a speaker of a language that is not your L1, what language do you generally use at home? What language do you **argue** in?

33. Do you feel like a **different person** sometimes when you use your different languages?

34. Is it easier or more difficult for you to **talk about emotional topics** in your second or third language? If there is a difference, could you tell us about that and perhaps provide some examples?

35. Do you have any other **comments** and/or suggestions for the authors of this questionnaire?

References

Abello-Contesse, C., Chacon-Beltran, R., Lopez-Jiménez, M. D. and Torreblanca-Lopez, M. M. (eds.) (2006) *Age in L2 Acquisition and Teaching*, Bern: Peter Lang.

Abrahamsson, N. and Hyltenstam, K. (2008) "The robustness of aptitude effects in near-native second language acquisition", *Studies in Second Language Acquisition*, 30 (4): 481–509.

Abrahamsson, N. and Hyltenstam, K. (2009) "Age of onset and nativelikeness in a second language: Listener perception versus linguistic scrutiny", *Language Learning*, 59 (2): 249–306.

Abu-Rabia, S. (2004) "Teachers' role, learners' gender differences, and FL anxiety among seventh-grade students studying English as a FL", *Educational Psychology*, 24 (5): 711–720.

Aida, Y. (1994) "Examination of Horwitz, Horwitz and Cope's construct of foreign language anxiety: The case of students of Japanese", *The Modern Language Journal*, 78: 155–168.

Altarriba, J. (2003) "Does cariño equal 'liking'? A theoretical approach to conceptual nonequivalence between languages", *International Journal of Bilingualism*, 7: 305–322.

Altarriba, J. and Bauer, L. (2004) "The distinctiveness of emotion concepts: A comparison between emotion, abstract, and concrete words", *American Journal of Psychology*, 117: 389–410.

Altarriba, J. and Canary, T. M. (2004) "Affective priming: The automatic activation of arousal", *Journal of Multilingual and Multicultural Development*, 25 (2–3): 248–265.

Altarriba, J. and Santiago-Rivera, A. L. (1994) "Current perspectives on using linguistic and cultural factors in counseling the Hispanic client", *Professional Psychology: Research and Practice*, 25: 388–397.

Amati-Mehler, J., Argentieri, S. and Canestri, J. (1993) *The Babel of the Unconscious: Mother Tongue and Foreign Languages in the Psychoanalytic Dimension* (J. Whitelaw-Cucco, trans.), Madison, CT: International Universities Press.

Anooshian, J. and Hertel, T. (1994) "Emotionality in free recall: Language specificity in bilingual memory", *Cognition and Emotion*, 8: 503–514.

Arnold, J. (2011) 'Attention to affect in language learning', *Anglistik*, 22 (1), 11–22.

Auer, P. (ed) (1998) *Code-Switching in Conversation: Language, Interaction, and Identity*, London/New York: Routledge.

Averill, J. R. (1982) *Anger and Aggression: An Essay on Emotion*, New York: Springer-Verlag.

Ayçiçeği-Dinn, A. and Caldwell-Harris, C. L. (2009) "Emotion memory effects in bilingual speakers: A levels-of-processing approach", *Bilingualism: Language and Cognition*, 12: 291–303.

Baetens Beardsmore, H. (2003) "Who is afraid of bilingualism?", in J.-M. Dewaele, Li Wei, and A. Housen (eds.), *Bilingualism: Beyond Basic Principles*, Clevedon: Multilingual Matters: 10–27.

Baker, C. (2006) *Foundations of Bilingualism and Bilingual Education*, 4th edition, Clevedon: Multilingual Matters.

Baker, S. C. and MacIntyre, P. D. (2000) "The role of gender and immersion in communication and second language orientations", *Language Learning*, 50 (2): 311–341.

Bandura, A. (2002) "Social cognitive theory in cultural context", *Applied Psychology: An International Review,* 51: 269–290.
Barcelos, A. M. F., Kalaja, P. and Menezes, V. (2008) *EFL Narrativized: Learning and Teaching Experiences,* Basingstoke: Palgrave-Macmillan.
Barrett, L. F. (2006) "Are emotions natural kinds?", *Perspectives on Psychological Science,* 1: 28–58.
Barrett, L. F., Lane, R., Sechrest, L. and Schwartz, G. (2000) "Gender differences in emotional awareness", *Personality and Social Psychology Bulletin,* 26: 1027–1035.
Barrett, L. F., Robin, L., Pietromonaco, P. R. and Eyssell, K. M. (1998) "Are women the 'more emotional' sex? Evidence from emotional experiences in social context", *Cognition and Emotion,* 12 (4): 555–578.
Basnight-Brown, D. M. and Altarriba, J. (2007) "Code-switching and code-mixing in bilinguals: Cognitive, developmental, and empirical approaches", in A. Ardila and E. Ramos (eds.), *Speech and Language Disorders in Bilinguals,* Nova Science Publishers: 69–89.
Bayley, R., and Schecter, S. (2003) "Introduction: Towards a dynamic model of language socialization", in R. Bayley and S. R. Schecter (eds.), *Language Socialisation in Bilingual and Multilingual Societies,* Clevedon: Multilingual Matters: 1–6.
Belz, J. A. and Kinginger, C. (2002) "The cross-linguistic development of address form use in telecollaborative language learning: Two case studies", *Canadian Modern Language Review,* 59, 189–214.
Belz, J. A. and Kinginger, C. (2003) "Discourse options and the development of pragmatic competence by classroom learners of German", *Language Learning,* 53: 591–647.
Bernaus, M., Moore, E. and Cordeiro Azevedo, A. (2007) "Affective factors influencing plurilingual students' acquisition of Catalan in a Catalan-Spanish bilingual context", *The Modern Language Journal,* 91 (2): 235–246.
Berthele, R. (2011) "On abduction in receptive multilingualism. Evidence from cognate guessing tasks", *Applied Linguistics Review,* 2: 191–220.
Berthele, R. and Lambelet, A. (2009) "Approche empirique de l'intercompréhension: répertoire, processus et résultats", *Revue de linguistique et de didactique des langues (LIDIL),* 39: 151–162.
Besemeres, M. (2004) "Different languages, different emotions? Perspectives from autobiographical literature", *Journal of Multilingual and Multicultural Development,* 25 (2/3): 140–158.
Bialystok, E. (2002) "Cognitive processes of L2 users", in V. Cook (ed.), *Portraits of the L2 User,* Clevedon: Multilingual Matters: 145–165.
Bialystok E. and Martin M. M. (2004) "Attention and inhibition in bilingual children: evidence from the dimensional change card sort task", *Developmental Science,* 7 (3): 325–339.
Bialystok, E. and Shapero, E. (2005) "Ambiguous benefits: The effect of bilingualism on reversing ambiguous figures", *Developmental Science,* 8 (6): 595–604.
Birdsong, D. (2005) "Interpreting age effects in second language acquisition", in J. F. Kroll and A. M. D. de Groot (eds.), *Handbook of Bilingualism: Psycholinguistic Approaches,* Oxford: Oxford University Press: 109–127.
Birdsong, D. (2007) "Nativelike pronunciation among late learners of French as a second language", in O. S. Bohn and M. Munro (eds.), *Language Experience in Second Language Speech Learning: In honor of James Emil Flege,* Amsterdam: Benjamins: 99–116.

Birdsong, D. (2009) "Age and the end state of Second Language Acquisition", in W. C. Ritchie and T. K. Bhatia (eds.), *The New Handbook of Second Language Acquisition*, Bingley (UK): Emerald: 401–424.

Block, D. (2002) "Destabilized identities across language and cultural borders", *Hong Kong Journal of Applied Linguistics*, 7 (2): 1–19.

Block, D. (2009) "Identity in Applied Linguistics: The need for conceptual exploration", in V. Cook and Li Wei (eds.), *Language Teaching and Learning*, London: Continuum: 215–232.

Bond, M. and Lai, T. (1986) "Embarrassment and code-switching into a second language", *Journal of Social Psychology*, 126: 179–186.

Borg S. (2006) "The distinctive characteristics of foreign language teachers", *Language Teaching Research*, 10, 3–32.

Borod, J. (2000) *The Neuropsychology of Emotion*, London: Oxford University Press.

Bown, J. (2006) "Locus of learning and affective strategy use: Two factors affecting success in self-instructed language learning", *Foreign Language Annals*, 39: 640–659.

Bown, J. and White, C. J. (2010) "Affect in a self-regulatory framework for language learning", *System*, 38 (3): 432–443.

Brackett, M. A., Lopes, P. N., Ivcenic, Z., Mayer, J. D. and P. Salovey (2004) "Integrating emotion and cognition: The role of Emotional Intelligence", in D. Y. Dai and R. J. Sternberg (eds.), *Motivation, Emotion, and Cognition*, Mahwah, New Jersey: Lawrence Erlbaum: 175–194.

Breitborde, L. (1998) *Speaking and Social Identity: English in the Lives of Urban Africans*, Berlin-New York: Mouton De Gruyter.

Brown, H. D. (1973) "Affective variables in second language learning", *Language Learning*, 23: 231–243.

Brown, J. D. and Rodgers, T. S. (2002) *Doing Second Language Research*, New York: Oxford University Press.

Buchanan, T. (2001) Online Implementation of an IPIP Five Factor Personality Inventory. Available at http://users.wmin.ac.uk/~buchant/wwwffi/introduction.html (July 2009).

Buchanan, T., Johnson, J. and Goldberg, L. (2005) "Implementing a five-factor personality inventory for use on the internet", *European Journal of Psychological Assessment*, 21: 115–27.

Byram, M. (1997) *Teaching and Assessing Intercultural Communicative Competence*, Clevedon: Multilingual Matters.

Byram, M. (2009) "Politics, policies and political action in foreign language education", in V. Cook and Li Wei (eds.), *Language Teaching and Learning*, London: Continuum: 193–214.

Caldwell-Harris, C. L. and Ayçiçeği-Dinn, A. (2009) "Emotion and lying in a non-native language", *International Journal of Psychophysiology*, 71: 193–204.

Canale, M. (1983) "From communicative competence to language pedagogy", in J. C. Richards and R. W. Schmidt (eds.), *Language and communication*, London: Longman: 2–27.

Caspi, A. and Roberts, B. W. (1999) "Personality continuity and change across the life course", in L. A. Pervin and O. P. John (eds.), *Handbook of Personality: Theory and Research*, New York: Guilford Press: 300–326.

Cenoz, J. (2001) "The effect of linguistic distance, L2 status and age on cross-linguistic influence in third language acquisition", in J. Cenoz, B. Hufeisen and U. Jessner (eds.), *Cross-linguistic Influence in Third Language Acquisition: Psycholinguistic Perspectives*, Clevedon: Multilingual Matters: 8–20.

Cenoz, J. (2003) "The influence of age on the acquisition of English: General proficiency, attitudes and code-mixing", M. P. García Mayo and M. L. García Lecumberri (eds.), *Age and the Acquisition of English as a Foreign Language,* Clevedon: Multilingual Matters: 77–93.

Cenoz. J. and Jessner, U. (2009) "The study of multilingualism in educational contexts", in L. Aronin an B. Hufeisen (eds.), *The Exploration of Multilingualism,* Amsterdam: Benjamins: 121–138.

Cenoz, J. and Hoffman, C. (2003) (eds.) *The effect of bilingualism on third language acquisition.* Special issue of *The International Journal of Bilingualism,* 7 (1).

Chambers, G. (1999) *Motivating Language Learners,* Clevedon: Multilingual Matters.

Chamorro-Premuzic, T., Bennett, E. and Furnham, A. (2007) "The happy personality: Mediational role of trait Emotional Intelligence", *Personality and Individual Differences,* 42: 1633–1639.

Chandler, P. M. (2006) "Critical period or language learning difficulties: Are there two types of adult foreign language learners?", in C. Abello-Contesse, R. Chacon-Beltran, M. D. Lopez-Jiménez and M. M. Torreblanca-Lopez (eds.), *Age in L2 Acquisition and Teaching,* Bern: Peter Lang: 59–77.

Cheshire, J. and Gardner-Chloros, P. (1998) "Code-switching and the sociolinguistic gender pattern", *International Journal of the Sociology of Language,* 129: 5–39.

Chomsky, N. (1965) *Aspects of the Theory of Syntax,* Cambridge, MA: MIT Press.

Cook, V. (1991) "The poverty of the stimulus argument and multicompetence", *Second Language Research,* 7: 103–117.

Cook, V. (1999) "Going beyond the native speaker in language teaching", *TESOL Quarterly,* 33 (2): 185–209.

Cook, V. (2002) "Introduction: Background of the L2 user", in V. Cook (ed), *Portraits of the L2 User,* Clevedon: Multilingual Matters: 1–28.

Cook, V. (2003) (Ed.) *Effects of the Second Language on the First,* Clevedon: Multilingual Matters.

Cook, V. (2007) "The nature of the L2 user", *Eurosla Yearbook,* 7: 205–220.

Cook, V. (2008) *Second Language Acquisition and Teaching,* 4th edition, London: Hodder Education.

Costa, B. (2010) "Mother tongue or non-native language? Learning from conversations with bilingual/multilingual therapists about working with clients who do not share their native language", *Journal of Ethnicity and Inequalities in Health and Social Care,* 3 (1): 15–24.

Costa, B. and Dewaele, J.-M. (2012) "Psychotherapy across languages: beliefs, attitudes and practices of monolingual and multilingual therapists with their multilingual patients", *Language and Psychoanalysis,* 1: 19–41.

Crystal, D. (1997) *The Cambridge encyclopedia of language,* 2nd edition, Cambridge: Cambridge University Press.

Csizér, K. and Kormos, J. (2008) "Modelling the role of inter-cultural contact in the motivation of learning English as a foreign language", *Applied Linguistics,* 30 (2): 166–185.

Curran, C. A. (1976) *Counselling-Learning in Second Languages,* Apple River, IL: Apple River Press.

Dai, D. Y. and R. J. Sternberg (2004) (eds.), *Motivation, Emotion, and Cognition: Integrative Perspectives on Intellectual Functioning and Development,* Mahwah, NJ: Lawrence Erlbaum.

Dalgleish, T., Dunn, B. D. and Mobbs, D. (2009) "Affective neuroscience: Past, present, and future", *Emotion Review,* 1 (4): 355–368.

De Angelis, G. (2007) *Third or Additional Language Acquisition*, Clevedon: Multilingual Matters.
De Bot, K, Lowie, W. and Verspoor, M. (2007) "A dynamic view as a complementary perspective", *Bilingualism: Language and Cognition*, 10 (1): 51–55.
DeKeyser, R. (2000) "The robustness of critical period effects in second language acquisition", *Studies in Second Language Acquisition*, 22: 499–533.
DeKeyser, R. (2006) "A critique of recent arguments against the critical period hypothesis", in C. Abello-Contesse, R. Chacon-Beltran, M. D. Lopez-Jiménez, and M.M. Torreblanca-Lopez (eds.), *Age in L2 Acquisition and Teaching*, Bern: Peter Lang: 49–58.
DeKeyser, R. and Larson-Hall, J. (2005) "What does the Critical Period really mean?", in J. F. Kroll and A. M. D. de Groot, (eds.), *Handbook of Bilingualism: Psycholinguistic Approaches*, Oxford: Oxford University Press: 88–108.
Derné, S. (1994) "Structural realities, persistent dilemmas, and the construction of emotional paradigms: Love in three cultures", *Social Perspectives on Emotion*, 2: 281–308.
Dewaele, J.-M. (2000) "Trilingual first language acquisition: Exploration of a linguistic miracle", *La Chouette*, 31: 77–86.
Dewaele, J.-M. (2001) "Tongue-tied in a foreign language", *The Linguist*, 40 (5): 153–155.
Dewaele, J.-M. (2002) "Psychological and sociodemographic correlates of communicative anxiety in L2 and L3 production", *The International Journal of Bilingualism*, 6: 23–39.
Dewaele, J.-M. (2004a) "Blistering barnacles! What language do multilinguals swear in?!", *Estudios de Sociolinguistica*, 5: 83–106.
Dewaele, J.-M. (2004b) "The emotional force of swearwords and taboo words in the speech of multilinguals", *Journal of Multilingual and Multicultural Development*, 25 (2–3): 204–223.
Dewaele, J.-M. (2004c) "Perceived language dominance and language preference for emotional speech: The implications for attrition research", in M. S. Schmid, B. Köpke, M. Kejser and L.Weilemar, L. (eds.), *First Language Attrition: Interdisciplinary Perspectives on Methodological Issues*, Amsterdam: Benjamins: 81–104.
Dewaele, J.-M. (2005a) "Sociodemographic, psychological and politico-cultural correlates in Flemish students' attitudes toward French and English", *Journal of Multilingual and Multicultural Development*, 26 (2): 118–137.
Dewaele, J.-M. (2005b) "The effect of type of acquisition context on perception and self-reported use of swearwords in the L2, L3, L4 and L5", in A. Housen and M. Pierrard (eds.), *Investigations in Instructed Second Language Acquisition*, Berlin: Mouton De Gruyter: 531–559.
Dewaele, J.-M. (2005c) "Investigating the psychological and the emotional dimensions in instructed language learning: Obstacles and possibilities", *The Modern Language Journal*, 89: 367–380.
Dewaele, J.-M. (2005d) The effect of order of language acquisition on self-perceived proficiency in adult polyglots and the theoretical implications of labeling languages L2, L3, L4... Paper presented at the Fourth International Conference on Third Language Acquisition and Trilingualism in Fribourg, Switzerland, 2005.
Dewaele, J.-M. (2006a) "Expressing anger in multiple languages", in A. Pavlenko (ed), *Bilingual Minds: Emotional Experience, Expression, and Representation*, Clevedon: Multilingual Matters: 118–151.
Dewaele, J.-M. (2006b) Multilinguals' inner code-switching. Paper presented at the Sociolinguistics Symposium, Limerick, July 2006.
Dewaele, J.-M. (2007a) "Interindividual variation in self-perceived oral communicative competence of English L2 users", in E. Alcón Soler and M. P. Safont Jordà (eds.), *Intercultural Language Use and Language Learning*, Berlin: Springer Verlag: 141–165.

Dewaele, J.-M. (2007b) "Context and L2 users' pragmatic development", in Z. Hua, P. Seedhouse, L. Wei and V. Cook (eds.), *Language Learning and Teaching as Social Inter-Action,* Basingstoke: Palgrave-Macmillan: 162–183.

Dewaele, J.-M. (2007c) "Multilinguals' language choice for mental calculation", *Intercultural Pragmatics,* 4 (3): 343–376.

Dewaele, J.-M. (2007d) "Diachronic and/or synchronic variation? The acquisition of sociolinguistic competence in L2 French", in D. Ayoun (ed), *Handbook of French Applied Linguistics,* Amsterdam: John Benjamins: 208–236.

Dewaele, J.-M. (2007e) "Becoming bi- or multi-lingual later in life", in P. Auer and Li Wei (eds.), *Handbook of Multilingualism and Multilingual Communication,* Berlin: Mouton De Gruyter: 89–118.

Dewaele, J.-M. (2007f) "The effect of multilingualism, sociobiographical and situational factors on communicative anxiety and foreign language anxiety of mature language learners", *The International Journal of Bilingualism,* 11 (4): 391–410.

Dewaele, J.-M. (2008a) "Appropriateness in foreign language acquisition and use: Some theoretical, methodological and ethical considerations", *International Review of Applied Linguistics,* 46 (4): 235–255.

Dewaele, J.-M. (2008b) "Dynamic emotion concepts of L2 learners and L2 users: A Second Language Acquisition perspective", *Bilingualism: Language and Cognition,* 11: 173–175.

Dewaele, J.-M. (2008c) "The emotional weight of 'I love you' in multilinguals' languages", *Journal of Pragmatics,* 40: 1753–1780.

Dewaele, J.-M. (2009a) "The cognitive perspective: The age factor", in K. Knapp and B. Seidlhofer (eds.), *Handbook of Foreign Language Communication and Learning,* Berlin: Mouton De Gruyter: 279–306.

Dewaele, J.-M. (2009b) "The effect of age of acquisition on self-perceived proficiency and language choice among adult multilinguals", *Eurosla Yearbook,* 9: 245–268.

Dewaele, J-M. (2009c) "Perception, attitude and motivation", in V. Cook and Li Wei (eds.), *Language Teaching and Learning,* London: Continuum: 163–192.

Dewaele, J-M. (2009d) "Individual differences in second language acquisition", in W. C. Ritchie and T. K. Bhatia (eds.), *The New Handbook of Second Language Acquisition,* Bingley (UK): Emerald: 623–646.

Dewaele, J-M. (2010a) "The perception of French by native speakers and advanced L2, L3 and L4 learners", in V. Regan and Chasaide, N. (eds.), *Language Practices and Identity Construction in French,* Bern: Peter Lang: 133–156.

Dewaele, J.-M. (2010b) "Multilingualism and affordances: Variation in self-perceived communicative competence and communicative anxiety in French L1, L2, L3 and L4", *International Review of Applied Linguistics,* 48: 105–129.

Dewaele, J.-M. (2011a) "The differences in self-reported use and perception of the L1 and L2 of maximally proficient bi- and multilinguals: A quantitative and qualitative investigation", *International Journal of Sociology of Language,* 208: 25–51.

Dewaele, J.-M. (2011b) "'Christ fucking shit merde!' Language preferences for swearing among maximally proficient multilinguals", *Sociolinguistic Studies.* 4 (3): 595–614.

Dewaele, J.-M. (2011c) "Reflections on the emotional and psychological aspects of foreign language learning and use", *Anglistik,* 22 (1), 23–42.

Dewaele, J.-M. (2011d) "Variation in self-reported frequency of use of French swearwords among L2 and L3 users of French", in F. Martineau and T. Nadasdi (eds), *Le français en contact: Hommages à Raymond Mougeon,* Quebec: Presses de l'Université Laval: 87–116.

Dewaele, J.-M. (2012) "L'acquisition et l'usage de scripts dans les différentes langues de multilingues adultes" in N. Auger, C. Béal and F. Demougin (eds.), *Interactions et interculturalité: variété des corpus et des approaches*, Berlin: Peter Lang: 195–222.

Dewaele, J.-M. (2013a) "Affect and Language learning", in C.A. Chapelle (ed), *The Encyclopedia of Applied Linguistics*, Oxford, UK: Wiley-Blackwell: 1–5, DOI: 10.1002/9781405198431.wbeal0011

Dewaele, J.-M. (2013b) "Multilingualism and Emotions", in C.A. Chapelle (ed), *The Encyclopedia of Applied Linguistics*, Oxford, UK: Wiley-Blackwell: 1–7. DOI: 10.1002/9781405198431.wbeal0795

Dewaele, J.-M. (2013c) "Communicating emotions in a foreign language. Plenary talk at AESLA May 2012", in A. Llances Baro, L. A. Ciro, L. Gallego Balsa, R.M. Matea Serra (eds), *La Lingüística Aplicada en la era de la globalización, Applied Linguistics in the age of globalisation*. Lleida: Edicions de la Universitat de Lleida, CD-Rom: 16–26.

Dewaele, J.-M. (2013) The link between Foreign Language Classroom Anxiety and Psychoticism, Extraversion, and Neuroticism among adult bi- and multilinguals. *The Modern Language Journal*, 97 (3): 670–684.

Dewaele, J.-M. and Edwards, M. (2004) "Tense/aspect, verb meaning and perception of emotional intensity by native and non-native users of English", *Eurosla Yearbook*, 4: 231–252.

Dewaele, J.-M. and Furnham, A. (1999) "Extraversion: the unloved variable in applied linguistic research", *Language Learning*, 49: 509–544.

Dewaele, J.-M. and Furnham, A. (2000) "Personality and speech production: A pilot study of second language learners", *Personality and Individual Differences*, 28: 355–365.

Dewaele, J.-M. and Shan Ip, T. (2013) "The link between Foreign Language Classroom Anxiety, Second Language Tolerance of Ambiguity and self-rated English proficiency among Chinese learners", *Studies in Second Language Learning and Teaching*, 3 (1): 47–66.

Dewaele, J.-M. and Li Wei (2012) "Multilingualism, empathy and multicompetence", *International Journal of Multilingualism*, 9 (4): 352–366.

Dewaele, J.-M. and Li Wei (2013a) "Is multilingualism linked to a higher tolerance of ambiguity?", *Bilingualism: Language and Cognition*, 16 (1): 231–240.

Dewaele, J.-M. and Li Wei (2013b) Intra- and inter-individual variation in self-reported codeswitching patterns of adult multilinguals. Unpublished manuscript.

Dewaele, J.-M. and Nakano, S. (2013) Multilinguals' perceptions of feeling different when switching languages. *Journal of Multilingual and Multicultural Development*, 34 (2): 107–120.

Dewaele, J.-M. and Pavlenko, A. (2001–2003) Web questionnaire Bilingualism and Emotions. University of London.

Dewaele, J.-M. and Pavlenko, A. (2002) "Emotion vocabulary in interlanguage", *Language Learning*, 52: 265–324.

Dewaele, J.-M. and Pavlenko, A. (2003) "Productivity and lexical diversity in native and non-native speech: A study of cross-cultural effects", in V. Cook (ed.), *The effects of the second language on the first*, Clevedon: Multilingual Matters: 120–141.

Dewaele, J.-M. and Stavans, A. (2012) "The effect of immigration, acculturation and multicompetence on personality profiles of Israeli multilinguals", *The International Journal of Bilingualism*, DOI: 10.1177/1367006912439941

Dewaele, J.-M., Petrides, K. V. and Furnham, A. (2008) "The effects of trait Emotional Intelligence and sociobiographical variables on communicative anxiety and foreign language anxiety among adult multilinguals: A review and empirical investigation", *Language Learning*, 58 (4): 911–960.

Dewaele, J.-M. and Thirtle, H. (2009) "Why do some young learners drop Foreign Languages? A focus on learner-internal variables", *International Journal of Bilingual Education and Bilingualism*, 12 (6): 635–649.

Dewaele, J.-M. and van Oudenhoven, J.P. (2009) "The effect of multilingualism/ multiculturalism on personality: No gain without pain for third culture kids?", *International Journal of Multilingualism*, 6 (4): 443–459.

Dörnyei, Z. (2001) *Motivational Strategies: Creating and Maintaining Student Motivation in the Foreign Language Classroom*, Cambridge: Cambridge University Press.

Dörnyei, Z. (2003) *Questionnaires in Second Language Research Construction, Administration and Processing*, Mahwah, NJ: Lawrence Erlbaum.

Dörnyei, Z. (2005) *The Psychology of the Language Learner. Individual Differences in Second Language Acquisition*, Mahwah, New Jersey: Lawrence Erlbaum.

Dörnyei, Z. (2006) "Individual differences in second language acquisition", *AILA Review*, 19: 42–68.

Dörnyei, Z. (2007) *Research Methods in Applied Linguistics*, Oxford: Oxford University Press.

Dörnyei, Z. and Clément, R. (2001) "Motivational characteristics of learning different target languages: Results of a nationwide survey", in Z. Dörnyei and R. Schmidt (eds.), *Motivation and Second Language Acquisition*, Honolulu, HI: The University of Hawai'i, Second Language Teaching and Curriculum Center: 391–424.

Dörnyei, Z. and Kormos, J. (2000) "The role of individual and social variables in oral task performance", *Language Teaching Research*, 4: 275–300.

Dörnyei, Z. and Ushioda, E. (eds.) (2009) *Motivation, Language Identity and the L2 Self*, Bristol: Multilingual Matters.

Dörnyei, Z., Csizér, K. and Németh, N. (2006) *Motivation, Language Attitudes and Globalisation*, Clevedon: Multilingual Matters.

Doughty, C. J. and Long, M. H. (eds.) (2003) *The Handbook of Second Language Acquisition*, Malden, MA: Blackwell.

Drescher, M. (2000) "Eh tabarnouche! c'était bon. Pour une approche communicative des jurons en français québecois", *Cahiers de praxématique*, 34: 133–160.

Dromey, C., Silveira, J. and Sandor, P. (2005) "Recognition of affective prosody by speakers of English as a First or Foreign language", *Speech Communication*, 47 (3): 351–359.

Duff, P. A. (2003) "New directions in second language socialisation research", *Korean Journal of English Language and Linguistics*, 3: 309–339.

Duff, P. A. (2007) "Second language socialisation as sociocultural theory: Insights and issues", *Language Teaching*, 40 (4): 309–319.

Edwards, M. and Dewaele, J.-M. (2007) "Trilingual conversations: A window into multicompetence?" *The International Journal of Bilingualism*, 11: 221–241.

Eilola, T. M., Havelka J. and Sharma, D. (2007) "Emotional activation in the first and second language", *Cognition and Emotion*, 21 (5): 1064–1076.

Etienne, C. and Sax, K. (2009) "Stylistic variation in French: Bridging the gap between research and textbooks", *The Modern Language Journal*, 93: 584–606.

Evans, C. (1988) *Language People. The Experience of Teaching and Learning Modern Languages in British Universities*, Milton Keynes/Philadelphia: Open University Press.

Evans, M. and Fisher, L. (2005) "Measuring gains in pupils' foreign language competence as a result of participation in a school exchange visit: The case of Y9 pupils at three comprehensive schools in the UK", *Language Teaching, Research*, 9: 173–192.

Everett, D. L. (2008) *Don't Sleep, There are Snakes*, New York: Pantheon Books.

Ewald, J. (2007) "Foreign language learning anxiety in upper-level classes: Involving students as researchers", *Foreign Language Annals*, 40 (1): 122–143.

Eysenck, H. J. and Eysenck, M. W. (1985) *Personality and Individual Differences: A Natural Science Approach*, New York: Plenum.

Eysenck, M., Derakshan, N., Santos, R. and Calvo, M. (2007) "Anxiety and cognitive performance: Attentional control theory", *Emotion*, 7 (2): 336–353.

Fanselow, M. (1999) "Learning theory and neuropsychology: Configuring their disparate element in the hippocampus", *Journal of Experimental Psychology: Animal Behavior Processes*, 25 (3): 275–283.

Farrell, P. (2006) "Portuguese SAUDADE and other emotions of absence and longing", in B. Peeters (ed.) *Semantic Primes and Universal Grammar*, Amsterdam: John Benjamins: 235–258.

Firth, A. and Wagner, J. (1997) "On discourse, communication, and (some) fundamental concepts in SLA research", *Modern Language Journal*, 81: 285–300.

Firth, A. and Wagner, J. (2007) "On discourse, communication, and (some) fundamental concepts in SLA research", *The Modern Language Journal*, 91 (5): 757–772.

Flynn, S. and Foley, C. (2009) "Research methodology in second language acquisition", in W. C. Ritchie and T. K. Bhatia (eds.), *The New Handbook of Second Language Acquisition*, Bingley (UK): Emerald: 29–43.

Fouser, R. J. (2001) "Too close for comfort? Sociolinguistic transfer from Japanese into Korean as an L≥3", in J. Cenoz, B. Hufeisen, and U. Jessner (eds.), *Cross-linguistic Influence in Third Language Acquisition: Psycholinguistic Perspectives*, Clevedon: Multilingual Matters: 149–169.

Frantzen, D. and Magnan, S. S. (2005) "Anxiety and the true beginner-false beginner dynamic in beginning French and Spanish classes", *Foreign Language Annals*, 38: 171–190.

Freed, B. F. (1995) "Language learning and study abroad", in B. Freed (ed.), *Second Language Acquisition in a Study Abroad Context*, Philadelphia: John Benjamins: 3–33.

Furnham, A. and Heaven, P. C. L. (1999) *Personality and Social Behaviour*, London: Arnold, New York: Oxford University Press.

Fussell, S. R. (2002) "The verbal communication of emotion: Introduction and overview", in S. R. Fussell (ed), *The Verbal Communication of Emotions: Interdisciplinary Perspectives*, Mahwah, NJ: Lawrence Erlbaum: 1–22.

Gal, S. (1979) *Language Shift: Social Determinants of Linguistic Change in Bilingual Austria*, New York: Academic Press.

García Mayo, M. P. and García Lecumberri, M. L. (eds.) (2003) *Age and the Acquisition of English as a Foreign Language*, Clevedon: Multilingual Matters.

Gardner, R. C. (1985) *Social Psychology and Second Language Learning: The Role of Attitudes and Motivation*, London: Edward Arnold.

Gardner, R. C. (2006) "The socio-educational model of Second Language Acquisition: A research paradigm", *EUROSLA Yearbook*, 6: 237–260.

Gardner, R. C. and Lambert, W. E. (1959) "Motivational variables in second language acquisition", *Canadian Journal of Psychology*, 13: 266–272.

Gardner, R. C. and MacIntyre, P. D. (1992) "A student's contribution to second language learning: Part I, Cognitive Factors", *Language Teaching*, 25: 211–220.

Gardner, R. C. and MacIntyre, P. D. (1993) "A student's contributions to second language learning: Part II. Affective variables", *Language Teaching*, 26: 1–11.

Gardner, R. C. and Tremblay, P. F. (1998) "Specificity of affective variables and the Trait/State conceptualisation of motivation in second language acquisition", in R. Agnihotri, A. L. Khanna and I. Sachdev (eds.) *Social Psychological Perspectives on Second Language Learning*, New Delhi: Sage: 187–203.

Gardner-Chloros, P. (2009) *Code-switching*, Cambridge: Cambridge University Press.
Gardner-Chloros, P. (2009) "Sociolinguistic factors in code-switching", in B. E. Bullock and A. J. Toribio (eds.), *The Handbook of Code-switching*, Cambridge: Cambridge University Press: 97–114.
Gardner-Chloros, P., McEntee-Atalianis, L. and Finnis, K. (2005) "Language attitudes and use in a transplanted setting: Greek Cypriots in London", *International Journal of Multilingualism*, 2: 52–80.
Gardner, R. C., Smythe, P. C., Clément, R. and Gliksman, L. (1976) "Social and psychological factors in second language acquisition", *Canadian Modern Language Review*, 32: 198–213.
Garrett, P. and Young, R. (2009) "Theorizing affect in foreign language learning: An analysis of one learner's responses to a communicative-based Portuguese course", *The Modern Language Journal*, 93 (2): 209–226.
Gass, S. M. and Selinker, L. (2008) *Second language acquisition: An introductory course*, 3rd edition, Mahwah, NJ: Erlbaum.
Gibbs, R. W., Leggitt, J. S. and Turner, E. A. (2002) "What's special about figurative language in emotional communication", in S. R. Fussell (ed), *The Verbal Communication of Emotions: Interdisciplinary Perspectives*, Mahwah, NJ: Lawrence Erlbaum: 125–149.
Gibson, J.J. (1979) *The Ecological Approach to Visual Perception*, Boston: Houghton Mifflin.
Goetz, T., Frenzel, A. C., Pekrun, R. and Hall, N. (2005) "Emotional intelligence in the context of learning and achievement", in R. Schulze and R. D. Roberts (eds.), *Emotional Intelligence: An International Handbook*, Cambridge, MA: Hogrefe, 233–253.
Goldberg, E. (2006) *The Wisdom Paradox*, New York: Gotham Books.
Gonzalez-Reigosa, F. (1976) "The anxiety arousing effect of taboo words in bilinguals", in C. D. Spielberger and R. Diaz-Guerrero (eds.), *Cross-cultural Anxiety*, Washington, DC: Hemisphere: 89–105.
Gosling, S. D., Vazire, S., Srivastava, S. and John, O. P. (2004) "Should we trust Web-based studies? A comparative analysis of six preconceptions about Internet questionnaires", *American Psychologist*, 59: 93–104.
Grabois, H. (1999) "The convergence of sociocultural theory and cognitive linguistics: Lexical semantics and the L2 acquisition of love, fear, and happiness", in G., Palmer and D. Occhi (eds.), *Languages of Sentiment: Cultural Constructions of Emotional Substrates*, Amsterdam/Philadelphia: Benjamins: 201–233.
Graham, C. R., Hamblin, A. W. and Feldstein, S. (2001) "Recognition of emotion in English voices by speakers of Japanese, Spanish and English", *International Review of Applied Linguistics*, 39: 19–37.
Green, D.W. (1986) "Control, activation, and resource: A framework and a model for the control of speech in bilinguals", *Brain and Language*, 27: 210–223.
Gregersen, T. (2003) "To err is human: A reminder to teachers of language-anxious students", *Foreign Language Annals*, 36: 25–32.
Gregersen, T. (2007) "Breaking the code of silence: A study of teachers' nonverbal decoding accuracy of foreign language anxiety", *Language Teaching Research*, 11: 209–221.
Gregersen, T. and Horwitz, E. K. (2002) "Language learning and perfectionism: Anxious and non-anxious language learners' reactions to their own oral performance", *The Modern Language Journal*, 86: 562–570.
Gregersen, T. and MacIntyre, P. (2013) *Capitalizing on Individual Differences: From Premise to Practice*. Bristol: Multilingual Matters.
Gregg, K. V. (2006) "Taking a social turn for the worse: The language socialisation paradigm for second language acquisition", *Second Language Research*, 22, (4): 413–442.

Griessler, M. (2001) "The effects of third language learning on L2 proficiency: An Austrian example", *International Journal of Bilingual Education and Bilingualism*, 4 (1): 50–60.

Griffiths, C. (ed) (2008) *Lessons from Good Language Learners*, Cambridge: Cambridge University Press.

Grin, F., Sfreddo, C. and Vaillancourt, F. (2010) *The Economics of the Multilingual Workplace*, London: Routledge.

Grosjean, F. (1982) *Life with Two Languages: An Introduction to Bilingualism*, Cambridge: Harvard University Press.

Grosjean, F. (1989) "Neurolinguistics, beware! The bilingual is not two monolinguals in one person", *Brain and Language*, 36: 3–15.

Grosjean, F. (1992) "Another view of bilingualism", in R. J. Harris (ed.) *Cognitive Processing in Bilinguals*, Amsterdam: North-Holland: 51–62.

Grosjean, F. (2001) "The bilingual's language modes", in J. L. Nicol (ed.) *One Mind, Two Languages: Bilingual Language Processing*, Oxford: Blackwell: 1–22.

Grosjean, F. (2008) "Manipulating language mode", in *Studying Bilinguals* (Chapter 5), Oxford: Oxford University Press.

Grunwald, I. S., Borod, J. C., Obler, L. K., Erhan, H. M., Pick, L. H. and Welkowitz, J. (1999) "The effect of age and gender on the perception of lexical emotion", *Applied Neuropsychology*, 6: 226–238.

Gu, Y. (2002) "Gender, academic majors and vocabulary learning strategies of Chinese EFL learners", *RELC Journal*, 33: 35–54.

Guiora, A., Paluszny, M., Beit-Hallatimi, B., Catford, J., Cooley, R. and Yoder Dull, C. (1975) "Language and person studies in language behavior", *Language Learning*, 25 (1): 43–61.

Hamers, J. F. (1994) "Rôle des réseaux sociaux dans le maintien de la langue maternelle, dans le développement bilingue et dans le développement de la littéracie" [The role of social networks in maintaining the native tongue, in the development of bilingualism, and in the development of literacy], *Bulletin suisse de linguistique appliquée*, 59: 85–102.

Hammarberg, B. (2009) (ed.) *Processes in Third Language Acquisition*, Edinburgh: Edinburgh University Press.

Hampson, E., van Anders, S. M. and Mullin, L. I. (2006) "A female advantage in the recognition of emotional facial expressions: Test of an evolutionary hypothesis", *Evolution and Human Behavior*, 27 (6): 401–416.

Han, Zh. (2009) "Interlanguage and fossilization: Towards an analytic model", in V. Cook and Li Wei (eds.), *Language Teaching and Learning*, London: Continuum: 137–162.

Harré, R. (2009) "Emotions as cognitive-affective-somatic hybrids", *Emotion Review*, 1 (4): 294–301.

Harris, C. L. (2004) "Bilingual speakers in the lab: Psychophysiological measures of emotional reactivity", *Journal of Multilingual and Multicultural Development*, 25 (2–3): 223–247.

Harris, C. L., Gleason, J. B., and Ayçiçeği, A. (2006) "When is a first language more emotional? Psychophysiological evidence from bilingual speakers", in A. Pavlenko (ed), *Bilingual minds: Emotional experience, expression, and representation*, Clevedon: Multilingual Matters: 257–283.

Harris, C., Ayçiçeği, A. and Gleason, J. (2003) "Taboo words and reprimands elicit greater autonomic reactivity in a first than in a second language", *Applied Psycholinguistics*, 24: 561–579.

Heft, H. (2001) *Ecological Psychology in Context: James Gibson, Roger Barker, and the Legacy of William James's Radical Empiricism*, Mahwah, NJ: Lawrence Erlbaum Associates.

Herdina, Ph. and Jessner, U. (2002) *A Dynamic Model of Multilingualism. Perspectives of Change in Psycholinguistics*, Clevedon: Multilingual Matters.

Heredia, R. and Altarriba, J. (2001) "Bilingual language mixing: Why do bilinguals codeswitch?", *Current Directions in Psychological Science*, 10: 164–168.

Hesse-Biber, N. S. and Leavy, P. (2006) *The Practice of Qualitative Research*, Thousand Oaks: Sage.

Hewson, C., Yule, P. D., Laurent, D. and Vogel, C. (2003) *Internet Research Methods: A Practical Guide for the Social and Behavioural Sciences*, London: Sage.

Hoffman, E. (1989) *Lost in Translation: A life in a New Language*, New York: Penguin Books.

Horwitz, E. K. (1986) "Preliminary evidence for the reliability and validity of a foreign language anxiety scale", *TESOL Quarterly*, 20: 559–562.

Horwitz, E. K. (2000) "It ain't over 'til it's over: On foreign language anxiety, first language deficits, and the confounding of variables", *The Modern Language Journal*, 84: 256–259.

Horwitz, E. K. (2001) "Language anxiety and achievement", *Annual Review of Applied Linguistics*, 21: 112–126.

Horwitz, E. K., Horwitz, B. and Cope, J. (1986) "Foreign language classroom anxiety", *The Modern Language Journal*, 70 (ii): 125–132.

Housen, A. (2002) "Paramètres liés à l'environnement dans l'apprentissage guidé d'une langue seconde", *Acquisition et interaction en langue étrangère*, 16: 23–46.

Housen A., Schoonjans E., Janssens S., Welcomme A., Schoonheere E. and M. Pierrard (2011) "Conceptualizing and measuring the impact of contextual factors in instructed SLA. The role of language prominence", *International Review of Applied Linguistics*, 49: 83–112.

Howard, M. (2005) "Second Language Acquisition in the study abroad context: A comparative investigation of the effects of study abroad and foreign language instruction on the L2 learner's grammatical development", in A. Housen and M. Pierrard (eds.), *Current Issues in Instructed Second Language Acquisition*, Berlin: Mouton De Gruyter: 495–530.

Huston, N. and Sebbar, L. (1986) *Lettres Parisiennes*, Paris: Editions J'ai Lu.

Hyltenstam, K. and Abrahamsson, N. (2003) "Maturational constraints in SLA", in C. J. Doughty and M. H. Long (eds.), *The Handbook of Second Language Acquisition*, Malden, MA and Oxford, UK: Blackwell: 539–588.

Hymes, D. (1972) "On communicative competence", in J. B. Pride and J. Holmes (eds.), *Sociolinguistics*, Harmondsworth: Penguin: 269–293.

Jaffe, E. (2005) "How random is that?", *American Psychological Society*, 9: 17–30. Available online at http://www.psychologicalscience.org/observer/getArticle.cfm?id=1838 (July 2009).

Javier, R. (1989) "Linguistic considerations in the treatment of bilinguals", *Journal of Psychoanalytic Psychology*, 6: 87–96.

Javier, R. (2007) *The Bilingual Mind. Thinking, Feeling and Speaking in Two Languages*, New York: Springer.

Javier, R. A., Barroso, F. and Muñoz, M. A. (1993) "Autobiographical memory in bilinguals", *Journal of Psycholinguistic Research*, 22 (3): 319–338.

Javier, R. and Marcos, L. (1989) "The role of stress on the language-independence and codeswitching phenomena", *Journal of Psycholinguistic Research*, 18: 449–472.

Jay, T. B. (2000) *Why We Curse*, Philadelphia: John Benjamins.

Jay, T. B. (2009) "The utility and ubiquity of taboo words", *Perspectives on Psychological Science*, 4 (2): 153–161.

Jay, T. and Janschewitz, K. (2007) "Filling the emotion gap in linguistic theory: Commentary on Potts' expressive dimension", *Theoretical Linguistics,* 33 (2): 215–221.

Jay, T. and Janschewitz, K. (2008) "The pragmatics of swearing", *Journal of Politeness Research,* 4: 267–288.

Jessner, U. (1999) "Metalinguistic awareness in multilinguals: Cognitive aspects of third language learning", *Language Awareness,* 8 (3–4): 201–209.

Jessner, U. (2006) *Linguistic Awareness in Multilinguals,* Edinburgh: Edinburgh University Press.

Jessner, U. (2008) "A DST-model of multilingualism and the role of metalinguistic awareness. Second language development as a dynamic process", *The Modern Language Journal,* 92 (2): 270–283.

Johnson, J. S. and Newport, E. L. (1989) "Critical period effects in second language learning: The influence of maturational state on the acquisition of ESL", *Cognitive Psychology,* 21: 60–99.

Kalaja, P. and Barcelos, A. M. F. (eds.) (2003) *Beliefs about SLA: New Research approaches,* Dordrecht: Kluwer Academic Publishers.

Kaplan, A. (1993) *French Lessons: A Memoir,* Chicago: The University of Chicago Press.

Kasper, G. (2009) "L2 pragmatic development", in W. C. Ritchie and T. K. Bhatia (eds.), *The New Handbook of Second Language Acquisition,* Bingley (UK): Emerald: 259–293

Kasper, G. and Rose, K. R. (2001) "Pragmatics in Language Teaching", in K. R. Rose and G. Kasper (eds.), *Language Teaching,* Cambridge: Cambridge University Press: 1–9.

Kasper, G. and Rose, K. R. (2002) *Pragmatic Development in a Second Language,* Oxford: Blackwell.

Kellman, S. (2000) *The Translingual Imagination,* Lincoln-London: University of Nebraska Press.

Kemp, C. (2007) "Strategic processing in grammar learning: Do multilinguals use more strategies?", *International Journal of Multilingualism,* 4 (4): 241–261.

Keshavarz, M. H. and Astaneh, H. (2004) "The impact of bilinguality on the learning of English vocabulary as a foreign language (L3)", *International Journal of Bilingual Education and Bilingualism,* 7 (4): 295–303.

Kinginger, C. (2004a) "Alice doesn't live here anymore: Foreign language learning and renegotiated identity", in A. Pavlenko and A. Blackledge (eds.), *Negotiation of Identities in Multilingual Contexts,* Clevedon: Multilingual Matters: 219–242.

Kinginger, C. (2004b) "Bilingualism and emotion in the autobiographical works of Nancy Huston", *Journal of Multilingual and Multicultural Development,* 25: 159–178.

Kinginger, C. (2008) *Language Learning in Study Abroad: Case Studies of Americans in France,* Malden, MA and Oxford, UK: Wiley-Blackwell.

Kinginger, C. (2009) *Language Learning and Study Abroad. A Critical Reading of Research,* London: Palgrave Macmillan.

Kinginger, C. and Belz, J. A. (2005) "Socio-cultural perspectives on pragmatic development in foreign language learning: Microgenetic case studies from telecollaboration and residence abroad", *Intercultural Pragmatics,* 2 (4): 369–421.

Kinginger, C. and Blattner, G. (2008) "Histories of engagement and sociolinguistic awareness in study abroad. Colloquial French", in L. Ortega and H. Byrnes (eds.), *The Longitudinal Study of Advanced L2 Capacities,* Mahwah, NJ: Lawrence Erlbaum: 223–246.

Kinginger, C. and Farrell Whitworth, K. (2005) "Gender and emotional investment in language learning during study abroad", *CALPER Working Papers Series,* 2: 1–12.

Knickerbocker, H. and Altarriba, J. (2011) "Bilingualism and the impact of emotion: The role of experience, memory, and sociolinguistic factors", in V. Cook and B. Bassetti (eds.), *Language and Bilingual Cognition*, Ney York/London: Psychology Press/Taylor & Francis: 453–477.

Knowlson, J. (1996) *Damned to Fame. The Life of Samuel Beckett*, London: Bloomsbury.

Kormos, J. and Csizér, K. (2007) "An interview study of inter-cultural contact and its role in language learning in a foreign language environment", *System*, 35 (2): 241–258.

Kormos, J. and Csizér, K. (2007) "The relationship of intercultural contact and language learning motivation among Hungarian students of English and German", *Journal of Multilingual and Multicultural Development*, 29: 30–48.

Koven, M. (1998) "Two languages in the self/the self in two languages: French-Portuguese bilinguals' verbal enactments and experiences of self in narrative discourse", *Ethos*, 26 (4): 410–455.

Koven, M. (2006) "Feeling in two languages: A comparative analysis of a bilingual's affective displays in French and Portuguese", in A. Pavlenko (ed.), *Bilingual Minds: Emotional Experience, Expression, and Representation*, Clevedon: Multilingual Matters: 84–117.

Koven, M. (2007) *Selves in Two Languages. Bilinguals' Verbal Enactments of Identity in French and Portuguese*, Amsterdam: John Benjamins.

Kramsch, C. (2003) "Metaphor and the subjective construction of belief", in P. Kalaja and A.-M. Barcelos (eds.), *New Approaches to Research on Beliefs about SLA*, Dordrecht: Kluwer: 109–128.

Kramsch, C. (2006) "From communicative competence to symbolic competence", *Modern Language Journal*, 90 (2): 249–252.

Kramsch, C. (2009) "Third culture and language education", in V. Cook and Li Wei (eds.), *Language Teaching and Learning*, London: Continuum: 233–254.

Krashen, S. (1981) *Principles and Practice in Second Language Acquisition*, Hemel Hampstead, Hertfordshire: Prentice Hall International.

Kundera, M. (1990) *L'immortalité*, Paris: Gallimard.

Lantolf, J. P. (2007) "Sociocultural source of thinking and its relevance for second language acquisition", *Bilingualism: Language and Cognition*, 10 (1): 31–33.

Lantolf, J. P. and Pavlenko, A. (2001) "(S)econd (L)anguage (A)ctivity Theory: Understanding second language learners as people", in M. Breen (ed.), *Learner Contributions to Language Learning: New Directions in Research*, London: Longman: 141–158.

Lanza, E. (1997) *Language Mixing in Infant Bilingualism. A Sociolinguistic perspective*, Oxford: Clarendon Press.

Larsen-Freeman, D. (1997) "Chaos/complexity science and second language acquisition", *Applied Linguistics*, 18: 141–165.

Larsen-Freeman, D. and Cameron, L. (2008) *Complex Systems and Applied Linguistics*, Oxford: Oxford University Press.

Larsen-Freeman, D. and Long, M. (1991) *An Introduction to Second Language Acquisition Research*, London: Longman.

Larson-Hall, J. (2008) "Weighing the benefits of studying a foreign language at a younger starting age in a minimal input situation", *Second Language Research*, 24 (1): 35–63.

Lasagabaster, D. (2005a) "Attitudes towards Basque, Spanish and English: An analysis of the most influential variables", *Journal of Multilingual and Multicultural Development* 26 (4): 296–316.

Lasagabaster, D. (2005b) "Bearing multilingual parameters in mind when designing a questionnaire on attitudes: Does this affect the results?" *International Journal of Multilingualism*, 2: 26–51.

Lasagabaster, D. and Huguet, A. (eds.) (2006) *Language Use and Attitudes towards Multilingualism in European Bilingual Contexts*, Clevedon: Multilingual Matters.

LeDoux, J. (1996) *The Emotional Brain: The Mysterious Underpinning of Emotional Life*, New York: Touchstone.

Lenneberg, E. H. (1967) *Biological Foundations of Language*, New York: Wiley.

Le Pichon Vorstman, E., De Swart, H., Ceginskas, V. and Van Den Bergh, H. (2009a) "Language learning experience in school context and metacognitive awareness of multilingual children", *International Journal of Multilingualism*, 6 (3): 258–280.

Le Pichon-Vorstman, E. M. M., De Swart, H. E., Vorstman, J. A. S. and Van Den Bergh, H.H. (2010) "Influence of the context of learning a language on the strategic competence of children." *International Journal of Bilingualism*, 14(4): 447–465.

Leppänen, S. and Kalaja, P. (2002) "Autobiographies as constructions of EFL learner identities and experiences", in E. Kärkkäinen, J. Haines and T. Lauttamus (eds.), *Studia Linguistica et Litteraria Septentrionalia: Studies Presented to Heikki Nyyssönen*, Oulu: University of Oulu: 189–203.

Leventhal, H. and Scherer, K. (1987) "The relationship of emotion to cognition: A functional approach to a semantic controversy", *Cognition & Emotion*, 1: 3–28.

Levine, G. S. (2003) "Student and instructor beliefs and attitudes about target language use, first language use, and anxiety: Report of a questionnaire study", *The Modern Language Journal*, 87 (3): 343–364.

Levy, R.I. (1983) "Introduction: Self and emotion", *Ethos*, 11, 128–134.

Linden, D. (2007) *The Accidental Mind: How Brain Evolution Has Given Us Love, Memory, Dreams, and God*, Cambridge MA: The Belknap Press of Harvard University Press.

Liu, Meihua (2006) "Anxiety in Chinese EFL students at different proficiency levels", *System*, 34 (3): 301–316.

Liu, Meihua (2009) *Reticence and Anxiety in Oral English Lessons*. Bern: Peter Lang.

Li, Wei (2007) "Dimensions of bilingualism", in Li Wei (ed.), *The Bilingualism Reader* (2nd ed.), London: Routledge: 3–22.

Long, M. H. (1990) "Maturational constraints on language development", *Studies in Second Language Acquisition*, 12: 251–285.

Llanes, À. and Muñoz, C. (2013) "Age effects in a study abroad context: children and adults studying abroad and at home", *Language Learning*, 63, 63–90.

Lutz, C. (1986) "Emotion, thought, and estrangement: emotion as a cultural category", *Cultural anthropology*, 1 (3): 287–309.

MacIntyre, P. D. (1995) "How does anxiety affect second language learning? A reply to Sparks and Ganschow", *The Modern Language Journal*, 79: 90–99.

MacIntyre, P. D. (1999) "Language anxiety: a review of the research for language teachers" in D. J. Young (ed), *Affect in Foreign Language and Second Language Teaching: A Practical Guide to Creating a Low-anxiety Classroom Atmosphere*, Boston: Mc Graw-Hill: 24–45.

MacIntyre, P. D. (2002) "Motivation, anxiety and emotion in second language acquisition", in P. Robinson (ed.), *Individual Differences and Instructed Language Learning*, Amsterdam: John Benjamins: 45–68.

MacIntyre, P. D. (2007) "Willingness to communicate in the second language: Understanding the decision to speak as a volitional process", *The Modern Language Journal*, 91 (4): 564–576.

MacIntyre, P. (2012) "The idiodynamic method: A closer look at the dynamics of communication traits", *Communication Research Reports*, 29 (4): 361–367.

MacIntyre, P. D. and Charos, C. (1996) "Personality, attitudes, and affect as predictors of second language communication", *Journal of Language and Social Psychology*, 15: 3–26.

MacIntyre, P. D. and Gardner, R. C. (1989) "Anxiety and second language learning: Towards a theoretical clarification", *Language Learning*, 39: 251–275.

MacIntyre, P. D. and Gardner, R. C. (1991a) "Methods and results in the study of foreign language anxiety: a review of the literature", *Language Learning*, 41: 25–57.

MacIntyre, P. D. and Gardner, R. C. (1991b) "Language anxiety: Its relationship to other anxieties and to processing in native and second language", *Language Learning*, 41: 513–534.

MacIntyre, P. D. and Gardner, R. C. (1994) "The subtle effects of language anxiety on cognitive processing in the second language", *Language Learning*, 44: 283–305.

MacIntyre, P. and Gregersen, T. (2012) "Emotions that facilitate language learning: The positive-broadening power of the imagination", *Studies in Second Language Learning and Teaching*, 2 (2): 193–213.

MacIntyre, P. D., Noels, K. A. and Clément, R. (1997) "Biases in self-ratings of second language proficiency: the role of language anxiety", *Language Learning*, 47: 265–287.

Marian, V. and Kaushanskaya, M. (2004) "Self-construal and emotion in bicultural bilinguals", *Journal of Memory and Language*, 51: 190–201.

Marcos, L. R. (1976) "Linguistic dimensions in the bilingual patient", *American Journal of Psychoanalysis*, 36: 347–354.

Markus, H. R. and Kitayama, S. (1991) "Culture and self: Implications for cognition, emotion, and motivation", *Psychological Review*, 98: 224–253.

Markus, H. R. and Kitayama, S. (1994) "The cultural construction of self and emotion: Implications for social behavior", in S. Kitayama, and H. Markus (eds.), *Emotion and Culture: Empirical Studies of Mutual Influence*, Washington, DC: American Psychological Association: 89–130.

Martinez-Pons, M. (2001) *The Psychology of Teaching and Learning: A Three Step Approach*, New York: Continuum.

Martin-Jones, M. (1995) "Code-switching in the classroom: Two decades of research", in L. Milroy and P. Muyskens (eds.) *One Speaker, Two Languages: Cross-Disciplinary Perspectives on Code-switching*, Cambridge: Cambridge University Press: 90–111.

Matsuda, S. and Gobel, P. (2004) "Anxiety and predictors of performance in the foreign language classroom", *System*, 32: 21–36.

Matthews, G., Deary, I. J. and Whiteman, M.C. (2003) *Personality Traits*, 2nd edition, Cambridge: Cambridge University Press.

McCroskey, J. C. and McCroskey, L. (1988) "Self-report as an approach to measuring communication competence", *Communication Research Reports*, 5: 106–113.

McLaughlin, B. (1984) *Second Language Acquisition in Childhood: Volume 1. Preschool children*, Hillsdale, NJ: Laurence Erlbaum.

Mercer, S. (2006) "Using journals to investigate the learners' emotional experience of the language classroom", *Estudios de Linguistica Inglesa Aplicada*, 6: 63–91.

Mercer, S. (2009) "The dynamic nature of a tertiary learner's foreign language self-concepts", in M. Pawlak (ed), *New Perspectives on Individual Differences in Language Learning and Teaching*, Poznan-Kalisz: Adam Mickiewicz University Press: 205–220.

Mercier, P. (2007) *Night Train to Lisbon*, New York: Grove Press.

Mettewie, L. (2004) "Attitudes en motivate van taalleerders in België" (Attitudes and motivation of language learners in Belgium), Unpublished PhD dissertation, Free University of Brussels.

Mettewie, L., Van Mensel, L. and Belang, D. (2006) *Entreprises bruxelloises et language étrangères. Pratique et coût d'une main d'oeuvre ne maîtrisant pas les langues étrangères*, Brussels: TIBEL ASBL.

Meuter, R. and Orr, J. A. (2011) "Does bilinguality per se contribute to successful cognitive aging?" Paper present at the 8th International Symposium on Bilingualism, Oslo.

Milroy, L. and Muyskens, P. (eds.) (1995) *One Speaker, Two Languages: Cross-Disciplinary Perspectives on Code-switching*, Cambridge: Cambridge University Press.

Mitchell, R. and Myles, F. (1998) *Second Language Learning Theories*, London: Arnold.

Mondada, L. and Pekarek Doehler, S. (2004) "Second language acquisition as situated practice: Task accomplishment in the French second language classroom", *Modern Language Journal*, 88: 501–518.

Mougeon, R., Nadasdi, T. and Rehner, K. (2002) "État de la recherche sur l'appropriation de la variation par les apprenants avancés du FL2 ou FLE", *Acquisition et Interaction en Langue Etrangère*, 17: 7–50.

Mougeon, R., Nadasdi, T. and Rehner, K. (2010) *The Sociolinguistic Competence of Immersion Students*, Bristol: Multilingual Matters.

Mugford G. (2008) "How rude! Teaching impoliteness in the second-language classroom", *ELT Journal*, 62: 375–384.

Muñoz, C. (2006) (ed) *Age and the Rate of Foreign Language Learning*, Clevedon: Multilingual Matters.

Muñoz, C. (2008a) "Symmetries and asymmetries of age effects in naturalistic and instructed L2 learning", *Applied Linguistics*, 29 (4): 578–596.

Muñoz, C. (2008b) "Age-related differences in foreign language learning. Revisiting the empirical evidence", *International Review of Applied Linguistics*, 46 (4): 197–220.

Noels, K. A., Pon, G. and Clément, R. (1996) "Language, identity, and adjustment. The role of linguistic self-confidence in the acculturation process", *Journal of Language and Social Psychology*, 15 (3): 246–264.

Norris, J. and Ortega, L. (2000) "Effectiveness of L2 instruction: A research synthesis and quantitative meta-analysis", *Language Learning*, 50: 417–528.

Novakovich, J. and Shapard, R. (eds.) (2000) *Stories in the Stepmother Tongue*, Buffalo, New York: White Pine Press.

Ogarkova, A. and Borgeaud, Ph. (2009) "(Un)common denominators in research on emotion language: A postscript", Special issue "The language of emotion – conceptual and cultural issues", *Social Science Information*, 48 (3): 523–543.

Ogarkova, A., Borgeaud, Ph. and Scherer, K. (2009) "Language and culture in emotion research: A multidisciplinary perspective", Special issue "The language of emotion – conceptual and cultural issues", *Social Science Information*, 48 (3): 339–357.

Ohara, Y. (2002) "Finding one's voice in Japanese: A study of pitch levels of L2 users", in A. Pavlenko, A. Blackledge, I. Piller and M. Teutsch-Dwyer (eds.), *Multilingualism, Second Language Learning, and Gender*, Berlin: Mouton De Gruyter: 231–254.

Onwuegbuzie, A., Bailey, P. and Daley, C. E. (1999) "Factors associated with foreign language anxiety", *Applied Psycholinguistics*, 20: 217–239.

Onwuegbuzie, A., Bailey, P. and Daley, C. E. (2002) "The role of foreign language anxiety and students' expectations in foreign language learning", *Research in the Schools*, 9: 33–50.

Ożańska-Ponikwia, K. (2013) *Emotions from a Bilingual Point of View: Personality and Emotional Intelligence in Relation to Perception and Expression of Emotions in the L1*. Newcastle upon Tyne: Cambridge Scholars Publishing.

Panayiotou, A. (2004a) "Switching codes, switching code: Bilinguals' emotional responses in English and Greek", *Journal of Multilingual and Multicultural Development*, 25 (2/3): 124–139.
Panayiotou, A. (2004b) "Bilingual emotions: The untranslatable self", *Estudios de Sociolingüística*, 5 (1): 1–19.
Panayiotou, A. (2006) "Translating guilt: An endeavour of shame in the Mediterranean?", in A. Pavlenko (ed.), *Bilingual Minds: Emotional Experience, Expression, and Representation*, Clevedon: Multilingual Matters: 183–208.
Panksepp J. (1998) *Affective Neuroscience: The Foundations of Human and Animal Emotions*, London: Oxford University Press
Panksepp, J. (2000) "The neuro-evolutionary cusp between emotions and cognitions: Implications for understanding consciousness and the emergence of a unified mind science", *Consciousness and Emotion*, 1, 1: 15–54.
Panksepp, J. (2003) "At the interface of the affective, behavioral, and cognitive neurosciences: Decoding the emotional feelings of the brain", *Brain and Cognition*, 52, 1: 4–14.
Paradis, M. (2004) *A Neurolinguistic Theory of Bilingualism*, Amsterdam-Philadephia: John Benjamins.
Pavlenko, A. (1999) "New approaches to concepts in bilingual memory", *Bilingualism: Language and Cognition*, 2 (3): 209–230.
Pavlenko, A. (2002a) "Emotions and the body in Russian and English", *Pragmatics and Cognition*, 10 (1–2): 201–236.
Pavlenko, A. (2002b) "Bilingualism and emotions", *Multilingua*, 21: 45–78.
Pavlenko, A. (2002c) Poststructuralist approaches to the study of social factors in L2, in V. Cook, (ed), *Portraits of the L2 User*, Clevedon: Multilingual Matters: 277–302.
Pavlenko, A. (2003) "'Language of the enemy': Foreign language education and national identity", *International Journal of Bilingual Education and Bilingualism*, 6: 313–331.
Pavlenko, A. (2004) "'Stop doing that, la Komu Skazala!': Language choice and emotion in parent-child communication", *Journal of Multilingual and Multicultural Development*, 25 (2–3): 179–203.
Pavlenko, A. (2005) *Emotions and Multilingualism*, Cambridge, MA: Cambridge University Press.
Pavlenko, A. (2006) "Bilingual selves", in A. Pavlenko (ed), *Bilingual Minds: Emotional Experience, Expression and Representation*. Clevedon: Multilingual Matters: 1–33.
Pavlenko, A. (2007) "Autobiographic narratives as data in applied linguistics", *Applied Linguistics*, 28, (2): 163–188.
Pavlenko, A. (2008a) "Emotion and emotion-laden words in the bilingual lexicon", *Bilingualism: Language and Cognition*, 11: 147–164.
Pavlenko, A. (2008b) "Bi- and multilingualism as a metaphor for research", *Bilingualism: Language and Cognition*, 11: 197–201.
Pavlenko, A. (2008c) "Structural and conceptual equivalence in the acquisition and use of emotion words in a second language", *The Mental Lexicon*, 3 (1): 91–120.
Pavlenko, A. (2009) "Conceptual representation in the bilingual lexicon and second language vocabulary learning", in A. Pavlenko (ed.) *The Bilingual Mental Lexicon: Interdisciplinary Approaches*, Clevedon: Multilingual Matters: 125–160.
Pavlenko, A. (2012a) Affective processing in bilingual speakers: Disembodied cognition? *International Journal of Psychology*, 47 (6): 405–428.
Pavlenko, A. (2012b) "Multilingualism and emotions", in M. Martin-Jones, A. Blackledge and A. Creese (eds), *The Routledge Handbook of Multilingualism*. London: Routledge: 454–469.

Pavlenko, A. (2013) "The affective turn in SLA: From 'affective factors' to 'language desire' and 'commodification of affect'", in D. Gabrys-Barker and J. Bielska (eds), *The Affective Dimension in Second Language Acquisition*. Bristol: Multilingual Matters: 3–28.

Pavlenko, A. and Driagina, V. (2007) "Russian emotion vocabulary in American learners' narratives", *The Modern Language Journal*, 91 (2): 213–234.

Penfield, W. and Roberts, L. (1959) *Speech and Brain-Mechanisms*, Princeton, NJ: Princeton University Press.

Petrides, K. V. and Furnham, A. (2001) "Trait emotional intelligence: psychometric investigation with reference to established trait taxonomies", *European Journal of Personality*, 15: 425–448.

Petrides, K. V. and Furnham, A. (2003) "Trait Emotional Intelligence: Behavioural validation in two studies of emotion recognition and reactivity to mood induction", *European Journal of Personality*, 17: 39–57.

Petrides, K. V. and Furnham, A. (2006) "The role of trait Emotional Intelligence in a gender-specific model of organizational variables", *Journal of Applied Social Psychology*, 36: 552–569.

Petrides, K. V., Frederickson, N. and Furnham, A. (2004) "The role of trait Emotional Intelligence in academic performance and deviant behavior at school", *Personality and Individual Differences*, 36: 277–293.

Petrides, K. V., Furnham, A. and Frederickson, N. (2004) "Emotional intelligence", *The Psychologist*, 17: 574–577.

Petrides, K. V., Furnham, A. and Mavroveli, S. (2007) "Trait Emotional Intelligence: Moving forward in the field of EI", in G. Matthews, M. Zeidner and R. Roberts (eds.), *Emotional Intelligence: Knowns and Unknowns*. Oxford: Oxford University Press.

Petrides, K. V., Pita, R. and Kokkinaki, F. (2007) "The location of trait Emotional Intelligence in personality factor space", *British Journal of Psychology*, 98: 273–289.

Phillips, E. M. (1991) "Anxiety and oral competence: Classroom dilemma", *French Review*, 65: 1–14.

Phillips, E. M. (1992) "The effects of language anxiety on student oral test performance and attitudes", *The Modern Language Journal*, 76: 14–26.

Pike, K. L. (1954) *Language in Relation to a Unified Theory of the Structure of Human Behaviour*, The Hague: Mouton.

Pike, K.L. (1993) *Talk, Thought and Thing. the Emic Road toward Conscious Knowledge*, Dallas: Summer Institute of Linguistics.

Piller, I. (2002) *Bilingual Couples Talk: The Discursive Construction of Hybridity*, Amsterdam: John Benjamins.

Ping Li, Sepanski, S. and Xiaowei Zhao (2006) "Language history questionnaire: A web-based interface for bilingual research", *Behavior Research Methods*, 38: 202–210.

Planchenault, G. (2005) Utiliser des extraits des films en classe de français langue étrangère. Etude sur l'enseignement et l'acquisition des compétences socioculturelle et sociopragmatique (Using film sequences in the French classroom. A study on sociopragmatic awareness and the expression of sociolinguistic variants in French interlanguage). Unpublished PhD dissertation, Birkbeck, University of London.

Poarch, G. J. and Van Hell, J. G. (2012) "Cross-language activation in children's speech production: Evidence from second language learners, bilinguals, and trilinguals", *Journal of Experimental Child Psychology*, 111 (3): 419–438.

Powers, R. (2009) " 'I love you' in different languages: Acquisition, Use, and Culture – what factors affect emotional weight?" Unpublished MA thesis, Washington University.

Regan, V. (2004) "The relationship between the group and the individual and the acquisition of native speaker variation patterns: A preliminary study", *International Review of Applied Linguistics*, 42: 335–348.

Regan, V. (2005) "From speech community back to classroom: What variation analysis can tell us about the role of context in the acquisition of French as a foreign language", in J.-M. Dewaele (ed.), *Focus on French as a Foreign Language: Multidisciplinary Approaches*, Clevedon: Multilingual Matters: 191–209.

Regan, V., Howard, M. and Lemée, I. (2009) *Acquisition of Sociolinguistic Competence in a Study Abroad Context. Irish Learners of French*, Clevedon: Multilingual Matters.

Register, N. A. (1996) "Second-language learners and taboo words in American English", *English Today*, 12: 44–49.

Rimé, B. (2009) "More on the social sharing of emotion: In defence of the individual, of culture, of private disclosure, and in rebuttal of an old couple of ghosts known as 'cognition and emotion'", *Emotion Review*, 1 (1): 94–96.

Ringbom, H. (2001) "Developing literacy can and should be fun: But only sometimes is", in D. Belcher and U. Connor (eds.), *Reflections on Multiliterate Lives*, Clevedon: Multilingual Matters: 60–66.

Ringbom, H. (2007) *Crosslinguistic Similarity in Foreign Language Learning*, Clevedon: Multilingual Matters.

Rintell, E. (1984) "But how did you feel about that? The learner's perception of emotion in speech", *Applied Linguistics*, 5: 255–264.

Rintell, E. (1990) "That's incredible: Stories of emotion told by second language learners and native speakers", in R. Scarcella, E. Andersen and S. Krashen (eds.), *Developing Communicative Competence in a Second Language*, Boston, MA: Heinle and Heinle: 75–94.

Robins, R. W. and Pals, J. L. (2002) "Implicit self-theories in the academic domain: Implications for goal orientation, attributions, affect, and self-esteem change", *Self and Identity*, 1: 313–336.

Robinson, M. D. and Clore, G. L. (2002) "Belief and feeling: Evidence for an accessibility model of emotional self-report", *Psychological Bulletin*, 128: 934–960.

Rodriguez, M. and Abreu, O. (2003) "The stability of general foreign language classroom anxiety across English and French", *Modern Language Journal*, 87: 365–374.

Rosaldo, M. (1984) "Toward an anthropology of self and feeling", in R. Shweder and R. LeVine (eds.), *Culture Theory: Essays on Mind, Self, and Emotion*, Cambridge: Cambridge University Press: 137–157.

Rose, K. R. and Kasper, G. (eds.) (2001) *Pragmatics in Language Teaching*, New York: Cambridge University Press.

Rosenthal, N. (2002) *The Emotional Revolution: How the New Science of Feelings Can Transform Your Life*, New York: Citadel Press.

Rubenfeld, S., Clément, R. Lussier, D. Lebrun, M. and Auger, R. (2006) "Second language learning and cultural representations: Beyond competence and identity", *Language Learning*, 56: 609–631.

Rubin, J. (1975) "What the 'good language learner' can teach us", *TESOL Quarterly*, 9 (1): 41–51

Rubin, J. (2008) "Reflections", in C. Griffiths (ed.), *Lessons from Good Language Learners*, Cambridge: Cambridge University Press: 10–18.

Safont Jordà, M. P. (2005) *Third Language Learners. Pragmatic Production and Awareness*, Clevedon: Multilingual Matters.

Saito, Y. and Samimy, K. K. (1996) "Foreign language anxiety and language performance: a study of learner anxiety in beginning, intermediate, and advanced-level college students of Japanese", *Foreign Language Annals*, 29: 239–251.

Santiago-Rivera, A. L. and Altarriba, J. (2002) "The role of language in therapy with the Spanish-English bilingual client", *Professional Psychology: Research and Practice*, 33: 30–38.

Sapir, E. (1921) *Language: An Introduction to the Study of Speech*, New York: Harcourt, Brace.

Sbisa, M. (2001) "Illocutionary force and degrees of strength in language use", *Journal of Pragmatics*, 33 (12): 1791–1814.

Scherer, K. R. (2005) "What are emotions? And how can they be measured?", *Social Science Information Sur Les Sciences Sociales*, 44 (4): 695–729.

Scheu, D. (2000) "Cultural constraints in bilinguals' codeswitching", *International Journal of Intercultural Relations*, 24: 131–150.

Schmid, M. (2009) "On L1 attrition and the linguistic system", *Eurosla Yearbook*, 9: 212–245.

Schommer, M. (1998) "The influence of age and education on epistemological beliefs", *British Journal of Educational Psychology*, 68: 551–562.

Schrauf, R. W. and Hoffman, L. (2007) "Effects of revisionism on remembered emotion: The valence of older, voluntary immigrants' pre-migration autobiographical memories", *Applied Cognitive Psychology*, 21: 895–913.

Schumann, J. (1997) *The Neurobiology of Affect in Language*, Oxford: Blackwell.

Schumann, J. (2001) " Learning as foraging", in Z. Dörnyei and R. Schmidt (eds.), *Motivation and Second Language Acquisition*, University of Hawai'i at Manoa: Second Language Teaching and Curriculum Center: 21–28.

Schumann, J. (2004) "The neurobiology of aptitude", in J. Schumann, S. E. Crowell, N. E. Jones, N. Lee, S. A. Schuchert and L. A. Wood (eds.), *The Neurobiology of Learning. Perspectives from Second Language Acquisition*, Mahwah, NJ: Erlbaum: 7–21.

Scovel, T. (1978) "The effect of affect on foreign language learning: A review of the anxiety research", *Language Learning*, 28: 129–141.

Scovel, T. (2006) "Age, acquisition and accent", in C. Abello-Contesse, R. Chacon-Beltran, M. D. Lopez-Jiménez and M. M. Torreblanca-Lopez (eds.), *Age in L2 Acquisition and Teaching*, Bern: Peter Lang: 31–48.

Searle, J.R., Kiefer, F. and Bierwisch, M. (1980) "Introduction", in J.R. Searle, F. Kiefer and M. Bierwisch (eds.), *Speech Act Theory and Pragmatics*, Dordrecht: Reidel: vii–xii.

Segalowitz, N. (2001) "On the evolving connections between psychology and linguistics", *Annual Review of Applied Linguistics*, 21: 3–22.

Shoaib, A. and Dörnyei, Z. (2005) "Affect in life-long learning: Exploring L2 motivation as a dynamic process", in P. Benson and D. Nunan (eds.), *Learners' Stories: Difference and Diversity in Language Learning*, Cambridge: Cambridge University Press: 22–41.

Shweder, R. (2008) "The cultural psychology of suffering: the many meanings of health in Orissa, India (and elsewhere)", *Ethos*, 36 (1): 60–77.

Siegal, M. (1996) "The role of learner subjectivity in second language sociolinguistic competency: Western women learning Japanese", *Applied Linguistics*, 17: 356–382.

Singleton, D. (2003) "Critical Period or general age factor(s)?", in M. P. García Mayo and M. L. García Lecumberri (eds.), *Age and the Acquisition of English as a Foreign Language*, Clevedon: Multilingual Matters: 3–22.

Singleton, D. (2007) "The Critical Period Hypothesis: Some problems", *Interlingüistica*, 17: 48–56.

Singleton, D. and Aronin, L. (2007) "Multiple language learning in the light of the theory of affordances", *Innovation in Language Learning and Teaching*, 1: 83–96.

Singleton, D. and Ryan, L. (2004) *Language Acquisition: The age factor*, 2nd edition, Clevedon: Multilingual Matters.

Skehan, P. (1989) *Individual Differences in Second-language Learning*, London: Edward Arnold.

Solomon, R. C. (2003) *Not Passion's Slave*, Oxford: Oxford University Press.
Sparks, R.-L., Artzer, M., Patton, J., Ganschow, L., Miller, K., Hordubay, D. J. and Walsh, G. (1998) "Benefits of multisensory structured language instruction for at-risk foreign language learners: A comparison study of high school Spanish students", *Annals of Dyslexia*, 48: 239–270.
Spielberger, C. D. (1983) *Manual for the State-trait Anxiety Inventory (form Y)*, Palo Alto, CA: Consulting Psychologists Press.
Stavans, I. (2001) *On Borrowed Words. A Memoir of Language*, New York: Viking Penguin.
Stenstrom, A. B. (1995) "Taboos in teenage talk", in G. Melchers and B. Warren (eds.), *Studies in Anglistics*, Stockholm: Almqvist and Wiksell International: 71–79.
Stenstrom, A. B. (1999) "He was really gormless - she's bloody crap. Girls, boys and intensifiers", in H. Hasselgard and S. Oksefjell (eds.), *Out of Corpora: Studies in Honour of Stig Johansson*, Amsterdam: Rodopi: 69–78.
Sutton, T. M., Altarriba, J., Gianico, J. L. and Basnight-Brown, D. M. (2007) "The automatic access of emotion: Emotional Stroop effects in Spanish-English bilingual speakers", *Cognition and Emotion*, 21 (5): 1077–1090.
Swain, M. Lapkin, S., Rowen, N. and Hart, D. (1990) "The role of mother tongue literacy in third language learning", *Language, Culture and Curriculum*, 3 (1): 65–81.
Taguchi, N. (2005) "Comprehending implied meaning in English as a foreign language", *The Modern Language Journal*, 89: 543–562.
Taguchi, N. (2008) "Cognition, language contact, and the development of pragmatic comprehension in a Study-Abroad context", *Language Learning*, 58 (1): 33–71.
Ten Have, P. (2007) *Doing Conversation Analysis: A Practical Guide*, 2nd edition, London: Sage Publications.
Tett, R. P., Fox, K. E. and Wang, A. (2005) "Development and validation of a self-report measure of Emotional Intelligence as a multidimensional trait domain", *Personality and Social Psychology Bulletin*, 31: 859–888.
Towell, R. and Dewaele, J.-M. (2005) "The role of psycholinguistic factors in the development of fluency amongst advanced learners of French", in J.-M. Dewaele (ed), *Focus on French as a Foreign Language: Multidisciplinary Approaches*, Clevedon: Multilingual Matters: 210–239.
Toya, M. and Kodis, M. (1996) "But I don't want to be rude: On learning how to express anger in the L2", *JALT Journal*, 18 (2): 279–295.
Ushioda, E. (2001) "Language learning at university: Exploring the role of motivational thinking", in Z. Dörnyei and R. Schmidt (eds.), *Motivation and Second Language Acquisition*, Honolulu, HI: University of Hawaii Press: 91–124.
Ushioda, E. and Chen, S. A. (2011) "Researching motivation and possible selves among learners of English: The need to integrate qualitative inquiry", *Anglistik*, 22 (1), 43–61.
Van Daele, S. (2007) Linguïstische vlotheid, accuraatheid en complexiteit in de verwerving en de verwerking van een tweede taal [Linguistic fluency, accuracy and complexity in the acquisition and processing of a second language], Unpublished PhD dissertation, Free University of Brussels.
Vandenbussche, W. (2004) "Triglossia and pragmatic variety choice in nineteenth century Bruges: A case study in historical sociolinguistics", *Journal of Historical Pragmatics*, 5 (1): 27–47.
Van Essen, A. (2004) "The Rise and Role of English as an International Language. Some educational consequences", *Humanising Language Teaching*, 6 (4) www.hltmag.co.uk/nov04/mart.htm.

Van Lancker, D. and Cummings, J. L. (1999) "Expletives: Neurolinguistic and neurobehavioral perspectives on swearing", *Brain Research Reviews*, 31: 83–104.
van Praag, H. M. (2008) *God en Psyche. De redelijkheid van het geloven. Visies van een Jood*, Amsterdam: Uitgeverij Boom.
Walls R. T., Nardi, A. H. von Minden, A. M. and Hoffman, N. (2002) "The characteristics of effective and ineffective teachers", *Teacher Education Quarterly*, 29: 37–48.
Warga, M. (2007) "Interlanguage pragmatics in L2 French", in D. Ayoun (ed.), *Handbook of French Applied Linguistics*, Amsterdam: John Benjamins: 171–207.
Warwick, J. and Nettelbeck, T. (2004) "Emotional intelligence is...?", *Personality and Individual Differences*, 37: 1091–1100.
Watson-Gegeo, K. A. (1988) "Ethnography in ESL: Defining the essentials", *TESOL Quarterly*, 22: 575–592.
Wierzbicka, A. (2004) "Preface: Bilingual lives, bilingual experience", *Journal of Multilingual and Multicultural Development*, 25: 94–104.
Wierzbicka, A. and Harkins, J. (2001) "Introduction", in J. Harkins and A. Wierzbicka (eds.), *Emotions in Crosslinguistic Perspective*. Berlin: Mouton De Gruyter: 1–34.
Wiklund, I. (2002) "Social networks from a sociolinguistic perspective: the relationship between characteristics of the social networks of bilingual adolescents and their language proficiency", *International Journal of the Sociology of Language*, 153: 53–92.
Williams, K. (1991) "Anxiety and formal second/foreign language learning", *RELC Journal*, 22 (2): 19–28.
Williams, M. and Burden, R. L. (1997) *Psychology for Language Teachers*, Cambridge: Cambridge University Press.
Williams, M. and Burden, R. L. (1999) "Students' developing conceptions of themselves as language learners", *The Modern Language Journal*, 83 (2): 193–201.
Williams, M., Burden, R. and Lanvers, U. (2002) "'French is the language of love and stuff': Student perceptions of issues related to motivation in learning a foreign language", *British Educational Research Journal*, 28 (4): 503–528.
Williams, M., Burden, R. L., Poulet, G. and Maun, I. (2004) "Learners' perceptions of their successes and failures in foreign language learning", *Language Learning Journal*, 30 (1): 19–29.
Wilson, R. (2008) "Another language is another soul": The presentation of self through a foreign language, Unpublished PhD thesis, Birkbeck, University of London.
Wilson, R. (2013) "Another language is another soul", *Language and Intercultural Communication*, DOI: 10.1080/14708477.2013.804534
Wilson, R. and Dewaele, J.-M. (2010) "The use of web questionnaires in Second Language Acquisition and bilingualism research", *Second Language Research*, 26 (1): 103–123.
Woodrow, L. (2006) "Anxiety and speaking English as a second language", *RELC Journal*, 37 (3): 308–328.
Wörde von R. (2003) "Students' perspectives on foreign language anxiety", *Inquiry*, 8 (1): 21–40.
Wu, Y.J. and Thierry, G. (2012) "How reading in a second language protects your heart", *The Journal of Neuroscience*, 32, 19: 6485–6489.
Xiao-Lei Wang (2008) *Growing Up with Three Languages*, Clevedon: Multilingual Matters.
Yashima T., Zenuk-Nishide, L. and Shimuzu, K. (2004) "The influence of attitudes and affect on willingness to communicate and second language communication", *Language Learning*, 54: 119–152.

Ye, Veronica Zhengdao (2001) "An inquiry into 'sadness' in Chinese", In J. Harkins and A. Wierzbicka (eds.), *Emotions in Crosslinguistic Perspective,* Berlin: Mouton De Gruyter: 359–404.

Ye, Veronica Zhengdao (2004) "La Double Vie de Veronica: Reflections on my life as a Chinese migrant in Australia", *Life Writing,* 1: 133–146.

Young, D. J. (1990) "An investigation of students' perspectives on anxiety and speaking", *Foreign Language Annals,* 23: 539–553.

Young, D. J. (1991) "Creating a low-anxiety classroom environment: What does language anxiety research suggest?", *The Modern Language Journal,* 75: 426–439.

Author Index

Subject Index

Printed and bound in Great Britain by
CPI Group (UK) Ltd, Croydon, CR0 4YY